WOME   M

Both sides of the camera

E. ANN KAPLAN

METHUEN
NEW YORK AND LONDON

First published in 1983 by
Methuen, Inc.
29 West 35th Street, New York, NY 10001
Reprinted 1984 and 1985

Published in Great Britain by
Methuen & Co.
11 New Fetter Lane, London EC4P 4EE

Library of Congress Cataloging in Publication Data

Kaplan, E. Ann.
  Women and film.

  Bibliography: p.
  Includes index.
  1. Women in moving-pictures. 2. Women in the
motion picture industry. 3. Feminist motion pictures –
History and criticism. I. Title.
PN1995.9.W6K3 1983   791.43′09′09352042   83-8198
ISBN 0-416-31750-2 (pbk.)

British Library Cataloguing in Publication Data

Kaplan, E. Ann
Women and film.
1. Moving-pictures 2. Women in moving-pictures
I. Title
791.43   PN1994

ISBN 0-416-31750-2

For Brett and Marty

Contents

List of plates

The plates are selected from the following films; full details are given in the caption following each plate.

The cover illustration shows a still from Von Trotta's *Marianne and Juliane*, reproduced by courtesy of New Yorker Films.

Preface

The idea for this book arose out of the course on women in film that I have been teaching for exactly ten years. I ran my first class in 1972 when women's studies was just getting under way in America and before the influence of semiology, structuralism, or psychoanalysis had begun to be felt. Since then, the course has gone through many different incarnations as my ideas developed in accordance with my experiences in teaching, my reading of the work of other feminists, and my own writing and thinking that has contributed to ongoing debates. In a sense, this book brings together ideas that I have wrestled with over a long period of time as I reacted to the various phases of the women's movement, which could not help but influence my work.

When I began teaching the course, I was working in a void; now, with the growth of a substantial body of feminist film theory on both sides of the Atlantic, as well as in France and Germany, many resources are available and the course starts out with a brief "history" of feminist film criticism. One could say that, over the past ten years, women have created an entire field within film studies which is now producing some of the most stimulating, intelligent, and exciting work going on and which has dramatically influenced the criticism of male writers as well. Few books on film, whether written by men or women, can now ignore issues of female representation.

But clearly a great deal of work remains to be done; sometimes I think that we are really only just beginning. The tension between theory and practice remains, as do differences about the most useful theoretical approaches. The field is changing and taking new directions as a result of the many graduate film students doing research and writing dissertations on women in film. Often very much influenced by psychoanalysis and semiology, these students are nevertheless asking new questions and establishing new lines of thought. Some are turning to the still neglected study of important Hollywood women directors (like Lois Weber and Ida Lupino) or the many foreign ones (like Germaine Dulac or Marie Epstein). Others are beginning to mine the silent era for the history of female representations in the early film, which still needs writing.

Obviously, the field of feminist film theory and criticism will continue to expand in the 1980s. I hope that this book will aid in that expansion by bringing together, situating, and developing ideas that have emerged over the past decade and that provide the starting point for any new work. I hope that teachers unfamiliar with feminist approaches to film will be inspired to undertake courses on women in film, or to build the perspective into their current courses. Finally, I hope that the book will reach students at all levels, for it is they, after all, who will build on the work already done.

E. Ann Kaplan
New York
January 1983

Acknowledgements

I hardly know how to begin to thank all the people who have made this book possible. As always, I must thank my family in England for their support and for enabling me to work freely in the summers by taking care of my daughter. And I must thank my daughter, Brett, for putting up with a very preoccupied mother during time that was meant for her.

Many friends have given me invaluable advice and support. I want to thank especially Martin Hoffman, who saw me through many times when I despaired of ever finishing my project, and who gave me useful advice on a crucial chapter. I want to thank the many people (some unknown to me) who read this book at various stages of its development, from the initial proposal to complete drafts, and whose suggestions I followed as far as I possibly could. Particularly helpful were the comments of Judith Mayne, Lucy Fischer, and Beverle Houston. Miriam Hansen and Marianne DeKoven read, and made useful suggestions for, chapter 1, and Miriam also helped me with the glossary in the second part of the Introduction. Yvonne Rainer advised me on the chapter on her films and patiently answered my many questions about her work and about references I lacked. I have met and talked with nearly all the filmmakers whose works I analyze in part II of the book, and I want to thank them also for answering my questions. I am grateful to Bob Stam for giving me information about Third World films, and to Maurice Charney for encouraging me to work up and submit the book proposal to Methuen in the first place.

Various institutions and libraries facilitated my research. I should like to thank the Cinema Studies Department of New York University for generously allowing me to see several times the films discussed in part I that are in their collection; Rutgers Library Multi-Media Services personnel were always helpful in arranging showings of films in our collection and in obtaining information I needed. I worked many long hours in the Lincoln Center Library for the Performing Arts and in the Anthology Film Archives, where librarians helped me to track down needed materials. Unifilm kindly set up a viewing for Sara Gomez's *One Way or Another*, and Bioskop-Film Produktion sent me the German scripts of Von Trotta's films. Yvonne Rainer kindly lent me her personal copies of her films for me to study.

The many students who over the years have taken my course on women in film deserve thanks for patiently listening to my lectures as I developed my ideas; their stimulating questions and responses made me continually reassess my formulations. The enthusiasm of both graduate and undergraduate students at Rutgers University and New York University convinced me that the course was worth making into a book.

I am very grateful to the women who typed and retyped several times all the chapters in this book, especially Paula Horvath (who continued to type for me even when she was no longer my secretary at Rutgers), and the Rutgers English Department secretaries, Nancy Miller, Linda Tepedino, Linda Adams, and Vicki Brooks.

Acknowledgement is also due to all those who allowed me to reprint from previously published articles and reproduce photographs from films.

In this respect I would like to thank *Millenium Film Journal* for permission to reprint as chapters (or parts of chapters) and in revised form my following articles, which first appeared in *Millenium*: "Feminism, psychoanalysis and history in *Sigmund Freud's Dora*," (Nos 7, 8, and 9); "Night at the opera: investigating the heroine in Sally Potter's *Thriller*," (Nos 10 and 11); "Deconstructing the heroine: Mulvey/Wollen's *Amy!*," (No. 12); "Semiotics of the documentary: theories and strategies," (No. 12).

In addition, thanks go to *The Quarterly Review of Film Studies* for permission to reprint in revised form as part of a chapter my article "The avant-garde feminist film: its value and function in relation to Mulvey/Wollen's *Riddles of the Sphinx*," which first appeared in *QRFS*, Vol. 4, No. 2 (Spring 1979).

Thanks go also to *Social Policy* for permission to reprint in revised form my article "*Marianne and Juliane*: politics and the family," which first appeared in *SP* (Summer 1982, © 1982 Social Policy Corporation, New York, N.Y. 10036).

I would also like to thank the editors of the new journal *Persistence of Vision* for permission to reprint my article on *Looking for Mr Goodbar*, which appeared in their first issue in Summer 1983.

Stills for the four Hollywood films were obtained from the Museum of Modern Art, New York.

Thanks go to the French Consulate in New York for the still for Duras's *Nathalie Granger*.

New Yorker Films kindly sent the stills for Von Trotta's *Marianne and Juliane*.

Yvonne Rainer lent me the stills for her films *Lives of Performers* and *Film about a Woman Who . . .*, for which, thanks.

I was given stills for chapter 10 by: Joyce Choppra (*Joyce at 34*); New Day Films (*Union Maids*); Alimi Cinema 5 Films (*Harlan County, U.S.A.*). Thanks go to all concerned.

The filmmakers kindly provided most of the stills for chapters 11 and 12. Thanks go to McCall, Tyndall, Pajaczkowska, and Weinstock for the still for *Sigmund Freud's Dora*; to Sally Potter for the still for *Thriller*; and to Michelle Citron for *Daughter-Rite*.

The British Film Institute kindly provided the stills for *Amy!* and *Riddles of the Sphinx*.

Thanks go to Unifilm for providing the still for Sara Gomez's *One Way or Another*.

Finally, most of this book was written while on sabbatical from Rutgers University. I wish to thank the University for its generous support.

E. Ann Kaplan
New York
January 1983

Introduction

Part I

Let me make quite clear, at the outset, the parameters of this book. The book is being written at a time when we have behind us about ten years of feminist film criticism; this criticism evolved directly out of the women's movement and its preoccupations in the early 1970s and, quite naturally, began with a sociological, political methodology. As the inadequacies of this approach became clear, feminists began to use structuralism, psychoanalysis, and semiology in their theoretical analysis. While much of this newer work is familiar to a small circle of feminist film critics and graduate students, undergraduate film students rarely learn much about it and the work is virtually unknown to people in other, related liberal arts disciplines (literature, the fine arts, history, drama). One aim of the book is thus to make accessible to undergraduates and nonspecialists recent theoretical work that is often couched in obscure language as well as assuming a broad background in psychoanalysis and semiology.

I did not, however, want simply to write a book summarizing contemporary feminist film theory: first, because there are several long articles that already do this; and second, because it seemed more important to show the theories in action rather than merely to describe them. In addition, I wanted to include a specific perspective on new theory – to point out some of its dangers, limitations, and problems – while recognizing its genuine contribution to the development of feminist approaches to film. Again, it seemed easier and more responsible to develop such a critique (or, perhaps more accurately, a set of qualifications) through detailed analyses of films.

Given the limitation of space in the book, there are two main compromises that I have had to make. First, in relation to theory, rather than attempt to deal with all the complex issues that have arisen, I decided to focus on the much discussed question of the male gaze, which, in patriarchy, is viewed as dominating and repressing women through its controlling power over female discourse and female desire. The introductory chapter, which contains in embryo the arguments to be made in the detailed analyses of films that follow, charts the development of this concept of the gaze as it has emerged out of recent psychoanalytic, structuralist, and semiotic theories. Following Laura Mulvey, I argue that the male gaze, in defining and dominating woman as erotic object, manages to repress the relations of woman in her place as Mother – leaving a gap not "colonized" by man, through which, hopefully, woman can begin to create a discourse, a voice, a place for herself as subject.

Second, in relation to history, I have been unable because limited by space to locate films adequately in their specific historical and institutional context. Since it was impossible to develop my argument through an analysis of even the major films of each decade, I was forced to choose "representative" examples of female positionings that one can readily perceive as widespread, both within a particular decade and across decades. This is not to say, however, that I in any way ignore the specificity of a historical period, or of the particular studio in which a director was working, or even the importance of the particular director and star that each film involves; it is simply that my emphasis will be on the larger structuring of the narrative and on the placement of the woman within that narrative – a structuring that in any case transcends the historical and individual specificities. Where possible, I will place films in their sociopolitical context, and I will attempt at times to sketch in the broad lines of a historical situation that has a bearing on the positioning of women within a text. But the book is not intended to cover works in their historical dimensions: I have aimed merely to isolate certain configurations as they emerge in certain texts which illustrate them well.

Feminist film theorists have often (correctly) been criticized for their ahistoricism, and I am reluctant to lay myself open to a similar charge. However, let me say two things about history as it regards women. First, it seems to me that while certain patterns that involve women are linked to a specific historical context, other patterns in relation to marriage, sexuality, and the family – ones that I am focusing on here – transcend traditional historical categories; and this for a good reason, namely that women, in being relegated to absence, silence, and marginality, have thereby also to a degree been relegated to the outskirts of historical discourse, if not to a position totally outside of history (and of culture), which has been defined as the history of white (usually middle-class) men. This is not to deny that women have a history of their own which can, to some extent, be rediscovered; but it is to argue that in terms of dominant film narratives, of classic forms, women, as they have been represented by men in these texts, take on images that have an "eternal" status, and are repeated through the decades in their essentials: the representation changes superficially in accord with current styles and fashions – but scratch the surface and one finds a familiar pattern.

Second, feminist theorists have been redefining history with Foucault in mind. Foucault's distinction between "total" and "general" history in his *Archeology of Knowledge* was useful in that it questioned the very basis of traditional histories that had excluded women. "Total" history "drew all phenomena around a single centre – the principle, meaning, spirit, world-view, overall form of a society or civilization." On the other hand, "general" history speaks of "series, segmentations, limits, difference of level, time-lags, anachronistic survivals, possible types of relation."[1] This second type of history seems to some feminists appropriate to their situation, for to construct a feminist history alongside the traditional male one would be to fall into a form that has suited the male mind with its need for a certain logical coherence. It would be to create yet one more form of history as a discourse that establishes false cause–effect relations.

I agree that there may not be a form of history specific to women – such a position smacks of a dangerous essentialism.[2] But important here is the omission of the female experience from dominant art forms, so that we have recurring patterns reflecting the positioning of women within a patriarchal unconscious that, at one level, works independently of capitalism.

Yet established historical modes – including the Marxist one with its emphasis on the roles of class conflict, modes of production, and the division of labor – are relevant to the female as to the male experience. My critique of psychoanalytic and semiological theory – to the degree that I have one – emerges from a concern that the realm of the social formation is some-times assigned to a level of discourse outside of which it cannot be known. I will be arguing here for the possibility that sensual/physical experience can "break through" patriarchal discourses, leaving open the possibility for change.

I am aware that this belief creates a certain methodological tension in the book; it is a tension arising out of the way that feminist film theory evolved, as I explain in chapter 1, from a sociological to a psychoanalytic approach.[3] Elsewhere I have argued that the two methodologies each refer to a different aspect of the human being – sociology to people in social structures, psychoanalysis to people's psychic structures.[4] Although semiology has tried to bring these two spheres together through the mediating agency of language and the unconscious, for the most part I prefer to talk of them as parallel but not mutually incompatible realms. Each methodology – the sociological and the psychoanalytic – is relevant when applied to its relevant sphere. Lacanian and Freudian psychoanalytic concepts seem valid as applied to the construc-tion of women in the classic Hollywood film. As I explain in chapter 1, the tools of psychoanalysis and semiology enable women to unlock patriarchal culture as expressed in dominant representations. They expose the psychic and mythic forces inherent in patriarchy and account for female positionings as we have internalized them. (Since many of the semiological and psychoanalytic concepts are unfamiliar, I have included in the second part of this introduction a glossary of the main terms and, in chapter 1, I summarize briefly the main theories that have influenced feminist film criticism and underpin many of the analyses in this book.)

Sociological issues cannot be altogether excluded, however, and I speak in that discourse where appropriate. A similar movement between levels and types of discourse may be found in the second part of the book, where I am particularly concerned with feminist cinematic strategies and with the issues around realism that have emerged from the new theories. Chapter 10 discusses realism in early women's documentaries and lays the foundation for the following chapters on different types of recent women's films.

Given the limited space available, I decided, if somewhat reluctantly, to focus in part I on those recurring and basic patterns as we find them in Hollywood films at different moments. The choice of films is more or less arbitrary, although I made the decision to cover different decades. The fact that there are three films from the 1930s and 1940s and none from the 1950s is because films from the earlier decades reflect a period rigidly circumscribed by sexual and political ideologies, and yet the struggle over these constraining ideologies is evident in the very narrative structures of the films themselves: the films, that is, permit a "reading against the grain"[5] in which interesting contradictions emerge to expose the underlying working of patriarchy. In addition, if, because of limited space, I could discuss only three classical Hollywood films, I felt that the 1950s film, if not exactly expendable, at least had to take lower priority than the earlier films, which supplied the groundwork for both the 1950s and later works. The 1950s represent very much the *end* of something; the films are interesting because they show earlier codes straining at the seams, ready to give way, but holding on tight. Sexuality is splattered everywhere and yet nowhere *recognized*; the mechanisms that worked to control female sexuality in the earlier decades, and which I will be exploring in detail here, implicitly recognized the force and danger of female sexuality; in the 1950s, the fear of female sexuality seems to be repressed – hence it overflows everywhere. (I am thinking particularly of actresses like Marilyn Monroe or Natalie Wood, as against Dietrich, Lauren Bacall, or Rita Hayworth.) But since the fear has been repressed, the films pretend that female sexuality somehow isn't really there in all its actual explosiveness.

Given that 1950s films are in a sense an anomaly, a decade unto themselves, it seemed preferable to omit an example of that decade than to cut out any of the other films, however hard that decision may have been. I was overwhelmed with choices for the contemporary Hollywood film, but settled finally on *Looking for Mr Goodbar* because of its fascinating contradictions between traditional discourses about female sexuality and the new, post-1960s, discourses.

In order to demonstrate the theoretical structure of the domination of the male gaze in the classical Hollywood film, and attempts by female filmmakers to use the cinematic apparatus so as to avoid this domination, I have divided the book into two main parts. In the first part, using semiological and psychoanalytic methodologies, I analyze four Hollywood films in depth so as to reveal the way in which the dominating male gaze, carrying with it social, political, and economic as well as sexual power, relegates women to absence, silence, and marginality, using a series of increasingly vicious mechanisms. Putting Molly Haskell's notion of a change from idealization to violation in rather different terms, I will show a series of shifts that parallel those Haskell outlined ten years ago.[6]

We will see first, in *Camille* (1936), how the dominating power of the male gaze, while often, as in this case, adoring, carries with it an economic and social superiority which results in a demanding authority over women. Made to function as erotic object, woman must sacrifice her desire to that of the male Other, helping to preserve patriarchy by submitting herself to its Law. Both economically and sexually vulnerable, women, as *Camille* proves, need the protection of *certain* men against their vulnerability to *other* men. Any attempts at subjectivity must be at the cost of fulfilling desire, since, as Jacqueline Rose notes,[7] to be subject and to own the desire is impossible for women.

Blonde Venus (1932) reveals a second method of dominating women in a representational system and of lessening the threat that women's sexuality holds in patriarchy. Through fetishizing the female form, man attempts to deny its *difference*; he incorporates it into his own body in addition by dressing the female in male attire. Woman qua *woman* thus disappears, rendered as she now is in likeness to man. As we will see, however, this process sometimes backfires because of patriarchal narcissism: the masculinized female image can become a *resisting* image for the female spectator; the male attire "permits" female–female bonding because it pays lip service to a sexual difference we have all come to believe is necessary. It allows, then, a form of sexual relating that excludes men and that thus subverts patriarchal domination while acceding to its symbolic form.

Blonde Venus also shows the link between male attempts to fetishize woman and the repression of mothering in patriarchy. This is a theme that will be increasingly important as the book goes on, particularly when in part II we discuss films by women. The assignment of the Mother in patriarchy to silence, absence, and marginality has been perpetuated by women reacting against conventional bourgeois structures for complex reasons that I'll discuss further on. A close analysis of how the Mother has been constructed in the Hollywood film may give us insight into this parallel (but differently motivated) rejection of the Mother. The work of Julia Kristeva (one of the few female French theorists that the American male critical establishment has granted proper attention) may be useful here: complex and controversial though her thought is, Kristeva's theories about Motherhood suggest first, possible reasons for the repression of mothering in patriarchy, and second, ways in which the mother–daughter bond may be subversive. She usefully distinguishes between the symbolic and nonsymbolic aspects of Motherhood; the symbolic aspect is that which patriarchy insists on, and which involves the daughter's desire to bear a child of her own father; linked in a basic way then to the father, the child simply reflects the father's function as originating, and justifying, reproductive desire.[8]

Patriarchy, that is, will only permit the symbolic aspect of Motherhood, which is, in effect, a repression of the aspects that would bind woman to woman were they permitted release. For underlying the symbolic constraint on Motherhood is a nonsymbolic aspect which has homosexual components: as Kristeva notes, "The body of the mother . . . is one toward which women aspire all the more passionately because it lacks a penis. . . . By giving birth, the woman enters into contact with her mother; she becomes, she is her own mother; they are the same continuity differentiating itself."[9]

Blonde Venus sets up at the start the symbolic patriarchal form of mothering, and then briefly allows the heroine to search for the repressed, nonsymbolic level by running away. The fierce pursuit by patriarchal agents exposes the threat this offers, and necessitates Helen's reinscription at the end of the film into her place within the patriarchal family.

I will show next how *Lady from Shanghai* (1946) represents a more direct confronting of the threat that woman poses. Woman is now neither helpless victim nor phallic substitute. Rather, the threat that her sexuality poses emerges in projecting the hostility onto the female image. As in all noir films, the heroine is now a femme fatale, exuding her seductive sexuality directly. Man at once desires her and fears her power over him. Drawing man away from his goal, her sexuality intervenes destructively in his life. Marked as evil because of her open sexuality, such a woman must be destroyed. While in the victim pattern the heroine takes the suffering upon herself and usually dies (through sickness or poverty), and while in the fetishism pattern the woman is brought under control diegetically (see definition 14 below), usually through marriage, here through reunion, the femme fatale must be murdered. The gun or knife stands in for the phallus which must dominate her by eliminating her.

The noir film showed a greater openness about the threat that female sexuality poses since it allowed female sexuality, in all its dangerous difference, to be expressed. Hayworth, in *Shanghai*, resists domination by all the mechanisms that in the previous films worked to suppress female sexuality or to render it harmless. Female sexuality is here fully expressed, but the sexual woman's duplicity and betrayal mark her as evil, granting man the moral right to destroy her, even if such destruction means depriving himself of a much needed pleasure.

The contemporary film, of course, has gone even further than the noir film in the open representation of female sexuality. The causes for this are well known: the various 1960s movements produced radical cultural changes resulting in a loosening of rigid, puritanical codes, and the women's movement encouraged women to take possession of their own sexuality, gay or straight. The open display of female sexuality has been threatening to patriarchy and has forced a greater degree of directness about the underlying causes for relegating women to absence, silence, and marginality. The mechanisms that worked in earlier decades (i.e. victimizing, fetishizing, self-righteous murdering) to obscure patriarchal fears no longer worked in the post-1960s era: the sexual woman could no longer be designated "evil," since women had won their right to be "good" *and* sexual, and the need to use the phallus as the prime weapon for dominating women, no matter whom they are or whether or not they have done anything wrong, could no longer be hidden.

As Molly Haskell has noted, this resulted in an unprecedented number of films in the early 1970s showing women being raped.[10] The larger patriarchal hostility is now expressed in the notion that all women are yearning for sex all the time. The repulsion in this notion (for men) comes from being forced to recognize the vagina, and thus sexual difference. Man's reaction is to want to "give it to her," as painfully as possible and by force, in order first to punish her for this (imagined) desire; second to assert his control over her sexuality; and finally to prove his "manhood" by his ability to dominate with the phallus.

The discussion of *Looking for Mr Goodbar* (1977) will show first that, while the femme fatale used her sexuality to manipulate the man for her own (corrupt) ends, the contemporary sexually-liberated woman is looking to *satisfy herself*, thereby forcing man to confront his fears of female sexuality directly; and second that, while the femme fatale in noir films had to be killed for eliciting desire in the male (for fear of his succumbing to her desirability), the new sexual woman has to be dominated by the phallus as a way of man asserting control over the newly found sexual expressiveness.

But, complicating things even more, I will show that, despite the temptation to read *Mr Goodbar* as about a "liberated" woman (Teresa does, after all, have possibilities not available to earlier heroines), it has an underlying, tradition-ally psychoanalytic discourse that in fact "explains" all Teresa's actions as really motivated by the need for love and approval from her father. In other words, her supposed "liberation," turns out to be no more than "resistance" (once again) to her rightful positioning as subject to the Law of the Father. Her rape and death, then, are punishment for refusing to submit to the codes that define her place and limit her possibilities to what patriarchy demands. Like Marguerite, Helen, and Elsa before her (who all in their different ways dared to transgress the defining patriarchal codes), Teresa must be silenced for her temerity.

In Hollywood films, then, women are ultimately refused a voice, a discourse, and their desire is subjected to male desire. They live out silently frustrated lives, or, if they resist their placing, sacrifice their lives for their daring. In the second part of the book, I deal with independent women's films, which, in the wake of the women's movement, either attempt to discover for women a voice and a subjectivity, a place from which to speak, or try to define what the "feminine" might be in a system that has done everything to define femininity for women.

Given the enormous output of women's films in the past decade or so, selecting which films to focus on was hard. I again tried to choose films that had not been written about and to discuss works that represented certain broad tendencies or which raised issues that had been influential in independent filmmaking. The first chapter in this section of the book is an overview of the three main groups of independent women's films, distinguished in terms of cinematic strategies and, for the purposes of discussion, labeled: first, the formalist, experimental avant-garde film; second, the realist, political and sociological documentary; and third, the avant-garde theory film. I discuss the difficulty of categorizing the various avant-gardes and explain the roots of women's films in earlier cinematic traditions established by male directors. Precursors Germaine Dulac and Maya Deren, important for women filmmakers because offering rare models, are discussed briefly, and I deal (again briefly) with their influence on some experimental American lesbian filmmakers.

The theoretical position that focuses on the impossibility of knowing what the feminine might be outside of patriarchal constructions has been criticized by American lesbian women, who see such theorizing as perpetuating male domination. They see women-identified women, and female bonding, as ways of circumventing patriarchal domination. Lesbian filmmakers present female images that depart radically from representations in the dominant cinema, offering another kind of alternative, another theoretical position to those found in the independent films discussed.

Before turning to the American scene, I look briefly at films by European women directors who have, for complex reasons, managed to produce narrative feature films while American filmmakers have by and large been limited to the short (mainly documentary) film. The influence of French New Wave directors, particularly Godard and Resnais, on European women filmmakers is well known; less well known may be the fact that a woman filmmaker, Marguerite Duras, was an important part of that movement (both influencing and influenced by it). The chapter on an early Duras film, *Nathalie Granger* (1972), is there partly to trace the influence of the French New Wave on women filmmakers, but also because the film reflects the particular way in which questions about the possibility for a female discourse have been articulated in France and developed into theoretical positions. It is also an important example of an effort to subvert the patriarchal, symbolic construction of mothering (where the child symbolizes the mother's desire for the father); the film represents a mother's attempt to "save" her child from the destructive symbolic realm that the child is apparently rebelling against.

Duras's film is placed in the context of work by women like Julia Kristeva, Luce Irigary, Hélène Cixous, and Monique Wittig, whose theories have influenced feminist film critics in Britain, and, more recently, in America also. In *Nathalie Granger*, Duras demonstrates a politics of resistance to male domination through the power of silence; since the realm of the symbolic is able to express only male concerns and ways of being, women must find ways to communicate outside of, or beyond, the male sphere. The women in *Nathalie Granger* find ways to solve a dilemma with a child through a politics of silence that at once exposes their oppressed situation as women within patriarchy and suggests gaps through which change may begin to take place.

Working in Germany eight years or so later, Margarethe Von Trotta developed an entirely different politics in relation to women, showing their struggle to survive in a male order which seeks to constrain them and which has locked them into destructive and competitive bonding. Von Trotta's relentlessly realist style, which does not, however, draw attention to itself, reveals her concern to find a form that fits her themes rather than an interest in processes of cinema. Here she aligns herself with east European realist directors rather than with a filmmaker like Godard who, in his late phases, has pioneered work questioning cinematic representation.

In America, a more important influence than the New Wave on filmmakers not interested in the documentary was that of the early 1960s avant-garde movements in dance, music, and sculpture. For obvious reasons, these co-op and minimalist trends were little concerned with explicitly feminist issues, and so it was interesting to look at the work of Yvonne Rainer, who emerged out of this art context.

I decided to concentrate on two early works, *Lives of Performers* and *Film about A Woman Who* . . . (1972–4), since they were made before any real feminist film community existed within the New York art world and yet were taken up by feminist film theorists because they represented the kind of cinema theorists had been envisaging. The differences between Rainer and the feminist theorists (revealed in a *Camera Obscura* interview[11]) is illuminating and raises many crucial issues to do with classical versus avant-garde cinema, with narrative, representation, and the cinematic apparatus. I argue that Rainer's film is less an anti-illusionist than an antinarrative one, for she employs a whole range of distancing devices for the deliberate end of generalizing about the female experience and leaving the film open to the spectator's speculations. We have to work to construct the film for ourselves, and in so doing we learn a lot about how relationships position women in certain ways and about the pain that women endure.

Having looked briefly at some developments in France and America, I move in the next chapter to an extended overview of the debate about the realist women's documentary which originated in Britain in the early 1970s. I survey the theories underlying the critique of realism and discuss realist cinematic strategies with a view to evaluating their effectiveness; I then go on to analyze the strategies in (what I call) the avant-garde theory film, which emerged in direct response to the critique of the realist documentary.

Influenced by French and other European theories, it was the British feminist film critics and filmmakers who first argued strongly for a feminist cinema as a counter-cinema. The first three avant-garde theory films discussed here, *Sigmund Freud's Dora* (1979), *Thriller* (1979), and *Amy!* (1980), as well as those discussed in the following chapter, represent a reaction to the marginality assigned women by the symbolic functioning of patriarchy, particularly as this is evident in the Hollywood film. The filmmakers explore the problem of defining the feminine in a situation where women have no voice, no discourse, no place from which to speak, and they examine the mechanisms through which women are relegated to absence, silence, and marginality in culture, as well as in classic texts and dominant discourses. Sally Potter's *Thriller* looks back to Cukor's *Camille* in its deconstruction from a feminist point of view of a classic text very similar to one that Cukor based his film on. *Sigmund Freud's Dora* takes on the discourses of history, cinema, and psychoanalysis in order to show how ideologically complicit female representations are, and how the discourse of psychoanalysis can be used to keep women subject to the Law of the Father.

Chapter 12 offers a case study on films dealing with mothers and daughters through an analysis of Mulvey and Wollen's *Riddles of the Sphinx* (1976) and Michelle Citron's *Daughter-Rite* (1978). As well as being an avant-garde theory film, Laura Mulvey and Peter Wollen's film looks back to Sternberg's *Blonde Venus* in its attempt to grapple with the reasons for the repression of mothering that I examine in that film. Crucial here is the fact that Mulvey/Wollen situate the film in the mother's consciousness and language, looking from her position. Narratively, Mulvey/Wollen's film was new in moving away from the pragmatic/realist level, on which Motherhood had been treated earlier, to a theoretical analysis that combined Lacanian psychoanalysis with Marxist questions. Michelle Citron's film was unique first in confronting the problem of the daughter's relationship to the mother, second in dealing with both conscious and unconscious fears and fantasies about the mother, and finally in its attempt to bridge realist and avant-garde cinematic strategies that had, by 1980, become polarized.

It seemed important to include at least one Third World film to show what women are doing in a non-capitalist society: again the choice was difficult, but I finally opted for Sara Gomez's *One Way or Another* (1974). The contrast between female representations as they emerge within a capitalist, patriarchal system and those that arise within a socialist patriarchal system seemed important for a consideration of the next step to be taken in women's thinking about their own future and that of a feminist cinema.

The book ends with two short chapters. The first deals with problems of production, exhibition, and distribution of independent women's films. I focus here particularly on the contradiction inherent in the very notion of an "alternate" cinematic practice and raise questions that must be answered if we are to move out of the impasse that both feminist filmmakers and feminist critics have now reached. I suggest that we need to combine debate about the most "correct" cinematic strategy (theoretically) with consideration of the practical problems of how individual films are received (read) and of the contexts of production and reception as these affect what films can be made and how films are read.

The final chapter, a conclusion, looks at future directions in relation to the possibilities for challenging dominant patriarchal discourses. I suggest that the figure of the Mother offers a possible way to break through patriarchal discourses since, as critics have noted, she has not been totally appropriated by dominant culture. But this is clearly a problematic area in which much work remains to be done.

Part II

For the benefit of readers new to current film theory, I have listed below definitions of terms, concepts, and theoretical models that are used frequently throughout this book and are central to the theoretical arguments being developed. Readers already familiar with current theory should move on to chapter 1.

1   THE CLASSICAL (DOMINANT, HOLLYWOOD) CINEMA

A feature-length narrative sound film made and distributed by the Hollywood studio system. There is ambiguity about the precise dates for the classic period (people agree on roughly 1930–60). What is important is the concept of a classical model with fixed conventions of film practice that are repeated from product to product and that the audience comes to rely on and to expect.

Central to this classical cinema are:

(a) genres (e.g. the gangster genre, the western genre, the adventure film, the woman's film),
(b) stars,
(c) producers, and
(d) directors.

(a), (b), and (c) can be distinguished from (d) by the fact that they have to do with the *selling* of films. The public come to demand certain stars and desire certain genres (the demand for different genres varies in different periods). Producers try to satisfy their public and develop marketing strategies to this end.

2 DIRECTORS/AUTHORSHIP

(a) Directors are one variable element in the total Hollywood institution; they are responsible for some of the *contradictions* in the system, since their relationship is not *directly* tied to the commercialism of the whole. However, they are by and large implicated in the system (financially and ideologically), and their ideology reflects this (the ideology works *through* them).

(b) The concept of authorship implies a certain autonomy to specific directors; it arose in the late 1950s, originating in France (hence often the French word *auteur* is used); a director's work was now analyzed for its common elements, said to reflect the individual's special "world view." Many critics are now questioning the validity of this way of discussing directors because of the special way that cinema works, as an apparatus.

3 THE CINEMATIC APPARATUS

This concept refers to the cinema in its many dimensions – economic, technical, psychological, and ideological. Embedded in a particular social and insti-tutional context, the cinema works to suppress discourse, to permit only certain "speakers," only a certain "speech." What critics call the *énonciation* of the cinema (its processes of saying) cannot be distinguished from the *énoncé* (what is said). Jean-Louis Baudry has argued that the meaning (ideology) that is produced by the cinematic mechanism (projection) depends not only on the content of the images but also on the "material procedures by which an image of continuity, dependent on the persistence of vision, is restored from discontinuous elements" (Jean-Louis Baudry (1974–5) "Ideological effects of the basic cinematographic apparatus," *Film Quarterly*, Vol. 38, No. 2, p. 42). Other critics have focused on the position of the spectator as that of creating the film as s/he watches it. The meaning established in the interaction between viewer and screen image involves a particular type of pleasure that arises from the cinema's dependence on the psychoanalytic mechanisms of fetishism and voyeurism (see definitions 7, 8 below).

4 IDEOLOGY

While for Marx ideology referred to the ideological components of all bourgeois institutions and modes of production, recent film critics have rather followed Althusser for whom ideology is a series of representations and images, reflecting the conceptions of "reality" that any society assumes. Ideology thus no longer refers to beliefs people consciously hold but to the myths that a society lives by, as if these myths referred to some natural, unproblematic "reality," (For an interesting discussion of ideology, see Bill Nichols (1981) *Ideology and the Image*, Bloomington, Ind., Indiana University Press, pp. 1–4.)

5 REPRESENTATION

This concept indicates the "constructed" nature of the image (see definition 10 below), which Hollywood mechanisms strive to conceal. The dominant Hollywood style, realism (an apparent imitation of the social world we live in), hides the fact that a film is constructed, and perpetuates the illusion that spectators are being shown what is "natural." The half-aware "forgetting" that the spectator engages in allows the pleasurable mechanisms of voyeurism and fetishism to flow freely.

6 FREUD AND THE OEDIPAL CRISIS

Before going on to discuss the mechanisms underlying pleasure in the cinema, it is necessary to outline Freud's notion of the Oedipus complex, which provided the cornerstone for his (at the time) revolutionary psychoanalytic theory and on which the other phenomena relevant to film theory depend.

Freud took the name Oedipus from classical mythology, particularly the story, dramatized by Sophocles, of how Oedipus unwittingly killed his father and married his mother, a deed for which he was severely punished. The myth represents for Freud the inevitable fantasy of the growing child: first bound in illusory unity with his mother, whom he does not recognize as Other, separate, or different, the child exists blissfully in a pre-Oedipal phase; as he moves into the phallic phase, the child becomes aware of his father. At the height of his positive Oedipal phase, he loves his mother and hates his father who takes mother for himself. Successful resolution of this Oedipal phase takes place on the boy's discovery that his mother lacks the penis, i.e. is castrated (he can only imagine that all people must originally have had penises). This bitter discovery propels him away from his mother, since he fears that by identifying with the one who lacks the penis, he will endanger his own organ. He now identifies with his father, whom he longs to be like, and he looks forward to "finding someone like his mother" to marry.

Freud did not pay much attention to the girl's Oedipal crisis, but post-Freudians have generally agreed that it is a much more complicated one. They argue that the girl turns away from her mother through penis envy and the belief that her mother is responsible for her lack of a penis. The girl tries to get from the father what the mother could not provide, now equating "child" with "penis", and looking to bear the child with a man like her father. The best neo-Freudian analysis of the girl's Oedipal complex can be found in Nancy

Chodorow's *The Reproduction of Mothering: Psychoanalysis and the Sociology of Gender* (1978, Berkeley, Calif., University of California Press). Chodorow examines the much more difficult task for the girl in having to turn away completely from her first love-object, her mother, and place erotic interest in her father; she argues that since they cannot "replace" their mothers, as boys do with their wives, girls remain attached pre-oedipally to their mothers throughout adulthood.

7 FETISHISM

Another Freudian term, fetishism refers to the perversion whereby men strive to discover the penis in the woman in order to grant themselves erotic satisfaction (e.g. long hair, a shoe, or earrings stand in for the penis). Fear of castration underlies fetishism in that sexual excitement is impossible with a creature who lacks the penis, or something that represents it. In the cinema, the whole female body may be "fetishized" in order to counteract the fear of sexual difference, i.e. of castration.

8 VOYEURISM AND EXHIBITIONISM

Pleasure in the cinema is created through the inherently voyeuristic mechanism that comes into play here more strongly than in the other arts. A Freudian psychoanalytic term, voyeurism refers to the erotic gratification of watching someone without being seen oneself, i.e. the activity of the Peeping Tom. Exhibitionism refers in psychoanalysis to the erotic gratification derived from showing one's body – or part of it – to another person, as in the pleasure of being seen, or seeing oneself on the screen. Voyeurism is an active perversion, practiced primarily by men with the female body as the object of the gaze, while exhibitionism is its passive counterpart.

9 THE GAZE: THE THREE "LOOKS" IN THE CINEMA

(a) Scopophilia, or sexual pleasure in looking, is activated by the very situation of cinema: the darkened room, the way the gaze of the spectator is controlled by the aperture of first, the camera and second, the projector, the fact that the spectator is watching moving images rather than either static ones (painting) or live actors (theatre), all help to make the cinematic experience closer to the dream state than is possible in the other arts. Psychoanalytic critics argue that a kind of regression to the state of early childhood happens in the cinema.

(b) The act of gazing is played upon in dominant cinema, creating the pleasure that, in this argument, has ultimately erotic origins. The gaze is built upon culturally defined notions of sexual difference. There are three looks:

(i)   within the film text itself, men gaze at women, who become objects of the gaze;
(ii) the spectator, in turn, is made to identify with this male gaze, and to objectify the women on the screen; and
(iii) the camera's original "gaze" comes into play in the very act of filming.

10 THE IMAGE

The image can be discussed, broadly, in two main ways:
(a) Sociological critics discuss the image in terms of the types of role characters play (e.g. the image of the housewife, the macho male (hero), the homosexual, the villain (anti-hero), the prostitute, etc.). They compare the representation of these roles in film to people in these roles in society. The problem here is that such analysis ignores the *mediation* of film as an art form (i.e. that these images are constructed).
(b) A cinematic analysis keeps in mind the construction and talks about distance of subject from camera, point of view, editing, place, function of a character in a narrative, etc.

11 SOCIOLOGY AND SEMIOLOGY

These two ways of thinking about the image are reflected in two main approaches in feminist criticism: first, the *sociological* method refers to a study of people in society; film critics here use the terminology of sex roles, e.g. Virgin, Vamp; second, the *semiological* method refers to a science of signs; critics here use a terminology from linguistics, discussing film as a signifying system, in which woman functions as "sign."

The sociological approach was the one the early feminist film critics used, and it continues to be an important method. Concepts such as the distinction made between the domestic (private) sphere of the home, where the wife and/or mother is positioned, and the work (public) sphere, where the husband belongs, are useful but limited. They do not tell us *how* meaning is produced in film, and tend to blur distinctions between the realm of lived experience (the social formation) and that of representation (images on film).

Semiology, applied to film, attempts to explain how film communicates, how its meaning is produced in a manner analogous to the way a sentence in written language communicates meaning. Ferdinand de Saussure is credited with introducing semiology or the science of signs. The meaning of language, he said, is found not in the words or thoughts of an individual speaker, but in the relation of elements within the sign system itself. He used the word *langue* to refer to the whole complex language system with its structure of relationships, and *parole* to refer to the level of speech, where the abstract rules of the larger system are put into operation.

The basic level for Saussure is that of sounds made by the human voice (i.e. the phonetic level). Here items gain their significance only from their relationship to other items in the system, which are signalled by *difference*. The level of recognized difference is called the phonemic level. As Terence Hawkes puts it: "This is to say that the meaning of each word resides in a structural sense in the difference between its own sounds and those of other words. . . . The English language has registered the contrast or sense of 'opposition' between the sound of /t/ in *tin* and the sound of /k/ in *kin* as significant, that is, as capable of generating meaning" (*Structuralism and Semiotics* (1977) London, Methuen, pp. 22–3).

Saussure called the two aspects of the linguistic sign *concept* and *sound-image*, the *signified* and the *signifier*. The signifiers in the language system are phonemes which can be made up into words to represent certain objects in the world, i.e. the signified on the level of *denotation* (see definition 12 below). Thus, the sounds r-o-s-e make up the word *rose*, which is the *sign* for a flower that looks a certain way. But there is no inherent relationship between this sign and the flower. It is only an *arbitrary* connection and thus can never be questioned in terms of its fitness or suitability to anything in the sensual world. Furthermore, all that we can think and know is conditioned by the language system we must use; ideas and concepts do not exist outside of the system, but are bounded by it, shaped by what the sign system permits. Critics thus do not simply *use* language (discourse) but are positioned *in* discourse (see definition 14 below).

Important here is the decentering of a hitherto unquestioned, autonomous and individualistic Cartesian "I." "I" is now simply the subject in a subject-predicate linguistic system. Far from being the central actor, man is controlled by the laws that govern the language system in which he lives.

Such a position clearly undermines the whole tradition of thought introduced by Descartes; this tradition was first questioned in the international Romantic and Post-Romantic movements by the thinkers who most influenced the early twentieth century: Rousseau, Darwin, Nietzsche, Marx, and Freud. These thinkers represent a variety of discourses which all, in one way or another, began to question the unproblematic self; but the full force of their work was not generally felt in the culture until the impact of the First World War made many of their theories suddenly relevant.

Semiology needs to be placed in the line of reaction against nineteenth-century humanist habits of thought which remained despite the inroads made by the thinkers named above. The earlier thinkers did not question their own ability (methodologically) to analyze their subject matter "objectively," and it is this examination of the very tools of analysis (*signification*) that characterizes semiology and puts the nail in the coffin of the unified self.

Relevance of semiology to the analysis of women in film
Christian Metz extended Saussure's theories about language to film and wrote a semiotics of the cinema (Metz (1974) *Film Language*, trans. Michael Taylor, New York, Oxford University Press). For Metz, cinematic discourse, like that of language, entails a source of articulation ("I"), a speaker, and a person being addressed (spoken to), a "You." But, as in the language system, this "I" and this "You" are structured in relation to one another in filmic discourse: "I" is the subject (like the linguistic subject in a sentence), and "You" is the object (again, like the object position in the sentence).

The rules and conventions that structure a particular discourse are called *codes*; Roland Barthes established a series of codes which literature uses (Barthes (1975) *S/Z*, trans. Richard Miller, London, Cape), and film critics began to apply them in film analysis. They took the concept of "code" to analyze how a film works (see definition 15 below). Barthes is further important for film theory because he revealed that we live in a world comprised of a whole series of signifying systems of which language, while dominant, is only one. Sign systems range from clothing, eating habits, sexual habits, to the construction of photographs, advertisements, film images. For Barthes, film is a sign system that functions largely on the level of *myth* – it has lost its connection to any tangible reference, any object in the real world. (Barthes (1975) *Mythologies*, trans. Annette Lavers, New York, Hill & Wang). A sign (for example, the sign "rose") can be emptied of its denotative meaning and a new connotative meaning piled onto it. Thus "rose" becomes a signifier for "passion" (a signified), making a totally new sign, a sign on the second level.

Now, on this secondary level of significance it is *culture* that provides the new meanings, that drains original signs of their denotation and lifts them into a connotation that is culture-specific, fitting a certain *ideology*, a certain set of values, beliefs, ways of seeing.

Thus, Barthes (in *Mythologies*, p. 116) gives the example of a photograph in *Paris Match* of a black soldier saluting the French flag. On the denotative level, that is the meaning of the photo: the soldier is saluting the flag; but on the secondary level of signification, that of culture, ideology, connotation, we know that the meaning has to do with celebrating French colonialism: we are to praise the fact that the colonized people love their governors and willingly fight for their cause.

Or take the example that Godard uses in the film *Letter to Jane* of the *Life* front-page photograph of Jane Fonda with the Vietnamese. This photograph too is full of connotation (i.e. ideology); it is emptied of its denotative sign, a white woman with some Asian soldiers in a jungle setting, and built up into the second level that Barthes calls "myth". Fonda, with connotations of both filmstar and radical activist, is in the front of the photograph – large, important, given status – while in the rear are the anonymous Vietnamese – small, bunched together, with connotations of inscrutability, foreignness, the

Other. The photograph thus praises the liberality of Jane Fonda, with her position in American culture as sex object and star, in going to visit the "enemy," who is racially stereotyped.

Now, in cinema woman is likewise, as her actual self, a real woman, lifted onto the second level of connotation, myth; she is presented as what she represents for man, not in terms of what she *actually* signifies. Her *discourse* (her meanings, as she might produce them) is suppressed in favor of a discourse structured by patriarchy in which her real signification has been replaced by connotations that serve patriarchy's needs. For example, the sentence "A woman is undressing," or the image of a woman undressing, cannot remain at the denotative level of factual information, but immediately is raised to the level of connotations – her sexuality, her desirability, her nakedness; she is immediately objectified in such a discourse, placed in terms of how she can be *used* for male gratification. That is how our culture *reads* such sentences and images, although these meanings are presented as *natural*, as denotative, because the layering of cultural connotation is masked, hidden. Our task, then, in looking at Hollywood films is to unmask the images, the *sign* of woman, to see how the meanings that underlie the codes function.

(See the bibliography for a list of works about structuralism, psychoanalysis, and semiology relevant to film studies.)

12 DENOTATION AND CONNOTATION

On the level of the sign (image, word), ideology works by a sliding between connotative and denotative usages of words or images. The strict, literal definition of an expression (word, image, sign) is not always easy to distinguish from its connotative uses (i.e. the suggestive and associative levels). What passes itself off as denotative "natural" meanings may already carry a number of implicit connotations. (See the discussion of semiology in definition 11 above.)

13 ICONOGRAPHY

Another way in which ideology is communicated in film is through the specific properties of the shot, i.e. its iconography, which include mise-en-scène, composition, dress, gesture, facial expression, focus, and lighting.

14 NARRATIVE: DIEGESIS, AND DISCOURSE

The film narrative combines diegesis and discourse and represents a chain of events occurring in time, in a cause–effect relationship. The diegesis is the denotative material of film narrative (the story, i.e. actions, happenings, characters, items of setting), while the discourse refers to the means of expression (i.e. the use of language and other sign systems in a spatio-temporal order) rather than to content. Discourse also contains, as its points of reference, the conditions of expression, a source of articulation ("I") and an addressee ("You").

15 CODE

The discourse is structured through a set of rules or conventions that semioticians call the code. The cinema employs a complex system of codes pertaining to its heterogeneous levels of expression: codes of representation and editing, acting and narrative, sound, music, and speech. Some of these codes are specific to the cinema (e.g. editing), while some are shared with other forms of art and communication.

16 LACAN'S IMAGINARY AND SYMBOLIC

Some aspects of Lacan have been useful in film theory because he combined Freudian psychoanalysis with semiology, thus offering a means for linking semiotic and psychoanalytic readings of films. Lacan's insight was to rephrase Freudian theory by using a linguistic model for the movement between different stages, as against the non-linguistic, essentially biological and developmental Freudian model. Lacan's concept of the imaginary corresponds (roughly) to Freud's pre-Oedipal phase, although the child is already a signifier, already inserted in a linguistic system. But the world of the imaginary is nevertheless *for the child* a prelinguistic moment, a moment of illusory unity with the Mother, whom he does not know as Other. The Lacanian child is forced to move on from the world of the imaginary, not because of the literal threat of castration but because he acquires language, which is based on the concept of "lack". He enters the world of the symbolic governed by the Law of the Father and revolving around the phallus as signifier. Here, in language, he discovers that he is an object in a realm of signifiers that circulate around the Father (= phallus). He learns discourse and the different "I" and "You" positions. The illusory unity with the Mother is broken partly by the mirror phase, with the child's recognition of the Mother as a separate image/entity, and of himself as an image (ego-ideal), creating the structure of the divided subject; and partly by introduction of the Father as a linguistic Third Term, breaking the mother-child dyad. Although the child now lives in the symbolic, he participates in the world of the imaginary; it is this world that the experience of the cinema partly recreates, particularly in the sense of providing the more perfect selves (ego-ideals) evoked by the mirror phase and facilitating a regression to that phase. (I have deliberately used "he" here since both Freud and Lacan assume a male subject. Part of my task is to make sense of the systems for the female. For more complete summary, see Bill Nichols, op. cit., pp. 30–4.)

17 CINEMATIC VERSUS THE EXTRA-CINEMATIC

Keeping this distinction clearly in mind prevents us from falling into the trap of sociological critics, and linking screen image and lived experience too simplistically.

(a) The *cinematic* refers to all that goes on on the screen and to what happens between screen image and spectator (what results from the cinematic apparatus).

(b) The *extra-cinematic* refers to discussion about, for example:

(i)   the lives of the director, stars, producers, etc.,
(ii) the production of the film in Hollywood, as an institution,
(iii) the politics of the period when a film was made, and
(iv) the cultural assumptions at the time a film was made.

PART I

The classical and contemporary Hollywood cinema

1 | Is the gaze male?

Since the beginning of the recent women's movement, American feminists have been exploring the representation of female sexuality in the arts – in literature, painting, film, and television.[1] As we struggle towards meaningful theory, it is important to note that feminist criticism, as a new way of reading texts, emerged from the daily, ongoing concerns of women re-evaluating the culture in which they had been socialized and educated. In this sense, feminist criticism differs in basic ways from earlier critical movements which evolved out of reaction to dominant theoretical positions (i.e. out of a reaction which took place on an intellectual level). Feminism is unusual in its combination of the theoretical and (loosely speaking) the ideological (Marxist literary theory alone shares a similar dual focus, but from very different premises).

The first wave of feminist critics adopted a broadly sociological approach, looking at sex roles women occupied in various imaginative works, from high art to mass entertainment. They assessed roles as "positive" or "negative" according to some externally constructed criteria describing the fully autonomous, independent woman. While this work was important in initiating feminist criticism (Kate Millett's *Sexual Politics* was a ground-breaking text), feminist film critics, influenced by developments taking place in film theory at the start of the 1970s, were the first to point out its limitations. First, influenced by semiology, feminist theorists stressed the crucial role played by the artistic form as the medium for expression; second, influenced by psychoanalysis, they argued that Oedipal processes were central to the production of art works. That is, they gave increasing attention to *how meaning is produced* in films, rather than to the "content," which had preoccupied sociological critics; and they stressed the links between the processes of psychoanalysis and cinema.

Before summarizing in more detail the French theorists whose influence shaped currents in feminist film theory, let me deal briefly with the reasons for using psychoanalytic methodology in chapters 2 to 5 of this book, those devoted to the Hollywood film. Why, given many feminists' hostile rejection of Freudian and Lacanian theory, do I see psychoanalysis as a useful tool?

First, let me make clear that I do not see psychoanalysis as necessarily uncovering essential "truths" about the human psyche which exist across historical periods and different cultures. Making trans-historical generalizations about human psychic processes is difficult since the means for verifying those generalizations barely exist. Nevertheless, the history of literature in western civilization does show a surprising recurrence of Oedipal themes. We could say that Oedipal themes occur at those historical moments when the human family is structured in specific ways that elicit Oedipal traumas; for my purposes here, since I am concerned with a recent art form, film, and the recent theory of Oedipal problems (dating back to Freud), I am prepared to make claims for the relevance of psychoanalysis only to the state of industrial social organization characteristic of the twentieth century.[2]

One could argue that the psychic patterns created by capitalist social and interpersonal structures (especially the late-nineteenth-century forms that carried over into our century) required at once a machine (the cinema) for their unconscious release and an analytic tool (psychoanalysis) for understanding, and adjusting, disturbances caused by the structures that confine people. To this extent, both mechanisms (film and psychoanalysis) support the status quo; but, rather than being necessarily eternal and unchanging in the forms in which we have them, they are inserted in history, linked, that is, to the particular moment of bourgeois capitalism that gave both their birth.

If this is so, it is extremely important for women to use psychoanalysis as a tool, since it will unlock the secrets of our socialization within (capitalist) patriarchy. If we agree that the commercial film (and particularly the genre of melodrama that this book focuses on) took the form it did in some way to satisfy desires and needs created by nineteenth-century familial organization (an organization that produces Oedipal traumas), then psychoanalysis becomes a crucial tool for explaining the needs, desires, and male–female positionings that are reflected in film. The signs in the Hollywood film convey the patriarchal ideology that underlies our social structures and that constructs women in very specific ways – ways that reflect patriarchal needs, the patriarchal unconscious.

Psychoanalytic discourse may indeed have oppressed women, in the sense of bringing us to accept a positioning that is inherently antithetical to being a subject and to autonomy; but if that is the case, we need to know exactly *how* psychoanalysis has functioned to repress what we could potentially become; for this, we must master the terms of its discourse and ask a number of questions. First, is the gaze *necessarily* male (i.e. for reasons inherent in the structure of language, the unconscious, symbolic systems, and thus all social structures)? Could we structure things so that women own the gaze? If this were possible, would women want to own the gaze? Finally, in either case, what does it mean to be a female spectator? Only through asking such questions within the psychoanalytic framework can we begin to find the gaps and fissures through which we can insert woman in a historical discourse that has hitherto been male-dominated and has excluded women. In this way, we may begin to change ourselves as a first step toward changing society.

Using psychoanalysis to deconstruct Hollywood films enables us to see clearly the patriarchal myths through which we have been positioned as Other (enigma, mystery), and as eternal and unchanging. We can also see how the family melodrama, as a genre geared specifically to women, functions both to expose the constraints and limitations that the capitalist nuclear family imposes on women and, at the same time, to "educate" women to accept those constraints as "natural," inevitable – as "given." For part of what defines melodrama as a form is its concern explicitly with Oedipal issues – illicit love relationships (overtly or incipiently incestuous), mother–child relationships, husband–wife relationships, father–son relationships: these are the staple fare of melodrama as surely as they are largely excluded from the dominant Hollywood genres, the western and the gangster film, that melodrama compensates for.

Using the framework developed by Peter Brooks, we might say that the western and gangster genres aim to duplicate the functions that tragedy once fulfilled, in the sense of placing man within the larger cosmic scene. But Brooks points out that we are now in a period when "mythmaking [can] only be personal and individual" since we lack "a clear transcendent value to be reconciled to;" so that even these genres, broadly speaking, fall into melodrama. All Hollywood films, taking this large view, require what Brooks considers essential to melodrama, namely "a social order to be purged, a set of ethical imperatives to be made clear." [3]

It is important that women are excluded from the central role in the main, highly respected Hollywood genres; women, and female issues, are only central in the family melodrama (which we can see as an offshoot of other melodramatic forms). Here Brooks's definition of the way characters in melodrama "assume primary psychic roles, Father, Mother, Child, and express basic psychic conditions" [4] seems particularly relevant, as is also his explicit linking of psychoanalysis and melodrama at the end of the book. Psychoanalytic processes themselves, he notes, reveal the "melodrama aesthetic" (we will see in chapter 11 that the directors of a recent feminist film, *Sigmund Freud's Dora*, also view psychoanalysis as melodrama); but important for our purposes here is his comment that the melodramatic form deals with "the processes of repression and the status of repressed content." Brooks concludes that "the structure of ego, superego and id suggests the subjacent manichaeism of melodramatic persons." [5]

Laura Mulvey (the British filmmaker and critic whose theories are central to new developments) also views melodrama as concerned with Oedipal issues, but she sees it primarily as a female form, acting as a corrective to the main genres that celebrate male action. The family melodrama is important, she says, in "probing pent-up emotion, bitterness and disillusion well known to women." For Mulvey, melodrama serves a useful function for women who lack any coherent culture of oppression. "The simple fact of recognition has aesthetic importance," she notes; "there is a dizzy satisfaction in witnessing the way that sexual difference under patriarchy is fraught, explosive and erupts dramatically into violence within its own private stomping ground, the family."[6] But Mulvey concludes that if melodrama is important in bringing ideological contradictions to the surface, and in being made for a female audience, events are never reconciled at the end in ways beneficial to women.

So why is it that women are drawn to melodrama? Why do we find our objectification and surrender pleasurable? This is precisely an issue that psychoanalysis can help to explain: for such pleasure is not surprising if we consider the shape of the girl's Oedipal crisis. Following Lacan for a moment (see definition 16 on p. 19), we see that the girl is forced to turn away from the illusory unity with the Mother in the prelinguistic realm and has to enter the symbolic world which involves subject and object. Assigned the place of object (lack), she is the recipient of male desire, passively appearing rather than acting. Her sexual pleasure in this position can thus be constructed only around her own objectification. Furthermore, given the male structuring around sadism, the girl may adopt a corresponding masochism.[7]

In practice, this masochism is rarely reflected in more than a tendency for women to be passive in sexual relations; but in the realm of myth, masochism is often prominent. We could say that in locating herself in fantasy in the erotic, the woman places herself as either passive recipient of male desire or, at one remove, as *watching* a woman who is passive recipient of male desires and sexual actions. Although the evidence we have to go on is slim, it does seem that women's sexual fantasies would confirm the predominance of these positionings. (We will look shortly at some corresponding male fantasies.)

Nancy Friday's volumes provide discourses on the level of dream and, however questionable as "scientific" evidence, show narratives in which the woman speaker largely arranges events for her sexual pleasure so that things are done to her, or in which she is the object of men's lascivious gaze.[8] Often, there is pleasure in anonymity, or in a strange man approaching her when she is with her husband. Rarely does the dreamer initiate the sexual activity, and the man's large erect penis usually is central in the fantasy. Nearly all the fantasies have the dominance-submission pattern, with the woman in the latter place.

It is significant that in the lesbian fantasies that Friday has collected, women occupy *both* positions, the dreamer excited either by dominating another woman, forcing her to have sex, or enjoying being so dominated. These fantasies suggest either that the female positioning is not as monolithic as critics often imply or that women occupy the "male" position when they become dominant.[9] Whichever the case may be (and I will say more about this in a moment), the prevalence of the dominance–submission pattern as a sexual turn-on is clear. At a discussion about pornography organized by Julia LeSage at the Conference on Feminist Film Criticism (Northwestern University, 1980), both gay and straight women admitted their pleasure (in both fantasy and actuality) in being "forced" or "forcing" someone else. Some women claimed that this was a result of growing up in Victorian-style households where all sexuality was repressed, but others denied that it had anything to do with patriarchy. Women wanted, rightly, to accept themselves sexually, whatever the turn-on mechanism.[10] But simply to celebrate whatever gives us sexual pleasure seems to me both too easy and too problematic: we need to analyze *how it is* that certain things turn us on, how sexuality has been constructed in patriarchy to produce pleasure in the dominance–submission forms, before we *advocate* these modes.[11]

It was predictable that many of the male fantasies in Friday's book *Men in Love* show the speaker constructing events so that he is in control: again, the "I" of identity remains central, as it is not in the female narrations. Many male fantasies focus on the man's excitement in arranging for his woman to expose herself (or even give herself) to other men, while he watches.[12]

The difference between this male voyeurism and the female form is striking. For the woman does not own the desire, even when she watches; her watching is to place responsibility for sexuality at yet one more remove, *to distance herself from sex*. The man, on the other hand, *owns the desire and the woman*, and gets pleasure from exchanging the woman, as in Lévi-Strauss's kinship system.[13]

Yet, some of the fantasies in Friday's book show men's wish to be taken over by an aggressive woman, who would force them to become helpless, like the little boy in his mother's hands. A tour of Times Square in 1980 (the organization Women Against Pornography runs them regularly) corroborated this. After a slide show that focused totally on male sadism and violent sexual exploitation of women, we were taken to sex shops that by no means stressed male domination. We saw literature and films expressing as many fantasies of male as of female submission. The situations were the predictable ones: young boys (but sometimes men) seduced by women in a form of authority – governesses, nursemaids, nurses, schoolteachers, stepmothers, etc. (Of course, it is significant that the corresponding dominance–submission fantasies of women have men in authority positions that carry much more status – professors, doctors, policemen, executives: these men seduce the innocent girls or young wives who cross their paths.)

Two interesting things emerge here. One is that dominance–submission patterns are apparently a crucial part of both male and female sexuality as constructed in western civilization. The other is that men have a far wider range of positions available: more readily both dominant and submissive, they vacillate between supreme control and supreme abandonment. Women, meanwhile, are more consistently submissive, but not excessively abandoned. In their own fantasies, women do not position themselves as exchanging men, although a *man* might find being exchanged an exciting fantasy.[14]

The passivity revealed in women's sexual fantasies is reinforced by the way women are positioned in film. In an interesting paper on "The 'woman's film': possession and address," Mary Ann Doane has shown that in the one film genre (i.e. melodrama) that, as we have seen, constructs a female spectator, the spectator is made to participate in what is essentially a masochistic fantasy. Doane notes that in the major classical genres, the female body *is* sexuality, providing the erotic object for the male spectator. In the woman's film, the gaze must be de-eroticized (since the spectator is now assumed to be female), but in doing this the films effectively disembody their spectator. The repeated, masochistic scenarios effectively immobilize the female viewer. She is refused pleasure in that imaginary identification which, as Mulvey has shown, repeats for men the experience of the mirror phase. The idealized male screen heroes give back to the male spectator his more perfect mirror self, together with a sense of mastery and control. In contrast, the female is given only powerless, victimized figures who, far from perfect, reinforce the basic sense of worthlessness that already exists.[15]

Later on in her paper, Doane shows that Freud's "A child is being beaten" is important in distinguishing the way a common masochistic fantasy works out for boys and for girls. In the male fantasy, "sexuality remains on the surface" and the man "retains his own role and his own gratification in the context of the scenario. The 'I' of identity remains." But the female fantasy is first desexualized and second, "necessitates the woman's assumption of the position of spectator, outside of the event." In this way, the girl manages, as Freud says, "to escape from the demands of the erotic side of her life altogether."[16]

But the important question remains: when women are in the dominant position, are they in the *masculine* position? Can we envisage a female dominant position that would differ qualitatively from the male form of dominance? Or is there merely the possibility of both sex genders occupying the positions we now know as "masculine" and "feminine?"

The experience of films of the 1970s and 1980s would support the latter possibility, and explain why many feminists have not been excited by the so-called "liberated" woman on the screen, or by the fact that some male stars have recently been made the object of the "female" gaze. Traditionally male stars did not necessarily (or even primarily) derive their "glamor" from their looks or their sexuality but from the power they were able to wield within the filmic world in which they functioned (e.g. John Wayne); these men, as Laura Mulvey has shown, became ego-ideals for the men in the audience, corresponding to the image in the mirror, who was more in control of motor co-ordination than the young child looking in. "The male figure," Mulvey notes, "is free to command the stage . . . of spatial illusion in which he articulates the look and creates the action." [17]

Recent films have begun to change this pattern: stars like John Travolta (*Saturday Night Fever, Urban Cowboy, Moment by Moment*) have been rendered object of woman's gaze and in some of the films (e.g. *Moment by Moment*) placed explicitly as a sexual object to a woman who controlled the film's action. Robert Redford likewise has begun to be used as object of "female" desire (e.g. in *Electric Horseman*). But it is significant that in all these films, when the man steps out of his traditional role as the one who controls the whole action, and when he is set up as sex object, the woman then takes on the "masculine" role as bearer of the gaze and initiator of the action. She nearly always loses her traditionally feminine characteristics in so doing – not those of attractiveness, but rather of kindness, humaneness, motherliness. She is now often cold, driving, ambitious, manipulating, just like the men whose position she has usurped.

Even in a supposedly "feminist" film like *My Brilliant Career*, the same processes are at work. The film is interesting because it foregrounds the independently minded heroine's dilemma in a clearly patriarchal culture: in love with a wealthy neighbor, the heroine makes him the object of her gaze, but the problem is that, as female, her desire has no power. Men's desire naturally carries power with it, so that when the hero finally concedes his love for her, he comes to get her. However, being able to conceive of "love" only as "submission," an end to autonomy and to her life as a creative writer, the heroine now refuses him. The film thus plays with established positions, but is unable to work through them to something else.

What we can conclude from the discussion so far is that our culture is deeply committed to myths of demarcated sex differences, called "masculine" and "feminine," which in turn revolve first on a complex gaze apparatus and second on dominance-submission patterns. This positioning of the two sex genders in representation clearly privileges the male (through the mechanisms of voyeurism and fetishism, which are male operations, and because his desire carries power/action where woman's usually does not). However, as a result of the recent women's movement, women have been permitted in representation to assume (step into) the position defined as "masculine," as long as the man then steps into *her* position, thus keeping the whole structure intact.

It is significant, of course, that while this substitution is made to happen relatively easily in the cinema, in real life any such "swapping" is fraught with immense psychological difficulties that only psychoanalysis can unravel. In any case, such "exchanges" do not do much for either sex, since nothing has essentially changed: the roles remain locked into their static boundaries.

Showing images of mere reversal may in fact provide a safety valve for the social tensions that the women's movement has created by demanding a more dominant role for women.

We have thus arrived at a point where we must question the necessity for the dominance–submission structure. The gaze is not necessarily male (literally), but to own and activate the gaze, given our language and the structure of the unconscious, is to be in the "masculine" position. It is this persistent presentation of the masculine position that feminist film critics have demonstrated in their analysis of Hollywood films. Dominant, Hollywood cinema, they show, is constructed according to the unconscious of patriarchy; film narratives are organized by means of a male-based language and discourse which parallels the language of the unconscious. Women in film thus do not function as signifiers for a signified (a real woman), as sociological critics have assumed, but signifier and signified have been elided into a sign that represents something in the male unconscious.

Two basic Freudian concepts – voyeurism and fetishism – have been used to explain what exactly woman represents and the mechanisms that come into play for the male spectator watching a female screen image. (Or, to put it rather differently, voyeurism and fetishism are mechanisms the dominant cinema uses to *construct* the male spectator in accordance with the needs of his unconscious.) The first, voyeurism, is linked to the scopophilic instinct (i.e. the male pleasure in his own sexual organ transferred to pleasure in watching other people having sex). Critics argue that the cinema relies on this instinct, making the spectator essentially a voyeur. The drive that causes little boys to peek through keyholes of parental bedrooms to learn about their sexual activities (or to get sexual gratification by thinking about these activities) comes into play when the male adult watches films, sitting in a dark room. The original eye of the camera, controlling and limiting what can be seen, is reproduced by the projector aperture which lights up one frame at a time; and both processes (camera and projector) duplicate the eye at the keyhole, whose gaze is confined by the keyhole "frame." The spectator is obviously in the voyeur position when there are sex scenes on the screen, but screen images of women are sexualized no matter what the women are doing literally or what kind of plot may be involved.

According to Laura Mulvey, this eroticization of women on the screen comes about through the way the cinema is structured around three explicitly male looks or gazes: there is the look of the camera in the situation being filmed (called the pro-filmic event); while technically neutral, this look, as we've seen, is inherently voyeuristic and usually "male" in the sense that a man is generally doing the filming; there is the look of the men within the narrative, which is structured so as to make women objects of their gaze; and finally there is the look of the male spectator (discussed above) which imitates (or is necessarily in the same position as) the first two looks.[18]

But if women were simply eroticized and objectified, matters might not be too bad, since objectification, as I have already shown, may be an inherent component of both male and female eroticism as constructed in western culture. But two further elements suggest themselves. To begin with, men do not simply look; their gaze carries with it the power of action and of possession which is lacking in the female gaze. Women receive and return a gaze, but cannot act upon it. Second, the sexualization and objectification of women is not simply for the purposes of eroticism; from a psychoanalytic point of view, it is designed to annihilate the threat that woman (as castrated and possessing a sinister genital organ) poses. In her article "The dread of women" (1932) Karen Horney goes to literature to show that "Men have never tired of fashioning expressions for the violent force by which man feels himself drawn to the woman, and side by side with his longing, the dread that through her he might die and be undone."[19] Horney goes on to conjecture that even man's glorification of women "has its source not only in his cravings for love, but also in his desire to conceal his dread. A similar relief, however, is also sought and found in the disparagement of women that men often display ostentatiously in their attitudes."[20] Horney then explores the basis of the dread of women not only in castration (more related to the father) but in fear of the vagina.

But psychoanalysts agree that, for whatever reason – fear of castration (Freud) or in an attempt to deny the existence of the sinister female genital (Horney), men endeavor to find the penis in women. Feminist film critics have seen this phenomenon (clinically known as fetishism[21]) operating in the cinema; the camera (unconsciously) fetishizes the female form, rendering it phallus-like so as to mitigate woman's threat. Men, that is, turn "the represented figure itself into a fetish so that it becomes reassuring rather than dangerous (hence overvaluation, the cult of the female star)."[22]

The apparently contradictory attitudes of glorification and disparagement pointed out by Horney thus turn out to be a reflection of the same ultimate need to annihilate the dread that woman inspires. In the cinema, the twin mechanisms of fetishism and of voyeurism represent two different ways of handling this dread. As Mulvey points out, fetishism "builds up the physical beauty of the object, turning it into something satisfying in itself," while voyeurism, linked to disparagement, has a sadistic side, and is involved with pleasure through control or domination and with punishing the woman (guilty for being castrated).[23] For Claire Johnston, both mechanisms result in woman not being presented qua *woman* at all. Extending the *Cahiers du Cinéma* analysis of *Morocco*, Johnston argues that Von Sternberg represses "the idea of woman as a social and sexual being," thus replacing the opposition man–woman with male–non-male.[24]

With this look at feminist film theories and at the issues around the problem of the gaze and of the female spectator that psychoanalysis illuminates, we can begin to see the larger theoretical issues the psychoanalytic methodology involves,[25] particularly in relation to possibilities for change. It is this aspect of the new theoretical approaches that has begun to polarize the feminist film community.[26] For example, in a round-table discussion in 1978, some women voiced their displeasure with theories that were themselves originally devised by men, and with women's preoccupation with how we have been seen/placed/positioned by the dominant male order. Julia LeSage, for instance, argued that the use of Lacanian criticism has been destructive in reifying women "in a childlike position that patriarchy has wanted to see them in"; for LeSage, the Lacanian framework establishes "a discourse which is totally male."[27] And Ruby Rich objected to theories that rest with the apparent elimination of women from both screen and audience. She asked how we can move beyond our placing, rather than just analyzing it.[28]

As if in response to Rich's request, some feminist film critics have begun to take up the challenge to move beyond the preoccupation with how women have been constructed in patriarchal cinema. Judith Mayne, for example, in a useful summary of issues in recent feminist film criticism, argues that the context for discussion of women's cinema needs to be "opened up" to include the film spectator: "The task of criticism," she says, "is to examine the processes that determine how films evoke responses and how spectators produce them."[29] A little later on, Mayne suggests that the proper place for the feminist critic may well be close to the machine that is the agency for the propulsion of images onto the screen, i.e. the projector. By forcing our gaze to dwell on the images by slowing down or stopping the projection that creates patriarchal voyeurism, we may be able to provide a "reading against the grain" that will give us information about our positioning as spectators.

If Mayne's, LeSage's, and Rich's objections lead in a fruitful direction, those of Lucy Arbuthnot and Gail Seneca are problematic, but useful here for the purposes of illustration. In a paper on *Gentlemen Prefer Blondes* Arbuthnot and Seneca attempt to appropriate for themselves some of the images hitherto defined as repressive. They begin by expressing their dissatisfactions not only with current feminist film theory as outlined above, but also with the new theoretical feminist films, which, they say, "focus more on denying men their cathexis with women as erotic objects than in connecting women with each other." In addition, these films by "destroying the narrative and the possibility for viewer identification with the characters, destroy both the male viewer's pleasure and our pleasure."[30] Asserting their need for identification with strong, female screen images, they argue that Hollywood films offer many examples of pleasurable identification; in a clever analysis, the relationship between Marilyn Monroe and Jane Russell in *Gentlemen Prefer Blondes* is offered as an example of strong women, who care for one another, providing a model we need.

However, looking at the construction of the film as a whole, rather than simply isolating certain shots, it is clear that Monroe and Russell are positioned, and position themselves, as objects for a specifically male gaze. The men's weakness does not mitigate their narrative power, and the women are left merely with the limited control they can wield through their sexuality. The film constructs them as "to-be-looked-at," and their manipulations end up as merely comic, since "capturing" the men involves their "being captured." The images of Monroe show her fetishized placement, aimed at reducing her sexual threat,[31] while Russell's stance becomes a parody of the male position. The result is that the two women repeat, in exaggerated form, dominant gender stereotypes.

The weakness of Arbuthnot and Seneca's analysis is that it ignores the way that all dominant images are basically male constructs. Recognizing this has led Julia Kristeva and others to say that it is impossible to know what the "feminine" might be, outside of male constructs. Kristeva says that while we must reserve the category "women" for social demands and publicity, by the word "woman" she means "that which is not represented, that which is unspoken, that which is left out of meanings and ideologies."[32] For similar reasons, Sandy Flitterman and Judith Barry have argued that feminist artists must avoid claiming a specific female power residing in the body of women and representing "an inherent feminine artistic essence which could find expression if allowed to be explored freely."[33] The impulse toward this kind of art is understandable in a culture that denies satisfaction in being a woman, but it results in Motherhood being redefined as the seat of female creativity, while women "are proposed as the bearers of culture, albeit an alternative one."[34]

Flitterman and Barry argue that this form of feminist art, along with some others that they outline, is dangerous in not taking into account "the social contradictions involved in 'femininity'." They suggest that "A radical feminist art would include an understanding of how women are constituted through social practices in culture" and argue for "an aesthetics designed to subvert the production of 'woman' as commodity," much as Claire Johnston and Laura Mulvey had earlier stated that to be feminist a cinema had to be a counter-cinema.

But the problem with this notion of a counter-cinema hinges on the issue of pleasure. Aware that a feminist counter-cinema would almost by definition deny pleasure, Mulvey argued that this denial was a necessary prerequisite for freedom but did not go into the problems involved. In introducing the notion of pleasure, Arbuthnot and Seneca have located a central and little-discussed issue, namely our need for feminist films that at once construct woman as spectator without offering the repressive identifications of Hollywood films and that satisfy our craving for *pleasure*.[35] They have pinpointed a paradox in which feminist film critics have been caught without realizing it, namely our fascination with Hollywood films, rather than with, say, avant-garde films, because they bring us pleasure; but we have (rightly) been wary of admitting the degree to which the pleasure comes from identification with objectification.

Our positioning as "to-be-looked-at," as object of the (male) gaze, has come to be sexually pleasurable.

However, it will not do simply to enjoy our oppression unproblematically; to appropriate Hollywood images to ourselves, taking them out of the context of the total structure in which they appear, will not get us very far. As I suggested above, in order fully to understand *how it is* that women take pleasure in objectification one has to have recourse to psychoanalysis.

Christian Metz, Stephen Heath, and others have shown that the processes of cinema mimic in many ways those of the unconscious.[36] The mechanisms Freud distinguishes in relation to dream and the unconscious have been likened to the mechanism of film. In this analysis, film narratives, like dreams, symbolize a latent, repressed content, except that now the "content" refers not to an individual unconscious but to that of patriarchy in general. If psychoanalysis is a tool that will unlock the meaning of dreams, it should also unlock that of films.

The psychoanalytic methodology is thus justified as an essential first step in the feminist project of understanding our socialization in patriarchy. My analyses of Hollywood films amply demonstrate the ways in which patriarchal myths function to position women as silent, absent, and marginal. But, once we have fully understood our placing and the way that both language and psychoanalytic processes, inherent in our particular form of nuclear family, have constructed it, we have to think about strategies for changing discourse, since these changes would, in turn, affect the structuring of our lives in society. (I am not here excluding the possibility of working from the other end, i.e. finding gaps in patriarchal discourse through which to establish alternate practices, such as collective child-rearing, which might, in turn, begin to affect patriarchal discourse; but this approach requires constant vigilance about the effect on our thoughts and actions of dominant signifying practices.)

As we'll see in the second part of the book, some feminist filmmakers have begun the task of analyzing patriarchal discourses, including cinematic representation, with a view to finding ways to break through them. The analysis of *Sigmund Freud's Dora*, undertaken in chapter 11, shows the filmmakers' belief that the raising of *questions* is the first step to establishing a female discourse, or perhaps that asking questions is the only discourse available to women as a resistance to patriarchal domination. Since questions lead to more questions, a kind of movement is in fact taking place, although it is in a non-traditional mode. Sally Potter structured her film *Thriller* (also analyzed in chapter 11) around this very notion and allowed her heroine's investigation of herself as heroine to lead to some (tentative) conclusions. And Laura Mulvey has suggested that, even if one accepts the psychoanalytic positioning of women, all is not lost, since the Oedipus complex is not completed in women; she notes that "there's some way in which women aren't colonized," having been "so specifically excluded from culture and language."[37]

From this position, psychoanalytic theory allows us to see that there is a possibility for women to change themselves (and perhaps to bring about social change) just because they have not been processed, as have men as little boys, through a clearly defined, and ultimately simple, set of psychic stages. It is this possibility that we will discuss in the book's conclusion, after looking at responses by women directors to repressive Hollywood representations.

2 | Patriarchy and the male gaze in Cukor's *Camille* (1936)

Although virtually any Hollywood film could be used to demonstrate the relegation of women to silence, absence, or marginality through the controlling power of the male gaze, Cukor's *Camille* is particularly appropriate for my purposes. First, the film is based on a historically significant classic melodrama, *La Dame aux camélias* by Alexander Dumas *fils*, written in 1849 (first performed in 1852); we thus have the re-evocation in 1936 of patterns of male–female relating and of ideas about the family, class conflicts, and bourgeois ideology that go back to a phase of Romanticism but which have dominated mainstream melodrama ever since (or at least through the 1950s).[1] (The play's almost constant production over the decades since it was written, with star actresses in the leading role, together with the number of film versions,[2] testifies to a continuing fascination that transcends the specific historical moment.)

Second, the particular aspect of the Romantic period that the play focuses on (that of Parisian Bohemian life in the 1850s) is historically important as marking a moment when, as a result of the industrial revolution, western societies were in a state of transition that inevitably disturbed traditional sex roles. The virgin–whore split (evident in western representations of women at least since ancient times) now took on the form that has dominated classic melodrama.

Third, *Camille* provides an interesting link to Sally Potter's recent feminist film *Thriller* (1980), which, on one level, is a deconstruction of another classic melodrama similar to *La Dame aux camélias*. Although an opera, and written forty years or so after Dumas's play, Puccini's *La Bohème* reflects a similar positioning of the heroine as ultimately marginal. While Puccini's opera was influenced by Henri Murger's *La Vie de Bohème* (1845–8), and Dumas's play deals with a different kind of underworld, they show a similar dilemma for the heroine in a patriarchal world. A feminist reading of Cukor's film will look toward, and has gained from, the deconstruction of *La Bohème* in Potter's film, which I'll discuss in part II.

Fourth, *Camille* is interesting for extra-cinematic reasons; Cukor is an unusually sensitive women's director, having directed Judy Garland and Ingrid Bergman in two archetypal women's films.[3] Furthermore, Cukor worked at MGM, and *Camille* shares the lushness and polish typical of productions of that studio as well as showing the historical care with which Cukor approached his task.

Finally, as a film made in the 1930s, *Camille* reflects the desire for films that took people out of the depressing social and political realities of the time. Posters for the film build up the love between Marguerite and Armand in terms of a romance between Garbo and Taylor; for example, one poster text reads "Greta Garbo loves Robert Taylor," while another has, underneath an image of Garbo and Taylor in a deep embrace: "Crush me in your arms until the breath is gone from my body" (words which do not, of course, occur in the play or film); Garbo is, in another poster, "the eternal woman ready to suffer and die for the man to whom she has given her affection." Yet another advertisement appeals directly to people's needs to be "taken away" from themselves on a tide of emotion: "Your heart will beat fast as its excitement overwhelms you; your emotions will flow back to Paris."[4] And the reviews are full of references to the weeping women in the audience, who, while they may cheer for Armand, suffer with Garbo.

The sentimentality of Cukor's film is the stock in trade of the melodramatic form which Dumas helped to develop into a viable form. His play represented in 1852 a departure from preceding dramatic forms in combining Eugène Scribe's theories of the well-made play with a new psychological realism.[5] *La Dame aux camélias* created a stir by its treatment of a theme not considered proper for the theatre, structured as it was for an elite audience who functioned according to specific notions of propriety.[6] The "loose woman" (courtesan or demimondaine) was not considered a proper subject for a play since she was barely tolerated socially. As Stanton points out:

> In 1852, courtesans were not accepted by the middle class, even in France. It had been a bold undertaking to show on the stage a courtesan who had been a public celebrity and to make her capable of unselfish love.[7]

And, as Schwarz has noted, Dumas made his realistic subject even less acceptable by daring to write about it in ordinary prose.[8] "What he did," Stanton notes, "was to bring the theatre into more direct touch with life and human problems than it had aspired to since before the Romantic movement."[9] And, of course, in so doing, he helped to develop a melodrama form that was ultimately to characterize and to speak explicitly to the bourgeois class.[10]

That critics see Dumas's work as reflecting "life and human problems" in an unmediated way underscores the need for readings of classic works that expose the construction of a "reality" dominated by bourgeois ideology and a patriarchal perspective. It is to Dumas's credit that he presented the drama from Marguerite Gautier's point of view (as against the more usual central positioning of the hero, as in Puccini's *La Bohème*), but he still accepts without question the necessity for female desire to be sacrificed to the needs of patriarchy. For Marguerite is seen to internalize patriarchal demands which require the sacrifice of herself and her happiness for the supposedly "higher" male ends.

That classical narratives in the mid-nineteenth century began to focus on the erring woman and her relationship to society is no accident; as I noted above, the industrial revolution inevitably produced a disturbance in sex roles as the whole fabric of society underwent dramatic change. By the start of the nineteenth century, a stolid, materialistic, bourgeois industrial class was firmly established in France and Britain, entailing a solidification of the nuclear family and a rigidifying of sex roles. The extreme materialism, together with the rigidity, produced a reaction in the "sons" of the new industrial magnates who turned to the artistic life as a way of rebelling against their fathers. Rousseau's hero in *La Nouvelle Héloise* (1761) was later given, in Goethe's *Werther* (1774), the form that would be repeated in many Romantic texts, such as those by Balzac, Stendhal and Flaubert. In England the Byronic hero, developed from Milton's figure of Satan, was a more glamorous and masculine version of the type,[11] while in Germany at the start of the twentieth century, the artistic son of the bourgeois industrialist is perhaps most sensitively treated by Thomas Mann. These sons flocked to the big cities to lead a carefree life, creating their art, playing with women, drinking, having fun; thus began the Bohemian life, described by Henri Murger and characterized by its irresponsibility – the men lived without wives and children, free to come and go as they wished. Although often starving and without money, they were carried along by the excitement and adventure of this form of existence which, for many, represented merely a rite of passage, a phase of what would ultimately be relatively regular, successful professional lives.

This form of rebellion against the materialistic bourgeois family was not available to middle-class women who were surrounded by codes that prevented their living in garrets or pursuing artistic, intellectual lives of this kind. As Stanton notes, however, in France in the 1860s there was a group of aristocratic women, daughters of officers killed in the wars of the Empire and "denied the marriages to which their background, training and tastes entitled them."[12] However, since these women could not pursue independent intellectual and artistic lives, they were forced to use their abilities and sexual endowments to win the affection and often friendship of suitable but married men, playing roles as mistresses but offering in fact much more than mere physical pleasures. Dumas coined the word "demimondaines" for these women.

Working-class women lacked the education to win men for more than their sexual attractions, and thus were driven either to prostitution proper (e.g. Musetta in Puccini's opera) or (like Mimi in the same work) to eking out a miserable existence by selling their labor – chiefly sewing skills – for a pittance. As we'll see later, in discussing Sally Potter's *Thriller*, it is precisely this contrast between the middle-class male artist "making something in his attic" (the investigating Mimi in Potter's film is never quite sure *what* exactly the artists are creating or even *why* they are creating) and Mimi, in her attic with no ambiguity about what she is "making" (she is sewing shirts and flowers out of necessity) that interests Potter. While the artists are safely outside of the chain of production, Mimi's labor is securely located within it: indeed, the chain relies for its profit on the exploitation of her labor.

Marguerite's link in the social chain is closer to that of the "demi-mondaines," despite her peasant background, than it is to that of laboring women. She maintains her luxurious lifestyle by prostituting herself to her rich admirers, most of whom she does not love and for whom she provides more than merely physical pleasure. But she becomes a threat to the economic system when she desires a young man, Armand Duval, on his way up the middle-class professional ladder. The satisfaction of her desire could mean the ruin of Duval: for on account of her class origins and promiscuous life Marguerite is unacceptable as a wife for such a man; she must renounce her desire in order for the bourgeois patriarchal system to remain intact.

In transferring the play to film, Cukor's scriptwriters did not offer a critique of the situation as outlined in Dumas's play; the film instead faithfully duplicates the meaning of the original. The following analysis will aim to show how *Camille* demonstrates the untenable position in which women are placed in patriarchy, from the point of view of subjectivity and desire. The dilemma has been summarized in the following way by Jacqueline Rose:

> What Freud's papers on femininity reveal, therefore, is nothing less than the emergence of this concept of desire as the question of sexual difference – how does the little girl become a woman, or does she? . . . Her desire . . . [is] the desire for an unsatisfied desire.[13]

Cukor's film falls into several distinct parts, each reflecting a different positioning of Marguerite in relation to subjectivity and desire, and to the male gaze. In the first section of the film, she is, in a sense, in the place of a cynical rebellion against her positioning as object of desire, as marginal, as Other. Marguerite embodies the perhaps inevitable psychology of prostitution, which involves split subjectivity, the woman becoming at once object of the male look, but also aware of presenting herself for the male look. She deliberately uses her body as spectacle, as object-to-be-looked-at, and manipulates the structures that privilege the male gaze for her own ends – i.e. money, gifts, admiration, worship (although the degree to which she any longer enjoys them is ambiguous); she is, in short, a fallen woman, a femme fatale as this figure has been represented over the decades. She is constructed at first as a castrating female, demonstrated, as we'll see, by the fact that she returns the look. But throughout this part of the film, where she appropriates subjectivity (controlling the action, seducing the men, dictating to her friends), her own desire is blocked; she fully illustrates the position of "her desire being the desire for an unsatisfied desire;" she does not want to change her way of life, but she is unhappy, bored, unfulfilled, lacking – paying the price, that is, for being subject and a woman.

The complex opening scene demonstrates the trap Marguerite is in. The impossibility for woman of subjectivity *and* desire is presented in an intricate series of misplaced looks involving Marguerite and her rival Olympe, on the one hand, and the Baron de Varville (whom Marguerite is supposed to seduce) and Armand Duval, long in love with Marguerite unbeknownst to her, on the other. Two parallel mistaken identities set the sequence in motion: first, the Baron de Varville, looking up at the box designated by Prudence, Marguerite's "friend," sees Olympe and mistakes her for Marguerite; then Marguerite, searching the crowd for the Baron, in order to seduce him, finds Armand gazing up at her in adoration and mistakes him for Varville. Marguerite is used to having to pretend to desire the men she knows can support her in style and is therefore overwhelmed to discover that a handsome young man is the rich lover she is to seduce. What happens is that for a moment Marguerite believes that her unblocked desire and her "prostitution" (in which she is subject, albeit in the only way in which women can be subject, namely to have a desire for an unfulfilled desire) have miraculously come together. It is this heady sense of possibility that gives those first exchanged glances with Armand their peculiar and wonderful intensity; for him too, of course, this is an unhoped-for moment – that the beautiful, desirable Marguerite Gautier would look lovingly on him, a mere banker's son. Thus for both of them it is a privileged moment, outside of the actual discourses and structures that bind each and that in fact make this an impossible love. We have a wonderful example here of how social codes, hierarchies, and economic practices define and limit desire and control what emotional connections are possible. The only way that this impossible love could begin was through mistaken identity.

As soon as Marguerite realizes who Armand is and that the Baron de Varville is in fact sitting opposite her with Olympe, she knows she must renounce Armand and return to her former position in the subject–desire dichotomy. She must return Varville's look, becoming at once castrating subject and, paradoxically, object of Varville's lascivious gaze; what develops as a result of this paradox is a tension/struggle between Varville's desire to possess Marguerite totally and her resistance to being possessed – a stance she can only maintain as long as she remains in the position of "prostitute" within the social hierarchy.

The next section of the film shows Marguerite's struggle to resist possession by the Baron de Varville, to retain the subjectivity she has won through her unfulfilled desire. The resistance is clear on the level of plot, for Marguerite refuses to go away with the Baron (pleading weakness from another bout of illness); and furthermore, she allows Duval to approach her while knowing full well that the Baron will not tolerate infidelity.

The first meeting with Duval in this section is important in establishing the facile imagery with which bourgeois society endows the "loose" woman. Duval gives Camille *Manon Lascaut*, telling her it is about a "woman who lived for love and pleasure" but who came to a sad end. Is Duval warning Marguerite about her possible end? Or does his action simply reflect the stance toward the "loose woman" characteristic of the bourgeoisie, for whom she is a scapegoat for repressed wishes and desires? On the surface, Marguerite lives like Manon, but though the spectator knows how false this bright exterior is, Duval has yet to learn it.

And learn it he does, in the famous party sequence, where Marguerite is at her most lush and beautiful, decked out in a white gown that highlights her fragility and spirituality, setting her off against her crass, vulgar friends. It is when she is at her apparently most gay and carefree that her physical and spiritual disease emerges; her coughing spell inflames Duval's passion and his desire to take care of her, and makes it impossible for Marguerite any longer to conceal her intense desire for him. In an extraordinarily powerful cinematic moment, Marguerite gives in to her desire and kisses Duval all over his face. Her sudden submission to her desire is emphasized by the mirror shot, which shows Garbo's frame leaning back, Taylor's body stretched over her. The image suggests a return to the imaginary, to the pre-Oedipal moment of a self merged with the Mother, and it gains its intensity from our awareness that this coming together is a violation of the discourses that in fact separate the lovers.

For it is only through a regression to the illusory, pre-symbolic realm of the imaginary that the lovers can free themselves from the constraints that in patriarchy prevent their union. The liberating sensation that accompanies all love called "romantic" in this culture comes from the freeing of symbolic limits, of the Oedipally induced repressions that happen as the child learns language and finds his/her place in a world defined by the Father, the Law. Armand and Marguerite at this moment stand outside of the Law, harmoniously united in reversion to the state before the entry of the Father, the Third Term, which forces the child away from the Mother and into the realm of the symbolic. Meanwhile, the mise-en-scène, with its claustrophobic drapery and fussy, crowding objects, suggests, in its crampedness, the trap the lovers are in: since their love is outside of the symbolic, it is an impossible love.

And indeed, moments after Armand has left with Marguerite's key, planning to return secretly later, the Baron appears, symbolizing the Law which forbids the newly declared love. It seems that Marguerite's love, having finally found its object, will nevertheless have to remain unfulfilled.

But the Law extends beyond the Baron to Duval's father – a much more formidable opponent since he has more at stake, namely his family lineage. In the scene where Duval visits his family, seeking money to travel since he thinks Marguerite has betrayed him, two important things are established: first, we meet Duval's sister and her fiancé, the "ideal" couple who, making the correct liaison, within the bosom of the patriarchal family, stand in contrast to Marguerite and Armand; second, we understand the economic relations binding Armand to his father. Armand depends on his father for money, since, although his grandfather left him a modest inheritance, his father forbids him to touch it. To violate his father's command in this matter would represent an irrevocable breach of trust.

Duval's threatened departure brings the lovers together in a scene that shows Marguerite's internalization of patriarchal norms, despite her marginal position which would seem to be subversive of those norms. Sitting cosily reconciled with Armand, Marguerite first admires the photographs of his family in his room: she is sentimental over the "idealized" family of the pictures – the lovely sisters, the happy husband and wife, the calm, settled existence that the photographs exude; second (here anticipating her later reactions to M. Duval), she tries to protect Armand from herself when he declares his love and his desire to take her away with him. Marguerite, we realize, half believes that she is "no good" since this is how society has constructed her.

It is because of Marguerite's and Armand's respective social constructions that their relationship is unacceptable to the bourgeoisie; they can thus only live out their love in a place apart – in, that is, the context of a deliberately created idyllic fantasy. The discourse of romantic love is anathema to bourgeois "reality" since it focuses on the loved one at the expense of the accumulation of wealth and the appropriation of property.[14] (It was for this reason "re-invented" in the Romantic period when the sons of bourgeois fathers were in revolt against the concern with the material level of existence.[15])

In moving the lovers away from the city, with its associations with culture, sophistication, and material wealth, to a rural setting, the film finds an apt metaphor for the realm of the imaginary, which is untouched by the discourses of bourgeois capitalism. The fake sets and artificial scenery here add to the film's meaning in that these cinematic elements underscore the "unreality" of the space the lovers are attempting to find, i.e. the space of the imaginary, outside of the public, symbolic discourses. The setting indicates the static, undialectical nature of the imaginary, since, as soon as there is movement, one is in the symbolic. The lovers attempt to regress to the illusory unified state of the pre-Oedipal stage.

Nurtured by Armand's loving and protective attention, Marguerite blossoms in this realm, freed from all social obligations. The mise-en-scène represents liberation in the extreme long shots, showing the lovers surrounded

Plate 1 The mise-en-scène here represents the liberation of nature as contrasted to the tight, claustrophobic city spaces. The extreme long shot shows the lovers surrounded by wide-open space, the unreality of the sets adding to the sense of a regression to the imaginary realm, outside of the symbolic that the public spaces represent. Armand gazes lovingly at Marguerite who now, virtuous, looks coyly down.

by wide-open space in contrast to the crowded, claustrophobic city spaces. But the Law threatens even here, symbolized by the Baron's castle looming on the skyline in the back of the frame; his presence is a reminder of the transitory nature of what they have, its "unreality", given the bourgeois capitalist construction of the world.

But once again the Baron is not the greatest threat; rather the hand of the Law descends on Marguerite in the form of M. Duval. A brief look at the key scene between Marguerite and M. Duval shows Marguerite moving from a position of opposition (where she attempts to assert her voice) to one of complete self-annihilation, of domination by the Law; she renders herself up to the place of object, Other – to silence, absence, and ultimately death. How does this happen? Why does it happen? Why is it necessary?

As I have noted, Marguerite begins by taking an oppositional stance, sensing that M. Duval's main reason for wanting to stop the marriage is his disapproval of Marguerite as a potential wife for Armand. But Duval's arguments are devious, taking three increasingly persuasive forms. First, he uses economic and social arguments: Armand is violating family codes in wanting to take his money out of his father's hands and, moreover, if he does this, the money will soon run out. Second, he uses arguments from the bourgeois discourses on family and marriage: a relationship that is not founded on marriage, children, and "sound ties," he says, cannot last. Armand's love will soon fade, since the human heart, outside of an institutional structure, is not to be trusted. It is at this point that Duval subtly shifts his argument to a third position in which he claims to be thinking of Marguerite's best interests. "No woman unprotected," he states, "can give the best years of her life to a man certain to leave her in the end," and he sweeps aside Marguerite's wise observation that "Any man can be lifted above self-interest."

Up to this point, Marguerite has listened but has not appeared to be won over. M. Duval has saved his trump card for the end, namely his appeal to what is best for Armand. Marguerite, he argues, is killing Armand's right to a "real" life in staying with him, since Armand will never be able to move within his natural circles. Under the weight of this awesome responsibility, Marguerite finally gives in, and as she does so she is internalizing values that function against her desire (and, for all we know, the desire also of her lover). She submits them *both* to the patriarchal Law, overwhelmed with a sense of her worthlessness as it has been defined to her and willing to sacrifice her own life for the man she loves. "I am not worth killing Armand," she says, oblivious to the fact that, paradoxically, her decision itself may "kill" him spiritually, as much as it will surely kill her physically.

What Marguerite really means is clear at the end of the interview with M. Duval when she pities *him*, for the pain she has caused him in having to ask this sacrifice of her! "Don't reproach yourself," she says. "You are only doing what Armand's father should have done." In other words, Marguerite is saying that

Plate 2 The hand of the Law descends on Marguerite in the form of M. Duval. The scene demonstrates the power of the bourgeois father over the destinies of the children. Marguerite is prey to victimization in a culture that denies her a voice and a place as subject in her own right. The tight framing and the dark lighting emphasize the blackness and rage of M. Duval's figure, which contrasts with Marguerite's light dress. Her innocence is stressed by the halo effect of the lighting on her hair.

neither she nor Armand are worth the act of going against the patriarchal Law that M. Duval represents and that she has, at this point, internalized as a value higher than herself.

The entire scene demonstrates, first, the power of the bourgeois father over the destinies of his children; and second, the manipulation that woman is subject to in a culture that denies her a voice, a place as subject in her own right, a legitimate position in the social order. Marguerite has no place from which to counter what M. Duval says; the precariousness of the idyllic realm that the lovers briefly inhabited is evident in that it all totally collapses in the face of the public (symbolic) sphere. Her pathetic "I have no one else but Armand" falls on deaf ears, of course, and she promises to send Armand back to his father.

Thus Marguerite has now to force herself to betray Armand, as earlier she had had to humiliate herself before the Baron de Varville in order to extricate herself to be with Armand. She deliberately returns to the "fallen woman" self that she had discarded in the country with Armand (Armand did not so much "redeem the prostitute" as bring out the "good" Marguerite lying buried in her). In a magnificent scene, Garbo convinces Duval that she no longer loves him, and then, again gorgeously decked in white, she sweeps through the open doors that look out on the Baron's castle far away on the skyline; the camera holds as her frail, translucent form moves further and further into the distance, signifying her loss of herself, her surrender to the abyss.

In this final section of the film, then, we see Marguerite placed in yet another relation to subjectivity and desire. We saw in the first section that she placed herself as subject, but at the cost of fulfilling her desire, and still very much bound by the limits of patriarchy; she was both object of the controlling male gaze and controlled men in turn with her gaze, so that a situation of tension prevailed. Socially, Marguerite was an outcast since she dared to violate the codes for women (i.e. to be virgins or wives) and to be promiscuous. In the second section, we saw that she was torn between her love for Armand, which would fulfill her desire, and her need for money and the luxurious life; in addition, socially, their love is an impossible one, there being no place for it within the social discourses available. The third section represents her choice for the "impossible" – a brief blissful return to the "unreal" imaginary world where subject and object are fused in a harmony that predates the symbolic.

This moment in the imaginary could not, of course, endure, and thus in the final section we find Marguerite renouncing all possibility for her voice, her subjectivity, and her desire; she succumbs to the demands of patriarchy and of bourgeois economic and class relations. This time she allows herself to be explicitly the Baron's victim for, broken-hearted, she no longer has any taste for the old games. She now has to endure the scorn, not only of Armand, but also of all but the most loyal of her friends. And the Baron takes delight in publicly humiliating her.

In relinquishing Armand and returning to the Baron, Marguerite is, in effect, desiring death. Her condition at this point represents that described by Freud in his "Mourning and melancholia" – melancholia being a condition that women are particularly susceptible to because of their positioning within patriarchy. From the start of the film, Marguerite showed a tendency toward the melancholia Freud describes as emerging from a lack of self-worth: "The patient represents his ego to us as worthless, incapable of any effort and morally despicable; he reproaches himself, vilifies himself, and expects to be cast out and chastised."[16] Talking to Armand early on in the film, Marguerite declares that she is worthless: "Why should you care for me?" she says. "I am always too sad or too gay." And we have seen already how hard it is for Marguerite to believe that Armand loves, and wants to stay with, her.

After she has let Armand go, Marguerite's melancholia moves into a new and more dangerous phase which is a direct result of her internalization of values antithetic to her real desires. Continually viewed as inferior (first because of her promiscuity, now because of her apparent betrayal of Armand), Marguerite would have had to possess an unusually strong ego to feel worthy. The supposed heroism of her self-sacrifice (i.e. leaving Armand because it is the best thing for him) is evidently not sufficient to sustain her. And yet the narrative is structured so as to put the spectator in the position of finding the "sacrifice" (with its suffering and subsequent death) "beautiful" and "admirable."

Since this is a type of sacrifice that women (both in art and in life) are often asked to make, it is worth exploring the degree to which such actions are indeed "noble." Freud helps us to see the deeply neurotic levels of suffering that women such as Marguerite undergo; we begin to see that it is through such representatiors that patriarchy ensures the construction of the feminine as "neurotic."

The mechanism of melancholia, as outlined by Freud, reveals the danger of sudden withdrawal of an intense erotic cathexis of the kind Marguerite had to Armand, and the deep sense of worthlessness that would motivate someone to subject herself voluntarily to such withdrawal:

> First there existed an object choice; the libido had attached itself to a certain person; then, owing to a real injury or disappointment concerned with the loved person, this object-relationship was undermined. The result was not the normal one of withdrawal of the libido from this object, and transference to a new one, but something different. . . . The free libido was withdrawn into the ego and not directed to another object. It did not find application there . . . but served simply to establish an identification of the ego with the abandoned object. Thus, the shadow of the object fell upon the ego, so that the latter could henceforth be criticized by a special mental faculty like an object, like the forsaken object.[17]

Once the object is withdrawn, Freud goes on to say, there is a danger of the subject regressing to narcissism; identification is substituted within the ego for the object-love (i.e. the ego is treated like an object and can launch against itself a hatred pertaining actually to the lost love-object). It is in this way that a person suffering loss becomes suicidal – killing the ego, as Freud puts it, instead of the lost object-love.

It is useful to see Marguerite's state of mind in the last section of the film as reflecting this kind of melancholia: her lover has, in effect, been taken from her by M. Duval, but instead of deflecting outward her hatred of Duval for his role in separating her from Armand, she turns the anger in upon herself, essentially committing suicide in not taking care of herself but rather living a life geared to aggravate her condition. She has allowed the patriarchal definition of herself as worthless to become her own definition of herself, not having any other discourse within which to evaluate herself differently.

It is thus only from the abstract, patriarchal position (that of M. Duval, for instance) that Marguerite's sacrifice can be seen as "noble." From Marguerite's position (masked in the film), her death is a pure waste of a life. But classical narratives of this kind require that the heroine die – as Sally Potter shows well in *Thriller* – because she offers a threat to the patriarchal order. In the play, Marguerite shows some understanding of the need for her death. She says:

> A while ago, I had a moment of anger against death; I regret this; death is necessary and I love it, because it waited until your return. If my death had not been certain, your father would not have written telling you to come back.[18]

Interesting from several points of view, this speech reveals Marguerite's awareness of the *necessity* of her death – and her passive acceptance of this necessity. She realizes that Armand's father would never have permitted him to return had her death not been certain. Similarly, in the film, the brief, tension-filled reunion with Armand is only possible because Marguerite will not live to threaten the patriarchal order with her passion for Armand, nor threaten it by trying to sustain in institutional mode a kind of love incompatible with bourgeois social organization in the nineteenth century.

Both film and play repress the essentially neurotic basis of Marguerite's "sacrifice" (her turning narcissistically in upon herself a hostility that legitimately belongs elsewhere), in favor of viewing as particularly "feminine" precisely this sort of abandonment of the self to male concerns perceived as basic to the organization of society. Produced as it was within Hollywood, a bourgeois institution, the film dare not suggest that there may be other possibilities, other ways of constructing society such that a love like that between Marguerite and Armand might indeed prosper.

Marguerite is victim of a culture that permits her only the desire for an unsatisfied desire; should she dare to pursue her own desire, the film shows, woman risks annihilation. By these mechanisms, woman in *Camille* is relegated ultimately to silence as the cost of continuing in a system that allows her no voice and no possibility for the fulfilment of her desire.

Fetishism and the repression of Motherhood in Von Sternberg's *Blonde Venus* (1932)

Although Cukor's film is not subversive (i.e. it does not provide a critique of the patriarchal positioning of women), it does expose the contradictory demands made on women by showing events from the heroine's point of view. On the one hand, *Camille* positions the female spectator so that she obtains a vicarious, sentimental satisfaction (often expressed by tears) from Marguerite's tragedy and leaves the theatre feeling that she has had a "beautiful" experience; yet, on the other hand, if the spectator were to dwell for a moment on *why* Marguerite had to die, the answers do lie within the film, as I have tried to show.

Thus, while in no way suggesting that any other social structure or mode of being is either possible or desirable, the film is ultimately sympathetic to the female plight. This is partly a result of Cukor's unique sensitivity as a "women's" director (i.e. as a maker of films geared specifically to a female audience and showing the pathos of women's situations).[1] To the extent that women see reflected in the films dilemmas that are indeed theirs (as a result of their positioning within patriarchy), the works speak to them. On this level, the films may have served in the 1930s very much the same function that soap operas serve today.[2] As we have already seen, the limitation of these kinds of work is that the figures women are asked to identify with are usually victims, so that the appeal is to the female spectator's socially engrained masochism (whether or not women in fact take up this position is another matter, about which we need more concrete information).

A further appeal in *Camille* is to the representation of Garbo and Taylor *together*, i.e. as lovers. They work well as a couple for two reasons. First, it is clear from reviews at the time that Taylor functioned as a sex symbol for many women, so that by identifying with Garbo the female spectator was vicariously "made love to" by Taylor. Second, Garbo's particular kind of fragile beauty, only subtly sexual, was not threatening to women since she does not seem overly invested in her own beauty and sexuality. She is somehow always "elsewhere;" and, in addition, Garbo's pathetic situations evoke women's pity, appealing to their nurturing, maternal part. The female spectator is on her side all the way through, hoping (a little ambivalently perhaps) that *she* at least will have her desire satisfied, to make up for the impossibility that the desire of those watching will be satisfied.

Von Sternberg's treatment of his most famous star, Marlene Dietrich, in the same decade reveals a classical Hollywood director who is the opposite of Cukor in sensibility. Where Cukor was sensitive both to his star and to her ideas on acting, Von Sternberg took total control over his, dominating her; where Cukor built scripts representing his heroine's point of view, Von Sternberg was totally uninterested in his heroine's roles or perspective. *Blonde Venus* is a film clearly constructed for the male spectator, using as its method of dominating women in its representational system that of fetishizing the female form. Having shown how this works, I will demonstrate that this method sometimes backfires as a result of male narcissism; the female spectator may read the masculinized female image as a *resisting* image in a way that no male spectator would suspect, since for him the male attire lessens the woman's sexual threat. For women, the male attire "permits" a form of female bonding that excludes men and thus subverts patriarchal domination, while acceding to its symbolic terms.

Von Sternberg was one of the directors singled out by Claire Johnston as relegating women to absence. She argues that woman as a sexual and social being is actually repressed in Von Sternberg's films, so that the man can remain at the centre of the world of the film, despite the fact that it ostensibly focuses on a woman:

> The woman as sign, then, becomes the pseudo-centre of the filmic discourse. The real opposition posed by the sign is male/non-male, which Sternberg establishes by his use of masculine clothing enveloping the image of Dietrich. This masquerade indicates the absence of man, an absence which is simultaneously negated and recuperated by man. The image of woman becomes merely the trace of the exclusion and repression of woman.[3]

For the first two-thirds of the film, this is largely true, for here we are never shown things from Helen's point of view, leaving the female spectator (who is trying to make some sense of Helen's actions) totally confused as to what she is about. But in the middle section of the film (when Helen is being "hunted"), while she is still constructed by the dominant discourse, we are *exposed* to this discourse as repressive because things are now seen from Helen's perspective.

Johnston, thus, goes too far in denying *any* presence to Dietrich. There are two ways – first, within the diegesis, as narrative figure, second, extra-cinematically, as historical figure (star) – in which Dietrich reveals awareness of her oppressive positioning through playing with it.

First, Dietrich as Helen positions herself in *Blonde Venus* as did Garbo in *Camille*, deliberately using her place as object of the male gaze and making the female spectator aware of this placing. For example, she quite self-consciously uses her body as spectacle, as object for the male gaze, when she is earning money by performing for male spectators; then, when she wants something from one of the men who have money or authority, she knows she can manipulate their desire for her own ends (the most comic version of this is in the Deep South section, where Dietrich "seduces" the detective, who has no idea whom she is, making him clay in her hands before she reveals herself to him).

Second, as historical figure in the pro-filmic event, Dietrich seems aware of how Von Sternberg is using her, of his fascination with her image. This awareness accounts for the extreme self-consciousness of her performance before the camera: she plays the scenes for Von Sternberg, it seems, deliberately making herself object of his gaze outside the frame, beyond the diegesis. This creates a certain tension in the image, since Dietrich's awareness

Plate 3 When Dietrich wants something from one of the men who have money or power, she knows she can manipulate their desire for her own ends. Here Dietrich tries to be sufficiently seductive to get the job she needs. Note how the position of her eyes, looking slantways in Smith's direction while leaving her head facing front, shows her awareness of his look at her as object of desire. (Compare the look here to that of Keaton in chapter 5, plate 7, p. 78.)

of how she is being used (despite her apparently passive, if slightly ironic, acceptance of this placing) alters in a significant way the effect of her objectification. Her understanding of the extra-cinematic discourse she is placed in permits a certain distance from what is being done to her, providing a gap through which the female spectator can glimpse her construction in patriarchy.

For the male spectator, on the other hand, Dietrich is constructed as the "ultimate fetish" (in Laura Mulvey's words). Her glamorous, sensuous, glossy eroticism, sign of her fetishized representation, comes from Von Sternberg's desire for Dietrich and his simultaneous need to repress the threat that her sexuality has for him. In other words, the processes that Von Sternberg is engaged in vis-à-vis Dietrich mimic those that take place in the culture at large vis-à-vis women in general. Cinematically, Von Sternberg achieves this (as Laura Mulvey points out) through breaking the powerful look of the male protagonist within the diegesis, which one finds in traditional narratives, "in favor of the image in direct rapport with the spectator." As Mulvey notes, the effect of this is that

> the beauty of the woman as object and screen space coalesce; she is no longer the bearer of the guilt but a perfect product, whose body, stylized and fragmented by close-ups is the content of the film and the direct recipient of the spectator's look.[4]

In this way, Von Sternberg is able to satisfy in a more powerful way than usual the need in the average male spectator for fetishized female images.

Von Sternberg's comments about his relationship to Dietrich indicate his fetishism of her. He has claimed total responsibility for how she appears on the screen, declaring not only that she is his creation, but that she *is* him:

> In my films, Marlene is not herself. Remember that, Marlene is not Marlene. I am Marlene, she knows that better than anyone.[5]

As a result of this stance, Von Sternberg's films narcissistically eliminate real consideration of his heroines or their points of view; he wants Dietrich merely for the spectacle that she can provide. Thus, those films that assign Dietrich a diegetic role as performer, where her position as "on display" has a narrative context, work better than those where the camera still forces her to be displayed but that lack any narrative motivation for the "display."

In *Blonde Venus*, we find both kinds of scene; in the first and last sections of the film, Dietrich is a performer, and in many sequences she is filmed so that she is, in Mulvey's words, "the direct recipient of the spectator's look," despite the fact that in the narrative there is an audience present. Fragmented in close-ups, her body becomes screen space, nothing else existing. In the odd voodoo number (disturbing because of its racist reading of the beauty and the beast configuration), Dietrich smiles confidently right at the camera, sure of her beauty and of her power over the spectator.

She is, however, most spectacularly fetishized in her final Paris performance; she emerges in a dazzling, white, male evening dress and top hat, seductive, confident, and cold as ice. Her spotless costume and flawless figure, together with her perfectly chiseled face and calculated gestures create a deliberately artificial, surreal image that is enhanced by the soft lenses and expressionist lighting. Isolated once more in the frame, Dietrich's image offers direct erotic connection for the male spectator, despite Nick's presence in the diegetic audience.

But Dietrich is also fetishized in the shots where she is with Nick, when again the camera refuses the mediation of the male protagonist, allowing the male spectator direct rapport with Dietrich's image. The extraordinary outfits signify Dietrich's fetishization here, particularly the heavily fur-collared coats with their long, slender, tapered line which hugs Dietrich's body. The huge collar frames Dietrich's head, which is made even tinier by the smooth, tight-fitting black hat. Close-ups of Dietrich in this outfit show her face framed by fur, deeply chiseled and a perfect mask. (Only her eyes move, darting back and forth, up and down, or circling around. The meaning of this is unclear: is the movement an effort to avoid the direct gaze of both camera and male spectator? Is it the one available (and very limited) form of resistance?)

The coat, hat, and gown that Dietrich wears on her return to the Faraday household at the end of the film is perhaps the most fetishistic and extraordinary outfit of all. The tight-fitting black hat is this time matched with a satin gown that leaves the shoulders bare but has sudden, puffy sleeves and a deeply décolleté neckline. The skirt is tight and narrow around Dietrich's body, and she wears high-heeled shoes. The coat has a sequined collar, and long sequined sleeves capped with fur. The camera first catches Dietrich outside the humble family door, peering, birdlike, over her shoulder, her figure incongruous in the context; and in the domestic scene that follows (during which Dietrich is again inserted in her place within the family unit), Dietrich's clothes betray the fundamental contradiction between fetishism and mothering that underlies the whole film (see plate 4, p. 54).

Extra-cinematic material is again significant in relation to this contradiction in showing processes at work within the larger patriarchal cultural context that are echoed through cinematic processes. Von Sternberg was strongly opposed to having Dietrich appear as a mother in *Blonde Venus*, and he did not want to include the long deterioration involved in the section in which she is hunted. Having fought to no avail with his producers over the script, and being so resistant to notions of Dietrich as Mother, Von Sternberg walked off and left the film. When Dietrich refused to work with the replacement director, Von Sternberg returned, but he always hated the film, despite the fact that the script was from his own story about his personal experiences.[6]

The resistance to having Dietrich portrayed as a mother is clearly linked to the fetishism involved in Von Sternberg's representation of her. For, if fetishism is partly designed to eliminate male fears of female sexuality, it is also a way of

Plate 4 In this shot, outside the humble family door, on her return from Paris, Dietrich's elaborate clothes betray the fundamental contradiction between fetishism and mothering that underlies the film. Note Grant's desiring look and Dietrich's averted eyes, although her face fronts the camera. *Her* desire is absent.

repressing Motherhood. Involved here is the contradiction between sexuality and mothering that has pervaded American film representations at least since Frank Powell's *A Fool There Was* (1914), and that has functioned as a way of recuperating both female sexuality and mothering in an effort to reduce woman's overall threat. Patriarchy has represented the Mother as outside of sexuality and therefore, within a certain definition, not threatening to man. But, as Kristeva has shown, the definition, to work, has had to focus only on the symbolic aspect of Motherhood; Motherhood, that is, is seen by patriarchy as "without fail a desire to bear a child of the father (a child of her own father)."[7] The father, according to Kristeva, is thus assimilated in the child, and the child reduced to an implementation of reproductive desire (which now becomes really a desire for the father). Thus, in this view, all female desire for the child, in and of itself, is eliminated. The whole process is recuperated for man in its complete repression of female sexuality and female desire for anything other than the father, which is a desire for the position of Other, object.

The other nonsymbolic aspect of Motherhood is repressed since it provides a gap through which woman might evade patriarchal domination. As Kristeva puts it, "The body of the mother . . . is one toward which all women aspire all the more passionately because it lacks a penis. . . . By giving birth, the woman enters into contact with her mother; she becomes, she is her own mother; they are the same continuity differentiating itself." [8] It is this subversive possibility that patriarchy (and patriarchal representation) must exclude.

Blonde Venus is particularly interesting in terms of its strategies for rendering Motherhood non-threatening because of its ambivalent attitude to the patriarchal (symbolic) conception of Motherhood which Kristeva outlines. While most classical Hollywood films triumphantly exhibit this symbolic view of mothering, Dietrich's status as fetishized object of desire makes the traditional representation problematic. While in no way, of course, supporting the nonsymbolic, subversive side of mothering (which, as always, must be thoroughly repressed), the film on one level unintentionally exposes the falseness of the ideal Hollywood family.

First, however, on the superficial narrative level, the film does try to assert the typical, ideal, Hollywood family complete with the perfect father, mother, and child, each in his/her correct place. In this conception, the mother is made into icon, the perfect, all-giving presence at the service of, and under the domination of, the father. She is object-for-the-other, rather than subject-in-herself; an empty signifier as subject, she embodies meaning for the Other as sign of safety, security, haven from the public sphere. Since the mother is seen only in relation to her husband and child, this symbolic patriarchal conception of Motherhood actually represses mothering as it relates to mother–child bonding and (particularly) as it relates to woman–woman bonding.

Thus, when Dietrich is, however awkwardly, in the mother position in the domestic sequences, she is in the traditional place, at the service of both husband and child. Faraday objects like any traditional husband to Helen's decision to go back to work (even though it is ostensibly to earn money for his operation); and when Helen prepares to leave for her first night at the Club, the camera frames husband and child, first, looking on dejectedly as she gathers her things and, second, standing forlornly at the top of the stairs as she departs. The shot of father and son alone at the supper table emphasizes the significance of the mother's absence, of Helen not being in her place. And throughout the rest of the film, the glum figure of Faraday will symbolize Helen's absence, the lack of what rightfully belongs to Faraday, and the child.

But this superficial support for the ideal Hollywood family is undercut in several ways. First, the visual awkwardness of Dietrich in the opening "domestic" sequence betrays both Von Sternberg's and Dietrich's extra-cinematic discomfort with the Mother role, which I have already mentioned, and accounts for the frequent critical complaint about Dietrich's "phoniness" as a mother. [9] Cinematically, the classical Hollywood iconography for

"Mother" – plain dress, apron, messy hair – is simply laid over Dietrich's already fetishized form (viz. the prologue sequence, where Faraday first glimpses Dietrich naked in a lake in Switzerland), with very odd results (in one scene, Dietrich actually looks like a maid, in black dress and apron).

Second, despite the narrative weight supposedly given to Faraday, as the poor, abandoned husband, the lighting actually favors Dietrich in several scenes, as Bill Nichols has pointed out.[10] Weight is not after all given to the family, but to Dietrich as the woman caught between the conflicting demands of two men. And Faraday's dour presence throughout casts a pall on the supposedly ideal family with his essential meanness and his extreme, intolerant behavior.

Third, the representation of the child undercuts the ideal family since he is far from the usual, cherubic Hollywood infant. Instead, Johnny is throughout associated with the mechanical and the destructive.[11] In the early shots of Dietrich bathing him, Johnny is aggressive, first trying to "kill" his toy crocodile and then blaring his trumpet in his mother's face. Before he goes to bed, the child is seen with a toy gun and then with a loud and ugly mechanical toy. As he falls asleep, listening to the narrative of his parents' meeting, he constantly pulls the eye of his bear out of its socket, letting it then plop back. Later shots show him similarly associated with noisy mechanical toys, and one eery scene opens up with a close-up of a frightening mask that turns out to be lodged on the back of Johnny's head. The film's distaste for the nuclear family and for the domestic emerges in this strangely perverse and aggressive child.

The child's unnatural involvement in his parents' sexuality may also reflect an unconscious exposure of the inner workings of the nuclear family. There is first the exposing of the Freudian family-romance syndrome, in which the child (here aided by his parents) exalts the parents to noble lineage; he thus remakes the family into a fairy-tale beauty belied by actual experience. But second, the inevitably incestuous workings of the nuclear family are revealed in the positioning of the child as voyeur in the retelling of the parents' first meeting as lovers and of their intercourse that resulted in the child.

But, as I noted above, all these ways of undercutting the ideal nuclear family do not arise from any wish to rephrase mothering (i.e. to define it in a way that is different from that of the dominant discourse), but rather emerge unintentionally from, first, the incompatibility, in dominant representation, of female sexuality and mothering and, second, from the film's focus on fetishism as a strategy for lessening male fears of female sexuality. It is this latter focus in particular that makes impossible for Von Sternberg the usual defense against hostility to the Mother in representation, i.e. hypostatization.

This lack of hypostatization of the mother in *Blonde Venus* permits more open expression of the need to repress mothering, but it is in the service of the film's constant attempt to reposition Dietrich in her familiar and preferred place as erotic object. The tension between the diegetic placing of Dietrich as

Mother and her fetishization are most evident in the long sequence where Dietrich is on the run with her child.

Narratively, Helen's running away is a violation of all the codes that have hitherto conditioned her placing – i.e. as object, as Other – first to her husband and second to Nick Townsend, her lover. As such, her deed evokes all the male rage one would expect from both her self-righteous, moralistic husband and from the State, signified by the police. For the first time in the film, we see events from Helen's perspective, allowing the extreme degree of male rage to be revealed. As Bill Nichols as noted, the mise-en-scène in this section of the film gathers together the jungle and slat motifs that symbolize the trap that Helen is in;[12] they signify the patriarchal codes that insist on confining her and depriving her of the motherhood that she has tried to appropriate to herself. A clear polarity is set up here between Helen as "performer," where indeed she continues, for the most part, to put her sexuality at the service of men, and her position as Mother, where she is no longer putting herself in a position of dependency on a man. This gap leaves room for female figures to move in as support for Helen – the (iconographically, "Hollywood lesbian") hotel manager who tips Helen off about the detective and later, in the South, the warm, supportive black maid. Both female types are, of course, those that patriarchy has defined as marginal and undesirable. It is this potentially subversive world of female bonding – a bonding that offers a threat to patriarchy – that the film has to disrupt, demolish, so as to bring Helen back into her rightful place as fetish object and, as is diegetically necessary, into her place as Mother within the circuit of the nuclear family.

This rupturing of her relationship with her child, presented as it is from Helen's point of view, exposes the cruelty of patriarchy's insistence on punishing the mother who deviates from her designated positioning. The scene at the railroad station expresses this cruelty in an unusually powerful visual manner; Dietrich's figure signifies loss in a dramatic way, and her shrunken frame on the railway bench, shrouded by the enormous hat and bent over in grief, suggests more about loss than could any dialogue. After the train leaves, she stands disconsolately on the railway track, hunched over, head bent, thin dress blowing in the wind, presenting a frail figure, helpless victim of forces stronger than herself. It is one of the rare moments in the film when Dietrich's figure is not set up for the male gaze, and where there is a moment of identification with Helen as victim.

A completely different moment of resistance to the dominant strategies of the film, which, in their various ways, seek to control and contain Dietrich's image, occurs in the final performance scene with which the "hunt" sequence culminates. Interestingly enough, it is in this performance that Dietrich dons male attire, producing an image with contradictory readings. On the one hand, the image connotes Dietrich's "masculinization" in living alone, outside of the family; on the other, the image allows subversive female–female bonding. For, as Dietrich enters the stage, she reaches out to fondle one of the departing chorus girls, using her masquerade to "legitimize" the attraction. At this moment, as women critics have noted, the female spectator may receive a powerful erotic charge through the combination of surface adherence to patriarchal codes (the male dress) and the subversive (illicit) female–female eroticism being shown.[13] This is not a response that the scene intends, constructed as it is for a narcissistic male spectator, and it demonstrates the availability of certain moments for female appropriation. For a second, Dietrich manages to combine being on display (as object for the male gaze both within the diegesis and in relation to the male spectator) with a subversive female–female bonding that functions in a mode quite other than the male objectification of the female.

But it is *only* a moment; and indeed, in terms of the entire flight, Helen has not really managed to escape from the structures that bind her. First, in relation to the child, she follows patriarchal codes in teaching him to remember his father, and their close physical relationship suggests that, following the symbolic patriarchal conception of mothering, he is a phallic replacement. That is, she never manages to break through to the nonsymbolic aspect of mothering (if, indeed, such a level is even possible, in Kristeva's terms, with a male child). Second, she continues to put her sexuality in the service of men through placing herself as object of the gaze, as spectacle, in the performances. All through the hunt sequence, the performances mitigate the "degraded" narrative role that Dietrich has been forced into. And, in fact, Dietrich remains glamorous even in her supposed "rags," since she is always on display. The camera refuses to relinquish fetishizing her, regardless of what she is engaged in diegetically and regardless of what she is wearing. And Dietrich continues to play for the camera, so that the spectator cannot even here really identify with her. We are forced to identify rather with the gazing camera, to observe/admire Dietrich, as from a distance.

Thus the "fall" is not so much visual, as far as Dietrich's own form is concerned, as purely diegetic; and even diegetically Dietrich cannot be allowed to remain as victim. As Nichols points out, Dietrich has descended so low only, of course, in order to turn around and ascend the stairs of the hovel, anticipating her phenomenal, meteoric rise to success and wealth. But it is a rise that serves only the purpose of providing more opportunity for fetishiz-ation: I do not agree with Nichols that this rise represents Helen achieving control over her actions and her life, as being in the position of "mastery." Or, to put it differently, I do not agree with the significance Nichols accords this rise, since Helen's rise is bought at such tremendous personal cost – a cost similar to that of Marguerite Gautier at the start of *Camille*. As I showed in discussing that film, the so-called "loose" woman *can* gain a degree of subjectivity (a subjectivity denied her married/betrothed/dependent sister), but only paradoxically, through manipulating the very position of erotic object conferred on her by patriarchy. Thus, the control is bounded by the terms of the system that defines the woman as "loose," and her existence continues in the service of men (i.e. to depend on men economically through the selling of the self to them).

Like the prostitute or demimondaine, Helen is, to a degree, free in her success at the end of the film. She has escaped the clutches of the two men who tried so hard to bind her to them, to possess and control her. But it is at the cost of love and intimacy. Male representational systems will not allow figures like Helen the female–female bonding, or mother–child bonding, which could replace that with man and lead to a full life. As it is, the film shows Helen in Paris cold, lonely, hard, and frigid. It is left to Nick to show her that she is really pining away for her son and the love of a man, and it is Nick who finally brings her home for reconciliation with her family. For the narrative cannot allow Helen to achieve wholeness outside of the family and apart from men.

The reconciliation is as unbelievable as the opening domestic sequences; for the diegetic requirement of Helen's reinscription in the family unit (complying with the ideology of classical Hollywood cinema in which the family is the privileged "natural" unit) is in direct contradiction with the mechanism of fetishism that is intended to exclude woman qua *woman* from the screen. Thus, in defiance of the classical Hollywood exclusion of sexuality from the family, Helen remains object of the camera's gaze in the last family sequence, dressed, as already noted, in her impossibly extravagant gown and making clear the contradiction between woman as erotic object (or narcissistic phallic replace-ment) and woman as Mother. The camera's gaze continues to eroticize her while at the same time she is object for the erotic gaze of both husband and son; it is, indeed, the child as erotic mover, as voyeur, who closes and secures the bonds that tie the Hollywood family together, bringing the film back full circle to the familiar narration of his parents' first meeting. Helen thus returns to her double confinement – by both the diegesis and the camera, never having, indeed, been able to stray away too far.

Nevertheless, the lesson of Dietrich's attempt at a degree of control is significant: her consciousness of her positioning both within the diegesis and extra-cinematically (as far as we can impute this), while not a liberation from controlling structures, reflects the one available form of resistance. Playing with her own objectification is a step beyond simply *being* objectified; and the momentary female–female bonding that subverts the dominant system while acceding to its symbolic terms is evidence of gaps in the system through which women may insert themselves.

4

The struggle for control over the female discourse and female sexuality in Welles's *Lady from Shanghai* (1946)

As Sylvia Harvey has noted, the world view presented in noir films reflects "a series of profound changes which, though they are not yet grasped or understood, are shaking the foundations of the established and therefore normal perceptions of the social order." [1] She goes on to show that it is "the strange and compelling absence of 'normal' family relations" in noir films that registers the shifts in the place women occupied in American society. [2] One of these shifts, according to Harvey, was the widespread introduction of women into the labor force in the Second World War, together with

> the changing economic and ideological function of the family that parallels the changing structure and goals of an increasingly monopolistic economy. These economic changes forced certain changes in the traditional organiz- ation of the family; and the underlying sense of horror and uncertainty in film noir may be seen, in part, as an indirect response to this forcible assault on traditional family structures and the traditional and conservative values they embodied. [3]

Christine Gledhill notes, in addition to these social forces accounting for the disturbed film-noir world, "the ongoing production of the private-eye/thriller form of detective fiction" and "the perennial myth of woman as threat to male control of the world and destroyer of male aspiration." [4]

While *Blonde Venus* sought on the one hand to control the threat of female sexuality by fetishizing the female form, and on the other to control female subjectivity by taking motherhood out of Helen's hands, returning it securely to its "rightful" place as subordinate to the father within the ideological circle of the nuclear family, Welles's film shows a heroine outside of the confines of the nuclear family altogether.

But this is not necessarily progressive, for, as Gledhill notes, the "in- dependent" woman has only two choices: work (usually as a performer in a night club) or living off a man. Any potentially progressive treatment of women is severely limited by the distasteful alternatives to marriage and motherhood. In addition, the "independent" woman often shares the cynicism of the male criminal world in which she is enmeshed, lessening further any sense of a viable alternative. And she is constantly subjected to the evaluation and moral judgement of the male investigator whose voice-over may shape our perceptions. "What this means for women," Gledhill concludes, "is the focusing of a number of contradictions, for the films both challenge the ideological hegemony of the family and in the end locate an oppressive and outcast place for women." [5]

The process of the male investigation of the female central character is highlighted in *Lady from Shanghai* because there is no other simultaneous investigation. Noir films usually begin with a murder that is the ostensible reason for the following investigative structure, but *Shanghai* starts with Michael O'Hara, in voice-over narration (the role is played charmingly, if somewhat artificially, by Welles himself), declaring his foolishness in pursuing his attraction for Elsa Bannister (Rita Hayworth). The work of the film is to recount, step by step, his increasing involvement with Elsa, his puzzlement as to the "state of her heart," and his final deception and betrayal by her.

While in the two Hollywood films previously discussed the male control over the female discourse and the female image was for the most part assured (there were, indeed, *fissures* in the patriarchal cloak through which the heroines briefly, and incompletely, strove for a subjectivity at great personal cost), in *Shanghai* there is no such nearly total control. This is the result of there being two distinct, if interconnecting, narrative levels in the film. Level I is that of Michael O'Hara's voice-over narration; level II is that of the Bannister-Elsa-Grisby triangle.

Let me look first at the O'Hara narration: in typical noir fashion, O'Hara is a hero on a quest for truth; Hayworth represents the snare in his quest, throwing him off balance, confusing him, and diverting him from the main preoccupation of his life, which in this case (and rather unusually) is presented directly as a search for purpose and identity. As in most noir films, the hero's success or not depends on whether he can extricate himself from the woman's manipulations. While sometimes the man is destroyed because he cannot resist the woman's lures, in this case the work of the film restores order through the exposure, and then destruction, of the sexual, manipulating woman.

On the first diegetic level, the female image escapes control through the device of the male voice-over narrative structure; in this case, the voice-over permits a gap to open up between sound and image, "within which an audience can judge between what they observe and the storyteller's account of it." [6] Since the Hayworth figure is completely ambiguous until the film's end, we can put what O'Hara says against what we see, resisting his account if we wish.

But we can also infer a struggle over the female discourse within the second diegetic level, which represents the world that Michael has to contend with. As an outsider to this world, Michael knows little about it; and since he is our narrative guide (nearly the whole film is presented from his point of view) we, as spectators, are similarly kept in the dark, a fact which helps to build the characteristically noir plot confusion, with its accompanying (deliberate) sense of loss, fear, alienation. For this reason, we cannot *perceive* the struggle that goes on between the men and Elsa, but we *infer* it from the glimpses we are given through Michael's interaction with the group and from the rare occasions on which we are privy to interactions between Bannister, Grisby, and Elsa when Michael is not present.

Let me begin with the struggle over the female image and discourse on the first narrative level, i.e. the voice-over narration of Michael's story. What is striking here (and what differentiates film noir from other genres) is the foregrounding of woman as enigma, mystery. A feminist re-reading of *Blonde Venus* revealed that, indeed, diegetic operations were such as to prevent the heroine from "being known" to the spectator. For varying reasons, she was not really present as herself, but stood in for something else (functioned as a sign, that is). But the narrative did not itself rely on this unknowability, or strive to point it out to the spectator. We could say that it was an unconscious effect of male fears and fantasies about women. But in *Lady from Shanghai*, the woman's unknowability provides the very impetus for the narrative: the hero's task is to discover the truth about the woman, a truth that constantly evades him, as it does therefore also the spectator, positioned as we are within his perspective. However, we constantly strive to know her from her image, and from what she says in the brief interactions with the protagonist, apart from what he says about her.

It may be useful at this point to speculate on the different positions of the male and the female spectator toward the heroine in *Lady from Shanghai*. As I discussed in chapter 1, some feminist film theorists, like Mary Ann Doane, are re-thinking Mulvey's tentative conclusion (in "Visual pleasure"[7]) that classical cinema is largely constructed for the male spectator. Doane, for instance, suggests that certain genres, like the woman's film, are in fact constructed explicitly for the female spectator. What has not yet been sufficiently explored are the ways in which the female spectator may be positioned differently from men in films clearly constructed for the *male* spectator. In *Lady from Shanghai*, for instance, it is possible that only the female spectator is able to "read" the ambiguity evident in Elsa's representation. Like *Blonde Venus*, *Lady from Shanghai* is constructed for the male spectator, but the female spectator may be able to avoid some of the positionings by *not necessarily* identifying with Michael O'Hara. The female spectator, that is, may alone be able to perceive the gap that Gledhill suggests opens up in the film between the male voice-over and the female image.

The male spectator would find it difficult in this film to occupy any position other than that of identification with O'Hara, thus experiencing the same phenomenon vis-à-vis Hayworth as that O'Hara describes. O'Hara's flashback narration of the couple's first meeting is significant in establishing the sexual discourse in which O'Hara is enmeshed; his opening words: "When I start to make a fool of myself, there's nothing will stop me," are accompanied by images of a carriage moving through the shadowed Central Park. A woman's lovely, starkly lit white face emerges from the darkness, gazing ahead confidently. O'Hara continues: "If I'd known how it would end, I'd never have started. But once I'd seen her, once I'd seen her, I was not in my right mind for quite some time."

The experience here is analogous to that described by Laura Mulvey, when, having summarized Lacan's theory of the mirror phase, she notes:

> Important for this essay is the fact that it is an image that constitutes the matrix of the imaginary, of recognition/misrecognition and identification, and hence of the first articulation of the I, of subjectivity. This is a moment when an older fascination with looking (at the mother's face, for an obvious example) collides with the initial inklings of self-awareness.[8]

In other words, at the moment of *seeing* Elsa, O'Hara regresses to the realm of the imaginary, which is governed by the memory of fusion with the Mother in illusory unity; he experiences a longing for *refusion*, together with a temporary loss of ego, characteristic of the merged stage (i.e. "I was not in my right mind for quite some time"). As Mulvey puts it: "The sense of forgetting the world as the ego has subsequently come to perceive it (I forgot who I am and where I was) is nostalgically reminiscent of that presubjective moment of image recognition."[9]

Only some such psychoanalytic phenomenon can explain O'Hara's total obsession with Elsa, against his reason, against his better judgement. He is a man driven with desire, acting almost against his will. He says: "I had nothing better to do than to get in trouble: some people would have smelled danger, but not me." A little later on he repeats his sense of being outside of himself: "That's how I found her," he says, "and then I was not myself for some time. I did nothing but think of her."

The "sense of forgetting the world," i.e. of O'Hara having entered some "other" space is emphasized by the cinematic techniques of the opening scene. The sets are strangely artificial – more so than in other noir films or than is usual in Welles (outside of *Touch of Evil*). The park scenes are darkly lit so as to highlight the harsh, glaring light (without any softening fill light) that falls on Hayworth's face as it emerges from the shadows of the carriage. This has the effect of isolating Hayworth's face, providing a separate space for it, as though it is in a vacuum. Making no pretense at realism, Welles allows the carriage to

Plate 5   At the moment of first *seeing* Elsa, O'Hara regresses to the realm of the imaginary which is governed by memory of illusory fusion with the Mother. Note Hayworth's starkly lit face, while Michael's face, framed in the carriage window, seems disembodied. Coded for sexuality (note her low-cut, tight-fitting dress, her flawless lips and face, her eyes that return O'Hara's fascinated gaze), Elsa is nevertheless strangely chaste.

seem to float in space, not secured to any surrounding environment, like the carriage that picks up Death in Fritz Lang's *Destiny*. We are given no sense of anything going on outside of the frame: the frame *is* the only space. The same effect governs the street and garage scenes, where the human figures stand as if frozen, like waxworks. This surreal quality adds to the sense of claustrophobia and nightmare characteristic of noir films a further feeling of being trapped. Clearly in a psychological rather than any other kind of space, we know that we are following an internal drama, a battle for knowledge, truth, identity, as well as for power and control. It is this atmosphere that will paradoxically pervade the boat, which, as outdoor space, could have reflected openness.

If for O'Hara things are happening at the level of primary identification, for the male spectator, identifying with him, they happen as secondary identification.[10] The male spectator gains satisfaction from the vicarious experience of a fusion he also (psychoanalytically) seeks; following the same processes as O'Hara, he is carried along in a similar return to the pre-symbolic.

A typical male spectator's response, described by Jean-Claude Allais, corroborates that the above is, indeed, happening. Allais says:

> For a long time, the spectator does not suspect the hideous reality hidden beneath the divine appearance of Rita. Blonde, magnificent, sculptural, she continues to incarnate an ideal founded above all on the physical fascination she exerts. Her beauty puts her above all suspicion. She is Rosalind. She is innocence and purity, Queen of an unknown universe (one which remains so because of the editing – we know only that the Chinese obey her with devotion), she is a goddess, surely, merely inhabiting an earthly body for a little while, remaining inaccessible.[11]

Hayworth is here idealized to the level of the Divine, her beauty evoking unremitting desire and longing while she yet remains inaccessible.

For the female spectator, however, not caught up necessarily in the same mechanism of desire for refusion with the Mother, the Hayworth figure appears ambiguous from the start. O'Hara himself makes us wary when he notes that others would have smelled danger on her, but there is something odd as well about the way Elsa is riding alone in the dark park. In typical noir fashion, she is coded for sexuality (viz. her low-cut, tight-fitting dress, her flawless lips and mouth, her seductive eyes), yet she seems strangely chaste, until she makes an open sexual play for O'Hara just before leaving him. The gun that O'Hara found in her bag makes us suspicious and adds a castrating power sufficient, at this point, to make O'Hara vow to stay away from her.

But any doubts about Elsa on O'Hara's part are apparently dispelled after the swimming scene. Having confronted Elsa, O'Hara is convinced by her tears of her innocence, and from then on is totally obsessed. But at least the female spectator, having more distance, has a chance to see her insincerity. Hayworth's glance, for instance, often seems clouded, indirect, impenetrable; and while she pretends to want to go away with O'Hara, somehow one is never convinced; the flicker in her glance at the very end, when he is participating in Grisby's plot in order to get money to live with her, gives away her true position. And the mise-en-scène here alerts the viewer that all is not well. As the lovers talk in the museum, supposedly vowing their passion for one another, large forms of fish and other monstrous creatures swim in the background, their huge jaws sometimes bigger than both human heads together.

But here, as throughout, Michael is unaware that he is being consumed by monsters, dazzled as he is by Hayworth's image. From the start, Hayworth refuses to be controlled, resisting and eluding O'Hara; her cool stance in the park scene marks her independence (for example, the assault ruffles her not a bit); and her possession of the gun, her wealth, and commanding position (she mentions her luxury boat that she "needs a man for") suggest a woman in authority; finally, her past (she was able to survive in Shanghai, a town where "you need more than luck") suggests her ability to take care of herself.

Yet, once Michael is hired and on the boat, Elsa plays another game; she now pretends to need Michael, to be the victim of her husband who is blackmailing her somehow – this is a position supported by her maid who calls Hayworth a "poor thing", someone who lives in a miserable situation. In other words, she *pretends* to surrender control of her discourse to Michael while in fact, of course, doing nothing of the sort. (Perhaps her masculine dress on the boat in a couple of scenes, recalling that of Dietrich in *Blonde Venus*, but used differently, is meant to suggest her underlying control of the narrative.)

From what we can infer about the second level of the narrative, i.e. the Bannister–Elsa–Grisby triangle, a similar struggle for control over Elsa's discourse and sexuality goes on, only in this case the battle-lines are more evenly drawn. Bannister and Grisby know who Elsa is, but they do not necessarily know at any point what in particular she is plotting. The world represented by Bannister and Grisby is ugly, cruel, twisted; both men are barely sane, and Bannister is bitter about his crippled legs. Presumably unable to satisfy Elsa sexually, he has hired a detective, Broom (masked as a cook), to ensure that she remains faithful. But Elsa is not only constantly watched by Broom; Grisby also keeps an eye on her, partly out of his own ugly lust, but also out of loyalty to his partner, Bannister.

In this level of the narrative, then, Elsa is positioned as object of the gaze of three men, who strive through the gaze to possess her, to control her sexuality, and to repress her discourse. That Elsa again refuses to be so bound is evident in the remarkable scene where she is sunbathing on the boat deck.

One of Bannister's strategies for controlling Elsa is sarcastic taunting that simultaneously degrades and provokes her. Her only weapon against her husband is her sexuality, and we see how she uses it in this scene. Bannister gets at Hayworth indirectly here by taunting Michael about his desire to leave the boat. As this discussion goes on, the camera keeps cutting to Hayworth's lovely form, laid out on the boat roof and decked in bikini-style swimsuit. The editing creates a kind of alternate space for Hayworth, since for much of the time she is not seen in the same frame with anyone else (even the strange cigarette-passing scene, which links her and Grisby surreptitiously, is done with a slow pan along her arm and hand to Grisby's hand, so that, while connected, it seems to be at great distance); she is isolated in her cold beauty, the shots functioning like inserts, unrelated to the narrative and creating a disturbing, surreal effect.

The editing reflects Hayworth's second strategy for resisting Bannister's control, which is withdrawal, distancing. She refuses to be provoked, remaining cool, unruffled, sure of her sexual appeal. To highlight this appeal, she begins to sing, in a husky, sexy voice, a luring song that underscores the symbolism of the boat's name, *Le Circe*. Hayworth is here the Siren, luring the sailors to their death. As her song gains strength, the four men connected to her – Bannister, Grisby, O'Hara, and Broom – all stop to listen, enticed by the desire it evokes. Above and below deck, the men all lean in the direction of the voice, unable to resist its power.

Structurally, of course, Hayworth *is* bound, in the second level of the narrative, through her marriage to Bannister and through whatever additional hold he has over her. We can infer that her manipulations and plotting are in part an effect of being controlled, although a sheer, corrupt motive of greed is presumably also involved. And O'Hara is the means through which she intends to liberate herself.

The second triangle – Bannister–Elsa–O'Hara – is the way in which the two levels of the narrative come together. This is a triangle full of deceit, for Elsa is deceiving both her husband and O'Hara by plotting with Grisby behind both their backs. O'Hara believes he is functioning to "save" Hayworth from her cruel, sadistic husband. The male spectator is constructed so as to believe in this image, along with Michael, for Elsa's behavior appears, on the surface, to support it.

The event which seals O'Hara's place in this triangle is the monstrous picnic that Bannister arranges, and which recalls the famous one in *Citizen Kane*. This picnic, like the one in that film, symbolizes the character's perversity: the jungle undergrowth, the crocodiles, the stagnant water, the vulture-like birds, all suggest the sickness of Bannister's soul, its brutal, twisted nature. The image of Hayworth gliding unconcerned through this lurid environment is again most likely read differently by the male and the female spectator: for the dazzled male spectator, who wants to believe in her innocence, the image seems to prove her purity; for the female spectator, more distant, the image suggests Elsa's toughness: she is a match for her environment and able to handle all that it involves.

The confrontation with Bannister at this picnic finally seals O'Hara's hatred of the man and what he stands for, and sets O'Hara up to play into Grisby's hands, lured by the money with which to win Elsa. He believes himself to be in a position to *possess* Elsa, while in fact it is she who "possesses" him through her underlying control of the narrative.

There is thus, on both levels of the narrative, an attempt to possess Elsa by controlling her sexuality and governing her discourse, but the opposite mechanisms are used in each case. We are reminded again of Karen Horney's observations (mentioned in chapter 1), where she notes the many artistic expressions by men of "the violent force by which man feels himself drawn to the woman, and side by side with his longing, the dread that through her he might die and be undone." [12] If the longing, with its accompanying idealization (glorification) is one way to conceal the dread, fetishizing the woman (as we've seen in the case of *Blonde Venus*) is another.

And both mechanisms come into play in *Shanghai*: O'Hara attempts to possess Hayworth through idealization, while Bannister and Grisby try to possess her through fetishism, achieved through the power of the gaze.

Bannister, because of his crippled state, can do little else *but* gaze (his necessary passivity makes fetishism inevitable); while Grisby must confine himself to gazing because Hayworth is unavailable. Archetypal voyeur, Grisby loves to watch the world secretively through his powerful binoculars, and the spectator is often positioned so as to be a voyeur with him, particularly as he picks up Hayworth's image.

These two mechanisms are the means through which the male spectator is sutured into the film's narrative – not, however, without a certain ambiguity, since the stance toward the female form, on the part of the men in the two narrative levels, is necessarily different (at least in some aspects; all the men desire Elsa and are dazzled by her beauty). While the female spectator may indeed take up one or other of these positions (standing then in the masculine position), she may also, as we've seen, remain more detached. In fact, the female spectator is free to watch the interplay of the two struggles to possess Elsa, across the diegesis, a position made possible by the opening up of the gap between voice-over and image, and also by the very existence of the two narrative levels.

As we've seen, the female spectator may also infer Elsa's resistance against domination by the male gaze in both the above forms. But it is important to note that Elsa is positioned so that her only available resistances are negative. Given the patriarchal structures that define and limit women, the woman who subordinates herself to the Law of the Father is the morally admirable one. Resistance, almost by definition then, when viewed from the masculine position, requires the woman becoming evil. In this case, Elsa's only weapons in her struggle are sexuality and deceit. She struggles against Bannister's fetishizing of her by seducing O'Hara, driving Bannister mad with jealousy; and she struggles against O'Hara's domination (through idealization) by manipulating and betraying him. The cost of her "independence" is moral degradation, since, given the male system in which she is embedded, she must be punished for her resistance to the codes laid down for women. The narrative, then, follows a pattern that first is a reflection of (unconscious) male fears and fantasies about women and second, offers a *warning* to men about the danger of the beautiful, sexual woman, should they give in to their desire for her.

The last section of the film represents, symbolically, the consequences of O'Hara's desire for, and idealization of, Hayworth. The crazy world of the fairground where Hayworth has, literally, transported O'Hara reflects the craziness of his obsession with her. Metaphorically, she had transported him to a "mad" space, so that he was willing to do almost anything, including risking his life, to win her. The horrific ride down the fairground chute, during which O'Hara is confronted with one terrifying image after another, symbolizes all the horrors that result from the kind of liaison O'Hara has entered into. The nightmare-like scene images the monstrous events that his misplaced trust has produced.

Plate 6　In a striking image, we see Hayworth's myriad reflections down the long line of mirrors, intertwined with those of the two men who have tried, in different ways, to possess her. Her gun points directly at the camera, while that of Bannister points first at Elsa and second at O'Hara within the frame. Michael is defenceless (as he has been, psychologically, throughout the film), and his image is inserted between those of the married couple in a suggestively Oedipal manner.

Paradoxically, by the time O'Hara wakes up in the crazy world of the fairground, he is "sane" about Elsa, as he tells us in voice-over narration. As a result of events at the trial, he finally "knew" about her. The knowledge is essential for the effect of the confrontation with Hayworth in the Hall of Mirrors that happens as soon as O'Hara finishes his ride. In a striking image, shot from O'Hara's point of view, we see Hayworth's myriad reflections down the long line of mirrors, mocking O'Hara's regression to the world of the pre-symbolic, which, as we saw, marked a return to the pre-Oedipal fascination with the Mother's face. The moment of mis-recognition that the mirror phase marks is also recalled here since the attempt at refusion with Hayworth was itself a mis-recognition, marking a fruitless effort to return to a phase that is in reality gone forever. The line of images suggests that while O'Hara has a thousand copies of Hayworth, he in fact has nothing; she is now what she has been throughout the film – an image, an empty signifier, a pure ego-ideal.

Bannister's entry into the scene marks the Oedipal nature of what is transpiring here; he is the Third Term, the Father, the Law (in both senses). His entry is visually dramatic since as he comes into the Hall of Mirrors he too is reflected many times. We see a long line of his white crutches, underscoring his castration. He is the crippled Father, the Law, weakened by insufficient manliness. Unable to possess his woman properly, and now assuming that she is plotting to elope with O'Hara, he has come to kill her, even though, as he says, to kill her is to kill himself.

The extraordinary image of Bannister surrounded by multiple images of Hayworth as he gets ready to shoot her suggests the multiple images that Hayworth has been funneled into throughout the movie; her body has been the site of fragmented, incoherent representations that never coalesced into a coherent whole. Seen by different men differently, Hayworth was a figure that could never be grasped, never understood.

Up to this point in this amazing scene, we have been given a series of mirror images, which, while providing multiple representations, have kept the body intact. Once the shooting starts everything is shattered, and again this shattering takes on different symbolic implications for the two male protagonists involved. (Significantly, Hayworth does not have a point of view here – the narrative has so positioned her as object that, in this denouement, there is no place for her perspective.) For O'Hara, the shattering of the mirrors signals a return to the realm of the symbolic, an end to his enmeshment in the imaginary. (This return will be underscored by the discussion he has with Hayworth about morality just before she dies.) For Bannister, the shattering of the mirrors symbolizes the end of his illusion about possessing her beauty: now that she apparently loves another, her sexuality must be recognized outside of himself, and for this she must die. In a scene that reminds one of O'Hara's tale of the sharks lusting after their own blood, husband and wife ludicrously shoot at the multiple images each now has of the other and of themselves: they have lost all sense of subject and object, self and Other, in a mad world of illusions and of mergings.

But the shattering of the mirrors has yet one more dimension. While for the characters within the film it represents a shattering of the world of the imaginary, for the spectator it represents a shattering of the world of the film. Just as the characters are made to realize, through the device of the broken mirror image, their participation in a world of illusory images (waking up, as it were, to "reality"), so the spectator now realizes that the film has been a dream from which s/he finally awakens as the mirrors are shattered. The screen, like the mirror, allowed the spectator to "regress," i.e. to participate in the film on the level of the imaginary.

One scene in particular marks this awakening on the part of both characters and spectator: it is the shot where the camera peeks through a piece of jagged glass into a blank, empty space, strewn with glass fragments. With its washed-out, overexposed look, the image appears like a desert or a wasteland. It is as though we have gone *through* the mirror, *through* illusion, and are standing on the barren, other side – the side divorced from the imaginary.

Significantly, the camera finds Hayworth standing in the wreckage; as she stumbles out, barely alive, we see that her composure has finally been broken by the imminence of death. With the collapse of her image, the "real" Hayworth emerges, ultimately vulnerable. But it is too late to remedy things with O'Hara: the discussion that reflects a return to the realm of the symbolic shows the huge moral gap between O'Hara and Elsa; for she believes that winning is all, while O'Hara claims to be disgusted by such a position.

Nevertheless, O'Hara's final action of refusing Elsa any comfort as she lies dying belies his self-righteous morality reflected throughout the movie. His behavior underscores the narcissistic Oedipal investment he had had in Elsa: bitterly disillusioned in his search for the ideal woman (refusion with the Mother), he cannot bear to go near her. His last words are to the effect that he will spend the rest of his life forgetting her.

Constructed for a male spectator, *Lady from Shanghai* ultimately presents an extremely complex and somewhat ambiguous view of woman. The subversive aspects have to do with demystifying the myth of the beautiful, pure, and innocent woman which has for so long captured men's imagination and arises out of the desire for refusion with the Mother – a regression that permits a lessening of the threat of sexual difference, and a return to a place that was safe for the little boy because it predated knowledge of difference.

At the same time, Welles undercuts the conception of the male hero; the typical male spectator cannot find in O'Hara that screen ego-ideal mentioned by Laura Mulvey who "can make things happen and control events better than the subject/spectator, just as the image in the mirror was more in control of motor coordination."[13] For O'Hara's voice-over constantly undercuts his ability to be in fact the hero the film requires. He is, from the start, disbelieving about the cinematic hero-mechanism, joking that he was only able to "play the hero" in the park because the men he was up against were amateurs (while he, we later learn, had been a professional killer in Franco's Spain). By the end of the film, we realize that O'Hara has in fact been the victim of the very object of his obsession: thinking himself the subject of the discourse and in control, he has in fact been out of control, unbeknownst to the male spectator; O'Hara is recounting the narrative after it has taken place, and is constantly sarcastic about his past illusions, warning the spectator not to believe in appearances. O'Hara is really an Othello type, too trusting and too honest himself to imagine the depth of deception others might be capable of.[14]

But if the film has certain subversive aspects, first, in Welles's destruction of a cloying, sentimental, and false female ideal and, second, in his deconstruction of the macho male protagonist, we cannot say that his treatment of Elsa is ultimately progressive. It is true that there is something subversive in the open presentation of female sexuality in the film, and in the fact that Elsa resists the men's attempts to dominate her. Refusing to be bound by male definitions and controls, Elsa, as we've seen, uses her sexuality in the only ways available to gain her "independence."

It is, however, an "independence" that no one can admire, since it is based on manipulation, greed, and murder. There is, thus, little that is progressive about a male director substituting for a form of structural repression (submission to the Law of the Father) an independence that, while permitting the woman freedom from the confines of family, is based on moral degradation. We will see in the next chapter how, when such an independence is granted without moral degradation (i.e. is seen from the female perspective), the full irrational force of male aggression toward the resisting woman is exposed.

5 Forms of phallic domination in the contemporary Hollywood film: Brooks's *Looking for Mr Goodbar* (1977)

As Molly Haskell and others have noted, two main cycles of films have dominated commercial cinema since the mid-1960s, in the wake of the women's movement. The first excluded women (these were the so-called "buddy-buddy" films) in an effort to avoid the problem of sexual difference altogether; while the second, emerging when the problem of sexual difference could no longer be avoided, showed women being raped and subjected to violence.

This latter cycle was prepared for in 1960 by a film which, while at that moment condemned for its unnecessary sadism, is now seen as ahead of its time – Michael Powell's *Peeping Tom*. This film, perhaps more than any other, brings together the mechanisms underlying all three of the earlier Hollywood films discussed, where we saw the attempt by patriarchy to eliminate woman's threat, first by dominating her through the controlling power of the gaze; second by fetishizing her; and finally through murder. The first two mechanisms depend very obviously on the camera as the apparatus for controlling and manipulating the look, and for objectifying woman. But the representation of woman murdered is, of course, equally the product of the camera used to control the female image, i.e. to oppress woman through representation itself. The camera is the means through which the feminine in representation is relegated to a male construct, so that women are deprived of owning "the feminine," and even of discovering what the feminine might be, outside of male constructs.

Ultimately a more complex and interesting work than the so-called "mad-slasher" movies emerging in the 1980s, *Peeping Tom* is also useful here in its dimension as a film that literalizes both the power of the camera to subdue women and the way the cinema constructs a masochistic female spectator. The psychopathic hero uses his camera, first, to seduce women. What is interesting here is that he relies paradoxically on the construction of women in patriarchy as to-be-gazed-at – a construction that women have internalized – to lure them into his realm. The desire of the women in *Peeping Tom* to be seen – to be objectified, made into spectacle – is what makes them vulnerable to his manipulation.[1]

But the hero secondly turns his camera into the destroying phallus (exposing here the link between the phallus/knife as murder weapon in noir films and the camera as phallic substitute for domination), since one of the tripod legs suddenly shoots out a knife (recalling the phallic/knife walking-stick in *Gilda*) as the hero begins the process of filming.

Finally, *Peeping Tom* exposes the way the cinema screen reflects women's masochistic identification with the female image as victim, through the device of the mirror attached to the hero's camera. Most brutally of all, his victims are forced to witness their own murder in the mirror placed so as to compel their vision. The woman spectator is thus in the position of experiencing a doubly masochistic identification: first, she identifies with the female figure and *her* construction as masochistic spectator; and second, there is her own position in the cinema as spectator identifying with the female victim.

The cycle that *Peeping Tom* prepares for is represented in the early 1970s by films like *A Clockwork Orange* and *Klute*, and a little later on by *Last Tango in Paris*, *Straw Dogs*, and *Lipstick*. The first two films show women treated brutally by men: in *Clockwork* women are abused, taunted, and finally raped; in *Klute*, the murderer's crazed final speech to the heroine exposes the underlying hostility toward female sexuality; women, for him, all want sex, and they titillate men to get it, the prostitute here simply expressing in a more overt form behavior that all women secretly aspire to.

Last Tango in Paris and *Straw Dogs* add a certain twist in that while women are again forcibly assaulted, they succumb to the rape finally because they become sexually aroused. Their behavior, in other words, corroborates the crazed murderer's notion that women all yearn for sex.[2] *Lipstick*, meanwhile, points toward a trend that has become fashionable in the 1980s, namely women first raped and brutally treated but then seen taking revenge on their rapists. Woman now has the phallus, in the shape of the gun, and her threat is diminished by dressing her in male clothes and in giving her the essentially male avenging role. Thus, the pattern fits the recent one of masculinizing women (which I mentioned in the Introduction) in that the dominant–submission pattern is kept intact but gender identification within the pattern has been altered.[3]

It is significant that in the 1980s the cycle of films showing brutality toward, and then on the part of, women has been relegated to the "B" film and to the horror genre. As the 1970s drew to a close, yet another cycle emerged in mainstream commercial film – a cycle geared specifically to a female audience and dealing explicitly with issues that the women's movement has raised. As Charlotte Brunsdon has noted, in an article on *An Unmarried Woman*, extra-cinematic factors provided the context for these films: these are the social, political, and economic events such as the changing patterns of women's employment and education, changing sexual patterns (brought about partly by the women's movement and the ready availability of contraception), and changes in the patterns of marriage and divorce.[4] As Brunsdon goes on to note, these films are concerned with the conflicting demands placed on women as they begin to undertake new roles within patriarchal structures barely ready for them – with, that is, "the contradictory and fragmented nature of femininities constructed within masculine hegemony"[5] and exposed by the new liberation.

In many ways, *Looking for Mr Goodbar*, made in 1977, is the film that provides the link between the mainstream cycle of films of the early 1970s showing violence toward women and the new cycle of "women's films" of the late 1970s which Brunsdon discusses. The threat elicited by the women's movement has lessened in the 1980s as American culture works towards integrating (at best), co-opting (at worst), demands made by women; so that a gap has opened up in which problems around sexual difference and gender roles can at least be addressed, even if the results are far from progressive.

And *Goodbar* does, like the later films, address the fundamental issue of female independence and the problems caused by it; but the film is still embedded in the extra-cinematic legacy of 1960s ideology, which has, by the 1970s, turned sour; the free-love and utopian idealism of the flower-children and the hippies, who took drugs to transcend bourgeois limitations, was transformed into middle-class wife-swapping and marijuana-taking, aimed at bolstering flagging sexual interest and boring corporate lives; or into the desperate search in the singles bars for drugs and the sexual "fix" that would mask the loneliness of alienated lives, spawned by increased mobility, the new industrial patterns of the computer age, and the further breakdown of community in the large urban centers.

In addition, *Goodbar* reflects the greater threat that the idea of female liberation still held for patriarchy in the mid-1970s. In this way it looks back not only to the early-1970s cycle of films showing violence to women but also to the dilemmas faced by heroines in the three Hollywood films just discussed. There is indeed the extra-cinematic historical specificity in the mid-1970s, which gives the film its particular coloring and special shaping, but beneath that we find conflicts and contradictions that refer to earlier patterns of female positioning within patriarchy. *Goodbar* is like *Camille* (and unlike the two other films) in being constructed for the female spectator; but it is like *Shanghai* in having a heroine who refuses to abandon her desire as the price for subjectivity. This combination of a film made from the heroine's position and containing a heroine who refuses to abandon her desire does, arguably, produce a relatively new situation in some respects; but since Teresa's position is still within a patriarchal structure that tries to control and dominate her, the novelty of her situation is ultimately reduced to a matter of degree.

Or perhaps we could say that Teresa's greater possibilities for leading her "own" life and for sexual satisfaction (as against those of the heroines in the three other Hollywood films) simply produces greater, more dangerous contradictions for her; her larger possibilities, that is, make her a more serious threat to patriarchal discourse and bring down even more hostility and rage on her head than most of the earlier heroines provoked. Even though her punishment "equals" that of Elsa in *Shanghai*, it is even more horrible in that she has been constructed as "good": narratively, she has done nothing to "earn" her murder, leaving even more exposed the rage she has aroused in the male figures by the sheer fact of her resistance to their domination.

The possibilities for independence available to Teresa, but not to the earlier Hollywood heroines, makes tempting a reading of the film as indeed about a "liberated" woman: one could see Teresa as trying to activate her desire and control her own life once she leaves her father's house. And many scenes in the film, taken on their surface level, would seem to justify such a reading. For instance, from the start Teresa is sexually aggressive: first, in her fantasy of a passionate embrace with Martin Engle, her professor, she marches confidently across the room and into his arms; then, once in his apartment as his assistant (in the film's present), she makes the first sexual advance. The love-making is shot this first time (as every subsequent time) to focus on *her* pleasure (we have close-ups of her face and hear her moans; she is the one who wants it to go on). In later scenes, we see her literally seduce Martin (bending over him with raised skirts), and on another occasion she rushes into Martin's car, already pulling up her skirt. So her eagerness is clearly shown. She does finally become disenchanted with Martin because of his coldness after the love-making, but nevertheless she has experienced pleasure with him.

We continue to see Teresa seeking out and enjoying physical pleasure with the men she meets; she is represented as eager for sex with Tony, and fully satisfied afterwards, and she rejects James at least in part because of his sexual gaucheness. As a woman eager for new experiences and refusing to be bound by the limits imposed by her father, she leaves home, gets a job to support herself by, and lives alone in her apartment, not depending on any one man in particular.

She is also fearless. The images present a woman unafraid of the "dangerous" night life: she remains cool throughout the meeting with the awesome drug-dealer and has no qualms about bringing totally strange men up to her apartment.

Nevertheless, to read the film as about a "liberated" woman would be to falsify its meanings by falling into the trap of relating to screen images as unified "essences," instead of looking at them as configurations in a total narrative system. Viewed in the latter manner, the meanings of the film can be seen to derive from the overall positioning of Teresa in the patriarchal world in which she moves. Such a reading reveals that the film is more complex and more ideologically conservative than the surface reading around "liberation" can allow.

Let me begin with the ideological conservatism: like many 1970s films dealing with the so-called "sexual liberation" of the 1960s and post-1960s, *Goodbar* constructs a basically negative view of the "singles" life; Brooks seems indeed to be drawing on films from Antonioni's *Blow Up* and Schlesinger's *Darling* to Pakula's *Klute* in his imagery of dark-lit bars, full of people drinking alcohol and taking drugs. The camera in these scenes is always in close-up, focusing particularly on female bodies, stressing cleavages and ample bosoms; on the sound track, the insistent jazz or disco music expresses an endlessly fast pace, a desperate hecticness. And the sordidness extends beyond the singles life to Teresa's unhappily married sister; Kathleen and her husband, doped out most of the time, watch pornography films and engage in sex orgies – so that no matter where Teresa turns, she is met with dope, sex, and drink.

In an earlier Hollywood film, the conservatism would have been underscored by providing a contrast between this sordid night life and an idealized Mother. *Looking for Mr Goodbar* is interestingly enough quite critical of the nuclear family that is here shown as far from ideal. Nevertheless, the film manages to introduce the idealized Mother in the shape of the heroine herself: in her daytime life, Teresa is a loving, nurturing teacher of deaf children. Warm and sensitive in this Mother role, Teresa is particularly helpful to the most needy child in her class, Amy, who is poor and black.

Through this clever device, we once again have a Hollywood film that separates the discourses of sexuality and Motherhood because of the difficulty patriarchy has in combining the two.[6] Throughout the second half of the film, there is cutting between Teresa's night-time sexual activities and her daytime "mothering" ones; the images are completely disconnected and contradictory, Teresa combining the traditional virgin-whore split within herself.[7] It is a split, moreover, that extends to all the women in the film: Teresa's two sisters are, on the one hand, Brigid, the mother (and unattractive) and, on the other, Kathleen, the "whore" (and sexually exciting). Mrs Dunn, the mother of all three girls, is totally subdued, beaten, and unattractive.

The combination of traditional cinematic discourses in relation to women and the newer discourse of liberation creates a series of contradictions in the film. The surface theme of liberation is, indeed, rendered problematic by the very presence of the traditional discourses. Because of the underlying traditional discourses, that is, the film is only able to conceive of liberation in its most popularized form, as it has filtered down through the media; and this is viewed critically as little more than self-indulgence or fanaticism. That Teresa's father links what she is doing to women's liberation is evident from his comment during their fight that he is not the tyrant that "the holy war of the bra-burning crusade" would no doubt dub him. And yet Teresa herself in no way associates what she is doing with women's liberation; her dissociation is clear in the scene when she is baby-sitting on New Year's Eve. The television announcer is heard saying that 1975 has been the "Year of the Dames," and there are shots of women demonstrating, but Teresa completely ignores the screen. (In the novel, her dissociation is more self-conscious, more self-destructive, for some teachers at her school actually invite her to participate in a consciousness-raising group. It is clear here that Teresa has little sense of female bonding, but the narrative does not explain the reasons directly.)

Clearly, to have had Teresa associate herself positively with the women's movement would have necessitated taking the movement seriously as offering alternatives for women. What the film does, rather, is to construct an ideology that *explains* Teresa's "liberation" (to the extent that it is shown as that) as a form of resistance to her "correct" placing (i.e. the traditional one of being subject to the Law of the Father). In this reading, far from having a "liberated" woman, or a woman owning the desire, we have a heroine still controlled by the patriarchal structures she grew up in. Although most of the film is shot from Teresa's point of view, as was *Camille* from Marguerite's, we see that the narrative is structured so as to reveal her need for male figures.

Plate 7 The film constructs an ideology that *explains* Teresa's "liberation" as a form of resistance to her "correct" placing as subordinate to the Law of the Father. Note here Teresa's slant-eyed "return" of Tony's look, signifying the "fallen" woman. (Compare with chapter 3, plate 3 of Dietrich.)

The ideology through which this need is inscribed is, not surprisingly, that of psychoanalysis. In other words, below the surface level, the narrative furnishes all the information necessary for exposing Teresa's behavior as motivated by her father's rejection. We learn, for instance, of Teresa's jealousy of her beautiful sister, much adored by their father; we see the repressed, absent mother, who never intervenes for her daughter; we discover that her father's difficulty in dealing with Teresa's scoliosis results from his repressing his own sister's death as a result of the same disease – he rejects Teresa because she reminds him of pain he cannot handle. From all of this, Teresa is seen as desperately needing her father's love and approval, but, unable to obtain it, she becomes what he most hates.

Thus, using psychoanalytic terms, the film constructs a family scenario of rejections and sibling rivalries that more than account for Teresa's problems in "adjusting" to her "rightful" role as a woman.[8] According to this discourse, her unresolved Oedipal crisis prevents her from establishing a healthy relationship with a suitable man like James, who loves her and wants to protect her. Her resistance to the idea of marriage and family comes partly from her rejection of her family, in turn for being rejected, but is compounded by her fear of having children because of her congenital scoliosis.

Thus, we can see how the film has explained her "liberation" as having no more meaning than her need for love from her father. She seeks her father in Professor Engle and once again is disappointed; thus, according to the film's discourse, she is ready to give up on love, marriage, permanent connecting. She rejects James just *because* he wants monogamy, just *because* he wants "protect" her; she can no longer believe in such ways of relating since she has been so disappointed before.

The final scene with her father before her death corroborates this aspect of the film's discourse. What happens in this scene is a sort of therapeutic release for Teresa, first from the burden of her father's lies about his sister Maureen; and second from the repression of his real feelings of repulsion for Teresa. She finally gets him to admit how painful it was to see his sister suffer and be tormented by her brothers, and his guilt in having his own child suffer in the same way through *his* genetic inheritance. Teresa forces the truth on him, crippling him with pain, but she is then freed from her bitter resentment towards him, and even finally pities him.

After this episode, she seems ready to begin a new life, affirming that the film's discourse about her rebellion has been the traditional psychoanalytic one. We see her cleaning her apartment for the first time, and she has it brightly lit, also for the first time. She flushes all her drugs down the toilet and ends the crazy relationship with Tony. Although she refuses to go out with James on New Year's Eve, she has not totally closed the door on him. The dialogue between them leaves possible her "adjustment" to the nice, stable, protective man who, according to the discourse, she ought to have. Refusing also to spend the evening with her sister and new boyfriend, Teresa finally decides to go to the bar. But, as she tells the barman, "this is my last night cruising bars," and we see indeed that she intends to begin a new life. A shot of James in the bar reminds us that she should have been with him; for subsequently we realize that her murder would not have taken place had she been ready a moment earlier to settle for what was "best" for her.

This psychoanalytic discourse, then, accounts for what happens to Teresa in the film: it accounts for her leaving home, her refusal to marry James, her sexual promiscuity, the desperation that leads her to drink and take drugs; and finally, it accounts for her murder. But while the film is almost successful in masking the reasons underlying the need for the psychoanalytic discourse, namely that patriarchy simply cannot tolerate a woman who transgresses the position prepared for her (i.e. as Other to the Law of the Father), it cannot quite do it. There are gaps through which the underlying rage against Teresa for refusing domination bursts out uncontrollably. These moments are over-determined in that they go beyond any narrative need. And they are, paradoxically, made possible by the fact that the film is shot largely from Teresa's point of view. Because of this positioning, the spectator experiences the uncontrolled rages that the men exhibit, and cannot help but be aware of their excess. To this small extent, then, the patriarchal need to possess and dominate women is exposed.

There are four main examples of an exaggerated rage by the male figures in Teresa's life. There is, first, the scene where Teresa's father over-reacts to her having spent one night away from home without telephoning. While her mother timidly, and with justice, comments: "We was afraid something had happened," her father sends the mother down to make the breakfast and then rages at Teresa: "You live by the rules of this house," he says; when she insists on leaving, because "I can't be myself and stay here," he cruelly comments that she's "not Kathleen, not by a long shot" (a terrible irony for Teresa since she was kept out for the night by Kathleen's own debauched party – this being a Kathleen totally unknown to the father). Finally, he tells her to go and "be alone in mugger's paradise" (the father is given a witty turn of phrase in the script) and warns "You'll never make it alone."

A second example is the scene where Teresa rejects Tony for the first time. After disappearing without saying anything, Tony suddenly reappears out of the blue, catching Teresa in the act of going to bed with a man she picked up at the bar. Puzzled by her "silent bit" (he amusingly characterizes it as "Bette Davis on the Late Show"), he tells her that she's "still his girl." When Teresa asserts that "I am my own girl," and that she is throwing him out, he gets into a rage and yells: "You and my mother – two biggest cunts in the world." (He exposes here the link between men's hatred of women and their resentment at the mother on whom they depended for so long.)

A third example is the rage James exhibits when Teresa also rejects him – a rage that is immediately echoed by her father who liked James and wanted her to marry him. This is significant because the representation of James has all along been problematic for the spectator. He has not really seemed to be "the nice man" that the narrative requires, and the father's endorsement of him makes him suspect. The scene where James invents the story about his parents' love-making makes him unattractive, so that the spectator has not experienced James as the viable alternative the narrative desires him to be.[9] In this way, the narrative subtly supports Teresa's ambivalence about James, while blaming her for not taking the one chance to get out of her "lost" existence.

James's view of himself dovetails with this level of the narrative: he cannot understand why she would refuse him when, from his point of view, she has absolutely nothing. He tells her that she needs him, but that "It has got to be me, and only me." When she walks out on him he flies into a rage and tears up her apartment, breaking a lamp and then pulling the bed apart – a rage that the situation itself in no way warrants. This is immediately followed by a scene at her parents' house where her father, having learned of the rejection, is seen following her down the stairs, his stick raised as if to beat her, yelling: "You're free to leave your family, free to leave the Church, free to go to hell;" he says he is unable to understand how she can give life to the deaf children she teaches, betraying again the patriarchal dichotomy that forces women into idealized mothers or "whores."

Of course, this series of rages at Teresa dotted throughout the text, and left "unexplained" by any of its discourses, culminates in the rage that George, her last lover, unleashes on her – a rage clearly linked to some basic, unalterable hostility to women "as cunts," i.e. very much as *sexual* beings. What we are dealing with here is again, in contemporary form, that "dread" of woman that Horney talked about, that distaste for the female organ because of its reminders of castration, of sexual difference.[10] In being sexually aggressive, Teresa transgresses her placing, and in this case it is fatal.

The nakedness of Teresa's desire together with her insistence on a certain distance (not letting men stay overnight) prove too much for George. He becomes impotent, and then confesses his weak sense of masculinity, describing his attempts to build a masculine body, his fears of being called a "fruit" in jail. George's homosexuality is, of course, simply an attempt on the part of the film to mask the sexual rage that many men, regardless of their chosen sexuality, have toward women. George's rage does not differ essentially from that of the three heterosexual males who raged at her; but, by locating the rage that leads to murder in a homosexual, the film permits the dominant class of men to avoid identification with the final, most brutal act.

The sexual resentment that George articulates just before he murders Teresa is similar to that of the murderer in *Klute*, mentioned earlier: "Goddam women," he says. "All you got to do is lay there. Guy's got to do all the work."

As his rage accelerates, he jumps on her and begins to rape her; while his rage makes him potent, he still has to kill her for the threat she offers. Phallus and knife coalesce here, the knife simply adding to the phallus instead of, as in *Shanghai*, standing in for it. The link between *Goodbar* and the cycle of films showing violence toward women, analyzed at the start of this chapter, is clear when George shouts as he rapes and kills: "That's what you want, bitch, right? That's what you want."

And in the electronically flickering light that renders both figures robot-like, unearthly, terrifying, suddenly Teresa's screams are silenced. In terms of the discourse that the film sets up, Teresa has received the punishment she deserves for not accepting her place in society; in terms of a feminist discourse, reading against the grain, patriarchy has punished Teresa for daring to transgress – that is, to own her sexuality and attempt to be her own person. This is revealed to be as much an impossibility in 1977 as it was in the 1850s, 1930s or 1940s. In symbolic systems there is simply no place for the single and sexual woman; patriarchal culture still fears the unattached woman, and Oedipal processes still lead men to expect woman's subjection to the Law of the Father.

PART II
The independent feminist film

6 | The avant-gardes in Europe and the USA

In part I, I examined in detail the way in which women in patriarchy have been constructed as silent, absent, or marginal because of the threat that woman, as woman, offers to man. I used the psychoanalytic discourse – a discourse that justifies woman's position as silent, absent, marginal – against itself; as a tool, psychoanalysis enabled us to decode Hollywood films so as to expose the abject placing of women that results from the psychoanalytic discourse underpinning the films. Understanding this placing and discourse may explain, first, the difficulties women have in assuming subjectivity; and second, the contradictions that, as feminists, we are often involved in.

While the Hollywood cinema I have been discussing often seems to be the *only* cinema, alternate practices have always existed in America. Historically, the well-known European avant-gardes (German expressionism, French surrealism and dadaism, French impressionism, Russian formalism, and the futurists) have been more active and visible than the American avant-gardes and independent filmmakers, but nevertheless, Pare Lorentz, Willard Van Dyke, and Ralph Steiner made their mark in the 1930s, as did Maya Deren in the 1940s. And in the recent period, from the 1960s onwards, the new American cinema has become one of the most talked-about avant-garde, including as it does people like Stan Brakhage, Michael Snow, Jonas Mekas, and Andy Warhol.

Categorizing these avant-gardes and explaining their differences is extremely difficult. In 1976 Peter Wollen attempted to distinguish two main avant-gardes: the first (the so-called "co-op" movement), he saw as largely confined to the USA and involved increasingly with the established art world and its values (Gidal, Cuyborns, the minimalists); the second (the so-called "political" avant-garde), he saw as deriving from the work of Godard, Gorin, and Straub-Huillet, and as barely represented within the USA. Wollen at that time believed that the two avant-gardes differed in aesthetic assumption, institutional framework, economic support, and kind of critical backing and historical/cultural origin.[1]

But in March 1981 Wollen revised his 1976 position, recognizing that the avant-garde was more complex than this simple division allows for. In a compact essay, Wollen notes that most avant-garde movements, whether in Europe or America, in fact contain several mutually inconsistent and contradictory trends, although two main opposing tendencies may be distinguished. These have been with modernism "ever since the 'natural' Renaissance scope of relations between signifier and signified was overthrown by Cubism."[2] Wollen goes on to say:

> One tendency reflects a preoccupation with the specificity of the signifer, holding the signified in suspense or striving to eliminate it. The other has tried to develop new types of relation between signifier and signified through the montage of heterogeneous elements.[3]

Of these two tendencies, Wollen prefers the second, which "is 'convergent'," he says, "with Godard and Straub-Huillet" (i.e. with the form of avant-garde Wollen had originally called "political"). Although Wollen is here much more careful in his terms, it is clear (even in this revised version of his theory) that he objects to the new disjunction between signifier and signified that led finally to the suppression of the signified altogether and has resulted in an art of pure signifiers, detached from meaning as much as from reference – in, that is, a self-reflexive cinema that takes its own formal properties as its subject.[4]

Some filmmakers, like Peter Gidal, see this use of the medium as the only way to avoid ideological contamination.[5] But in his revised essay, Wollen identifies as the problem of film semiotics its failure to develop a film theory in relation to the avant-garde:

> The problem of film semiotics has been twofold: the failure, building on the Saussurian base, to find flexible enough concepts to extend the scope of semiotics beyond the classical codes of Hollywood and art cinema . . . and secondly, a tendency to look for general theories of the cinematic sign (or "dispositif" or "imaginaire") rather than stressing the plurality and heterogeneity of film.[6]

At the end of his essay, Wollen notes (without going into detail) that it is feminist filmmaking and feminist film theory that has begun to break through the divisions in the avant-gardes. The reasons for this are not hard to find, given the kind of work that women have to do. Women have been forced to develop a semiotics of the cinema that would include a theory of reference, since our oppression in the social formation impinges on us daily. But as our oppression emerges from our (mis)representation in signification, how can we avoid dealing with representation? Since our voices have never been heard, how can we avoid attempting to locate a voice, a discourse, despite the difficulties involved in such a search in a patriarchal culture that excludes us? Further, how can we continue to tolerate, first, our exclusion from mainstream history (i.e. the repression of women's presence in history) and, second, left-activist omission of women's political issues?

If we take the above issues to characterize the various feminist film projects, independent women filmmakers have obviously gone about their tasks in a wide variety of ways. Despite the difficulties of creating satisfactory categories for women's films, for the purpose of organizing my discussion I will outline three broad groups of films, distinguished in terms of the cinematic strategies used: first, the formalist, experimental, avant-garde film; second, the realist political and sociological documentary; and third, what I call the avant-garde theory (political) film.

All three groups naturally have their roots in earlier historical traditions. The women's experimental film looks back to French surrealism and impressionism, German expressionism, and Russian formalism; more recently, there are influences from the 1960s avant-gardes – happenings, John Cage, minimalism. The realist film has its roots in the American and British documentaries of the 1930s, which in turn look back to Kuleshov in Russia and forward to Italian neo-realism and the British Free Cinema movement. The avant-garde theory film comes out of Brecht, Russian directors like Eisenstein and Pudovkin (who while remaining within realism and narrative cinema hoped to find a new realm of signifiers for their "new" (socialist) content),[7] and, most recently, the French New Wave movement, especially Godard, in his post-1968 phase, and Straub-Huillet.

But, for the most part, these traditions were initiated and developed by white men; and when women were involved (as in the notable exceptions of Germaine Dulac and Maya Deren, whom I will discuss shortly), they were not feminists in our contemporary sense.[8] This very exclusion has enabled women filmmakers to become especially sensitive to issues of form and style, and has prevented any blind following of previous conventions. While forced to rely on what are essentially male artistic traditions, we see women filmmakers in all three categories re-thinking conventions for themselves, shaping them so as to make them serve their particular projects as outlined above, obviously with varying degrees of success (as will be clear in chapter 10). It is in this way that women filmmakers find themselves, almost by accident, bridging what are for men distinct film forms.

For various reasons, many women filmmakers were early on attracted to the experimental cinema, animation or surrealist forms predominating. This may have been in part due to the influence of the only two available historical models of women directors in the independent cinema – Dulac and Deren – whose works were shown at all the early feminist film festivals. Dulac's most readily available film was *The Smiling Madame Beudet*, made in 1922, and shaped by French impressionism (which itself looked back to the nineteenth-century symbolist movement)[9] and surrealism. While not exactly a feminist film, *The Smiling Madame Beudet* uses surrealist techniques to present the inner pain and wish-fulfilment fantasies of a wife suffocating in a provincial marriage. While for much of the film, M. Beudet is seen as a vulgar, insensitive man, he is not *per se* the enemy: Dulac rather sees the entire institution of bourgeois marriage that the couple are locked into as at fault. In some ways, M. Beudet is as much a victim as his wife. Nevertheless, the presentation of things from the wife's perspective was innovative in a cinema that largely reflected male positions. And Dulac's often anti-illusionist cinematic techniques were perfectly adapted to this portrayal of the inner life of a severely frustrated woman.

Dulac's work serves the important function of *exposing* the positioning of women in patriarchy, even if she has no sense of alternatives. Equally important is the model she offers as a historical woman, who struggled to overcome prejudices against her; and who, as a woman in a male-dominated field, managed successfully to assert herself, to be visible, even if later her role was neglected by historians.

While Dulac works in a quiet, poetic manner, Deren's films are shocking, forceful, violent. Highly original in her techniques, Deren labored long and hard to perfect a style that corresponded to her image of what the cinema should be. An advocate, like Dulac, of the art film and of a "pure" cinema,[10] Deren strove to find acceptance for herself and her works in a period when there was little interest in the independent and avant-garde film and even less interest in work by women. Her sheer technical knowledge, of a precise, detailed kind, is impressive: at times, she reminds one of Eisenstein in her intense theoretical and formalist concerns. Focused on women, Deren's heavily surrealist films explore female splitting, alienation, jealousies, nightmares.

That Deren had a direct influence on contemporary feminist filmmakers is evident in Barbara Hammer's comment, quoted by Jaquelyn Zita in an article in the issue of *Jump Cut* devoted to "Lesbians and film:"

> I hadn't seen a film that I identified with until I saw Maya Deren's *Meshes in the Afternoon*, and then I felt I had discovered the Mother of American experimental film. She was working in a genre not often seen. It was like reading a poem in cinema, rather than a story or novel, which is what comes out of Hollywood. She was a great symbolist, who for the first time looked at the complexities of the female psyche, discovered the many inner selves of the feminine personality, and tried to project them into images.[11]

For many women, therefore, experimental cinema meant a liberation from illusionist representations that were oppressive and artificial in Hollywood films. If a similar experience also produced the documentary film, the directions were diametrically opposed. Women attracted to the experimental film were often searching for an outlet for their inner experiences, sensations,

feelings, thoughts, while those interested in documentary were more concerned with women's lives in the social formation, as will be clear later on.

If several lesbian filmmakers have used the experimental form (besides
Hammer, one thinks of Connie Beason, Jan Oxenberg, Barbara Jabaily, and
Ariel Dougherty, as well as many others mentioned in the excellent
filmography of lesbian works in the *Jump Cut* issue referred to), it may be in an
effort to avoid the co-optation of their images by male spectators reared to view
lesbian love-making as pornographic. Yet it is precisely their sexuality that
lesbians want to represent, for this is what patriarchy represses because it so
threatens the dominant order. How could illusionist representation of lesbian
love-making avoid co-optation by the male spectator for whom it would
represent, as it presumably does in pornography, an Oedipal regression (i.e. the
little boy has "the mommies" all to himself – there is no threatening daddy-like
male figure to intervene in the erotic arousal)?[12] If pornography has distorted
heterosexual love-making, lesbian love-making has been totally appropriated.

Thus the experimental form made sense for women interested in bringing
lesbian sexuality out of the closet. Barbara Hammer's *Multiple Orgasm* (1977)
conveys female ecstasy through sound and through the landscape images
superimposed on the clitoris (being manipulated) that fills the screen. Her
Double Strength (1978) goes further in showing the many levels of an
intimate lesbian relationship conveyed through experimental use of the film
form. Shots of a woman on a trapeze, first clothed, then naked, suggest
freedom, joy, spirituality, as well as sheer sensuality. The women's bodies
swinging together imply their closeness, their absorption in one another. Later
on, the words and the images referring to death suggest a crisis in the
relationship, but the film avoids working on the narrative level so that this
development is never made clear. The powerfully presented images of splitting
are also aesthetically stunning, as the woman's body is shown sometimes
doubled on a split screen, sometimes as the body superimposed on itself, doing
gymnastics. On the track, women's voices describe their pleasure in each
other's bodies, and also the pain of separation.

Other films about lesbians, particularly those focused on public lives (e.g.
Nancy Porter and Mickey Lemie's *A Woman's Place Is in the House* (1975), about
Ellen Noble), use the realist form and, like other women's documentaries, are
important in presenting new images of women that belie those that the
commercial cinema constructs out of its patriarchal position. Naturally, these
films reflect the same problems as those of other realist documentaries, to be
discussed in chapter 10. Let me say here simply that the difficulty surrounds
one's belief, or not, in the possibility of representing relationships that are not
constructed by the dominant order. To what degree are lesbians shaped by
their position as Other in a signifying system that has assigned a specific
(negative) sign to the "lesbian?" Can images of women-identified women and
of female bonding really subvert patriarchal domination? Can we create

representations of such relationships that escape their construction by the dominant order as marginal, ghettoized, co-optable? Or should we view lesbian relationships as we might mother–child bonding, i.e. as one area not colonized by men (at least on the non-symbolic level) and as therefore another possible gap through which to bring about change?

Perhaps answers to these questions will emerge from the many films about female bonding (sometimes sexual, sometimes not) being made in western and eastern Europe. Besides the two films about female bonding discussed here (Duras's *Nathalie Granger* and Von Trotta's *Marianne and Juliane*), there are works by Chantal Akerman, Nelly Kaplan, and Agnes Varda in France; by Marta Meszaros in Hungary; and, most recently, by Helke Sander, Ulrike Ottinger, and Jutta Brückner in Germany. Their work reveals a significant advance in female representations since women are seen finding a voice and a positioning that, despite the reliance in some cases on realism, looks different from that in Hollywood films.

In the following chapters, I focus first on the two European directors mentioned above, who, making films in very different political and cinematic contexts, reflect some dominant European trends and cinematic styles. In *Nathalie Granger*, based on a particular set of French feminist politics, Marguerite Duras uses aspects of the New Wave (which she herself helped to develop) for her own feminist ends. Margarethe Von Trotta, on the other hand, working in the political turmoil of 1980s Germany, looks in *Marianne and Juliane* at the interaction of personal and political choices for women living in a culture still struggling with the aftermath of Nazism.

Second I analyze the early films of an important American director, Yvonne Rainer, whom I see as bridging the avant-gardes outlined above while belonging predominantly in the experimental tradition. This is followed by a study of early women's documentaries in America, and of the issues around realism that emerged from the impact of new theory. I explore the reasons for the evolution of (what I call) the avant-garde theory film, which was developed specifically in reaction to the realist documentary, and provide three in-depth analyses of films that represent this category. Finally, I study a Third World film whose strategies are, in some degree, similar to those of the theory films while also concerned with realism. The book ends with two chapters in which I raise questions about the future of the independent feminist film in America and look at possible theoretical directions.

7 Silence as female resistance in Marguerite Duras's *Nathalie Granger* (1972)

For complex reasons, European women filmmakers began producing independent feature films long before women in the USA. Despite the proliferation of films by women in the wake of the recent women's movement, the output in the USA has been limited almost entirely to short films. The causes for this difference are too difficult to address here, but clearly they are related, first, to the particular structure of the American film industry where methods of financing and ideological hegemony made it difficult for women to direct; and second, to the different cultural positioning of middle-class women in Europe, which has made it easier for at least a few to obtain power. It has been possible in Europe to finance small independent film companies (something that is only now beginning to happen in America), and more recently television stations (especially in France, Germany, and Britain) have been willing to finance independent films, including films by women.

Marguerite Duras is important as a woman director who began working in film before the recent women's movement. Originally part of the (largely male-dominated) French New Wave movement (she wrote the script for Alain Resnais's *Hiroshima mon amour* (1959) and generally worked with him on the film), she began making her own films in the mid-1960s, after many years of writing avant-garde novels.[1] The political position that she had developed by the mid-1960s (as expressed in an interview with Jacques Rivette and Jean Narboni) anticipated in many ways the position taken by recent French feminist writers, except that then Duras was talking about the hippies and other oppressed groups while in the 1970s women were the focus.

For instance, talking about *Detruire, dit-elle* in the interview, Duras notes that "Faye is a man who reads. He wants to destroy knowledge but from *within* knowledge." But, she says, she "would like to destroy it in order to replace it with a void. The complete absence of man."[2] Rivette suggests that this creation of a vacuum might develop into a dangerous, purely passive state, but

Duras argues for this very passivity as a necessary stage before what *is* can be replaced with a new order:

> They [the Hippies] excel at not doing anything. Getting to that point is fantastic. Do *you* know how not to do anything at all? I don't. This is what we lack most. . . . They create a void, and all this . . . recourse to drugs . . . it's a means, I'm certain of that. . . . They're creating a vacuum, but we can't yet see what is going to replace what was destroyed in them – it's much too early for that.[3]

Later on, Duras argues that the hippies are "outside the circuit of production:"

> The hippie is a creature who has absolutely no ties with *anything*. He is not only outside every sort of security, every sort of social welfare, but outside of everything.[4]

Duras believes that this position "outside" is a useful one; it's a place that enables people to move from one situation to another without an abrupt change. As she puts it:

> It's not a rejection; it's a waiting period. Like someone taking his time. Before committing himself to act. . . . It's very hard to pass from one state to another. Abruptly. It is even abnormal, unhealthy. . . . It is necessary to wait. . . . You don't do something unless you *undo* what's gone before.[5]

A little further on, the position becomes clearer when Duras talks of "the gap between hope and despair. . . . A gap that can't be described." It is this gap that she calls "the void," or "the zero point," the place where "sensitivity regroups . . . and rediscovers itself."[6] It is a place Duras says that reflects "a sort of exemplary freedom," a freedom which the hippies are enjoying and using well.

It is important to see the politics being articulated here as arising out of Duras's disillusionment with an earlier political position. This earlier politics, an idealistic activism, involved going into factories and "taking them over." Duras already then objected to the imposition on workers by outside intellectuals of their view of things and had wanted to have the workers lecture to the action committee; but at the time of the interview with Rivette and Narboni she viewed that politics as a kind of paternalism, a nineteenth-century style of charity. Her new position involves a form of genuine communication between people that, once established, will radically change the social order, as opposed to what she calls the "false revolutions" which were imposed against people's will.[7]

For Duras, true communism involves a new kind of love – a love free from ego-investment, individualism, ownership, jealousy, competition, possession. The self would rather be given over to the larger community, transcended in the interests of the social whole. People would thus not be so clearly differentiated; there would be a sliding of personalities, an intermingling caused by the merging of self in the whole.[8]

Before the recent surge of theorizing about women, therefore, Duras had arrived at a critique of patriarchy in general. In *Nathalie Granger*, however, she explicitly locates the critique in an analysis of the specific oppression of women. Her film was made very much in the context of the revolutionary activities of French feminists that took place between 1970 and 1972,[9] and while preceding much of the theoretical writing on women (Gisèle Halimi's *La Cause des femmes* (1973) and Hélène Cixous's *Le Rire de la Méduse* (1975) were landmark publications), *Nathalie Granger* develops precisely the kind of feminist politics that was later articulated by French theorists. Let me briefly sketch in the broad outlines of this theory before looking at some of Duras's statements in 1975 and then showing how *Nathalie Granger* reflects the politics that women later advocated.

Influenced by Lacan, French theorists focused on language and on the fact that language, as the main tool of social progress and social organization, has an inherent male bias. It follows that if language is by definition "male" women who speak it are alienated from themselves. Using Lacan's distinction between the world of the imaginary (seen as pre-linguistic) and the world of the symbolic (the language-based order), they argued that women were forced to find their place within an essentially alien linguistic system which, linear and grammatical, orders the symbolic, the superego, and the law. A real contradiction faces women: as long as they remain silent, says Xavière Gauthier, "they will be outside of the historical process. But, if they begin to speak and write as men do, they will enter history subdued and alienated; it is a history that, logically speaking, their speech should disrupt."[10]

According to Claudine Herrmann, the only thing left for woman to do is to find, and speak from, the empty space, the no-man's-land, which she can at least call her own. "The *void* is for her, then, a respectable value."[11] Or, as Kristeva puts it, "Estranged from language, women are visionaries, dancers who suffer as they speak."[12]

Kristeva goes on to discuss the way that this estrangement is beginning to dissipate. Women, like the male avant-garde writers before them, are developing an extra sensitivity to language and creating a kind of under-ground, a sort of rupture through negativity. Although there is no "I" to assume this "femininity," Kristeva argues that "it is no less operative, rejecting all that is finite, and assuring in (sexual) pleasure the life of the concept. 'I,' subject of a conceptual quest, is also a subject of differentiation – of sexual contradictions."[13]

Discussing the problem for women writers of assuming "the name of father" (the no of the father),[14] which determines submission to the Law and to any "conventional language," Gauthier recalls asking Marguerite Duras "if a woman could write if she kept her father's name." Duras replied: "That's something which never seemed possible, not for one second. Like many women, I find this name so horrible that I barely manage to say it."[15]

We see here Duras's links to the theories that were being articulated in the mid-1970s. In an interview in *Signs* in 1975, Duras talked of the darkness and silence that have enveloped women living in male-dominated culture for centuries:

> The writing of women is really translated from the unknown, like a new way of communicating rather than an already formed language.[16]

She goes on to note that, because she is a woman trying to write "from the darkness" that is her feminine self, something inside her stops functioning, becomes silent:

> But everything shuts off – the analytic way of thinking, thinking inculcated by college, studies, reading, experience. I'm absolutely sure of what I am telling you now. It's as if I were returning to a wild country . . . men have gotten lost in, whereas women have never known what they were. So they aren't lost. Behind them, there is darkness. Behind men, there is distortion of reality, there are lies. . . . The silence in women is such that anything that falls into it has an enormous reverberation. Whereas in men, this silence no longer exists.[17]

Duras believes that it is the very virile force of men, including their words, that has rendered women silent and kept them silent. Women are like the proletariat in having been so oppressed that creativity was impossible:

> It is as if you asked me: "Why aren't there writers in the proletariat? Why aren't there musicians among the workers?" That's exactly the same thing. There are no musicians among the workers just as there are no musicians among women. And vice versa. To be a composer, you must have total possession of your liberty. Music is an activity of excess, it is madness, a freely consented madness.[18]

In another interview, Duras again denounces men's need to theorize, to speak from established positions, as being destructive of truly progressive change. She cites May 1968 as an example of men forcing women and minorities to keep silent and of the way they "enlisted the aid of the old way of theorizing, in order to relate, to recount, to explain this new situation: May '68." According to Duras, what was needed was a silence that would leave room for new formulations to emerge:

> This collective silence was necessary because it would have been through this silence that a new mode of being would have been fostered: it would have been from a common obscurity that collective actions would have sprung into being and found direction.[19]

Although *Nathalie Granger* was made in 1972, a year before this last interview, it seems closely related to the ideas expressed there. First, the film is about the politics of silence, as a female strategy to counter the destructive male urge to articulate, analyze, dissect; Duras shows in a powerful way how a crisis can be worked through without words which, given phallocentric culture, would permit only certain, male-style actions and understandings. Second, the form of the film itself expresses this politics: it is largely filmed as a silent movie would be, Duras relying on editing/montage and on her camera and the composition of the frames to convey her meanings. She employs sound judiciously, often contrapuntally, to underscore points made visually. Duras is using film form in the manner of the avant-garde that Kristeva has praised; like avant-garde writers (Joyce, Artaud, John Cage), Duras uses the form in new ways, trying, through negativity and rupture (refusing well-worn conventions) to get beyond the familiar representation of "reality." According to Kristeva, the ties that the avant-garde has always had to the underground offer a model for women to break through the limits of traditional (phallocentric) language and forms.[20] *Nathalie Granger* is structured like a poem, with a series of recurring motifs that gather increasing symbolic significance with each return.

The film opens with a series of shots from different parts of the film, establishing the freeing of conventional time–space relations which will continue throughout the film. Duras moves back and forth between past and present time, and inserts memories or fantasies (or what may be such) at various points. The effect is to liberate us from our normal relationship to time and space in conventional art works, and to situate us in a different kind of consciousness, one not controlled by rigid cause–effect relations. We have to suspend our usual modes of mental functioning, which constantly work to make us ask defensively (protectively): "Who is she? What did that mean? Why are they doing such and such?" In conventional art works, we are always given answers to such questions.

To the extent that we experience chronological time, the film seems to cover one afternoon in the life of the Granger family when a decision about Nathalie, the 8-year-old daughter, must be taken. At the start of the afternoon, the parents decide to send her away to another school, but as the day proceeds another solution emerges out of the situation: the important thing here is that the new decision is not arrived at by intellectual analysis – i.e. through language used in a linear, goal-oriented mode. It arrives rather from the non-verbal interactions of the women and the children, and particularly through what music means and symbolizes (of which more in a moment).

The recurring motifs replace the usual time–space and cause–effect relationships, creating another kind of structure, another coherence. In this structuring, what is important for the women's emotional lives is given emphasis. The repeated female voice-over (we presume it is Nathalie's school principal before this is confirmed), discussing the child's unruly and violent behavior in school, reflects Isabelle Granger's deeply felt concern about her daughter. This voice, although technically female, in fact embodies the male discourse of established institutions; it is cold, unfeeling, mechanical. We do not know for sure whether Isabelle is remembering the voice (as in flashback) or anticipating an interview that (apparently) takes place later on in the film. The time dimension is not important – only the fact that the child has been disruptive and is being taken out of school.

A similar device for setting up an outside (male) official world that is hostile to women is another repeated (disembodied) voice-over; this time a man is speaking, reporting periodically on the murder of two girls by teenagers in some woods not far from the Granger home. This outside voice establishes a public world which is male, and hostile to women (i.e. it is a place dangerous for women), and which becomes a counterpoint to the space within the Granger house and garden that is linked to the women, children, and animals (cat, bird); the male report repeatedly ruptures the quiet of the house with its disturbing message, all the more since the message parallels that (other) disturbing one about Nathalie; indeed, the suggestion is that somehow Nathalie's own "violence" is produced by and linked to the violence in the outside world.

Duras's camera emphasizes the separation of the female inner, and male outer, worlds; the house-versus-street polarity becomes a metaphor for the different modes of being that characterize women and men in current society (rather than reflecting an essentialist position, locating women specifically in the domestic, and men in the public (work) world). The camera constantly picks up the women staring out of, or into, windows. At the start, the husband is briefly in the house. As the camera pans the lunch table, we hear his voice talking about Nathalie. Isabelle responds quietly, while the others – her friend, the children – sit silent, still, their faces showing no expression. The children leave for school. Soon the husband is seen through the window, crossing the street and departing in his car, and suddenly quiet descends on the house. Silently and gravely, with slow, deliberate movements, the women clear the table. The garden can be seen beyond the windows, but nothing stirs; the black cat yawns and stretches, symbolizing the stillness and the sense that time has somehow stopped. The women together appear to create an Other space – they move similarly, but although they rarely speak to each other, they seem in harmony. They do not need words to know what each is feeling. Each seems totally aware of the other while going about her tasks quite independently.

Isabelle, for instance, telephones Nathalie's piano teacher, asking that Nathalie be allowed to continue her lessons. The voice replies that only Nathalie can decide that. Pained, Isabelle lets the telephone drop into her lap; her friend (played by Jeanne Moreau), meanwhile, has stopped clearing the table to listen to what is happening to Isabelle, sensing and sharing her trouble. As soon as the conversation is over, she resumes her actions.

Plate 8　This shot, like many others, is set up so that the women are seen in front of a window. The garden outside is glimpsed, but nothing stirs. The women together appear to create an Other space; they do not need words to know what each is feeling.

The conversation about the music lessons, together with an earlier statement by Isabelle at the lunch table that "If she doesn't study music, Nathalie is lost," shows that music signifies something extremely important for both child and mother. As the film develops, and as the piano-lesson refrain is repeated at specific moments, it appears that music symbolizes a means of expression beyond the oppressive limits of male language. Music is the last remaining connection for Nathalie with a world she has given up on, presumably in rebellion against the place male language has allotted her. It represents life, love, her mother, and without it she is lost to violence, destruction, aggression. Only this nonverbal mode can reclaim her and reinsert her in the values her mother (and her mother's friend) offer.

The mother and Nathalie are in some strange way in this together. It is not so much a conflict *between* them as a conflict between women and the patriarchal culture in which they are placed. Isabelle feels helpless in relation to the child's dilemma; it is a dilemma beyond them both, rather than a matter of one of them against the other. The music connects them in the only way left. At one poignant moment, Isabelle's friend tells her, "Forget Nathalie," and Isabelle, in pain, questions, "What, not touch my child?" The pain of this is presented in another poignant moment when Isabelle, ironing Nathalie's clothes, pauses, overwhelmed by silent tears, and holds a small garment up to her face.

The piano-lesson music, a well-known French exercise, comes to signify Nathalie, and is played whenever Isabelle thinks of her daughter. For instance, in a scene in the early afternoon, after the dishes are done, Isabelle wanders around the house, wondering what to do about Nathalie, and the music is heard; later on, she goes into Nathalie's room to pack her things for boarding school, and as the camera pans over the objects (including a sign that says "Nathalie's: do not touch"), the music occurs again. Shortly after this, Isabelle wanders into the room where the piano is and sits down, obviously wanting to play, to connect with her child this way, but she cannot bring herself to do it. The piano music occurs again as she gets up and moves away.

The introduction of the music in this first part of the film is carefully counterpointed with the other main parts of the sound track: first, the repeated male voice on the radio, discussing the murder of the two young girls, and second, the teacher's voice, talking about the unnatural violence of the little girl (Nathalie). These two discourses are set off against the music as being involved with the oppressive male order, while music comes to represent the female realm, beyond or outside of the language that can only judge, dissect, analyze.

Silence, however, is the main way in which women can resist the oppression of language, and Duras insists on this throughout the film in the cinematic use of silence – a use that violates normal cinematic conventions. For instance, we never hear any sound from the women's movements – the sound track, that is, picks up no noises from their footsteps or activities (like washing the dishes, ironing, making the fire, and raking leaves in the garden); in this way, a further distinction between the inside and outside realms is made, since noises from the street periodically intrude (blaring car horns, traffic sounds, voices); these noises startle (as do the male voice-overs) because of the silence within.

Other devices emphasize this silence: there is the use made of the cat – the shots of it lazily yawning (in close-up) and then idly slinking along the extended passageways provide a mood of reverie and timelessness; its movements stand as correlatives for those of the women who move equally silently, slowly, and gracefully.

In other ways, Duras links the women to nature; there is their work in the garden itself, but more than this is the reflection of movements in nature in those of the women; for instance, when the friend is standing by the pond, the wind moves her hair, and Duras cuts to the wind moving the surface of the water in an identical manner.[21]

The sound track reinforces what the image, camera work, and editing also show regarding the antagonism of the dominant male order to the female mode of being. The special nature of the female mode is established visually in several ways. To begin with, as already noted, Duras establishes the separation between male and female realms by the boundary she creates between the house and garden, on the one hand, and the street, on the other. There are frequent shots of the window frames through which the "other" territory can be seen, as for example at the start of the film when the husband leaves for work (we see him through the house window cross the street, get into his car, and drive off); later on, we watch the salesman through the window leave the house, try knocking on other doors, disappear, and finally reappear and go off in his car. We watch the friend cross the street, entering the alien territory momentarily to pick up the children from school; and at the end of the film, we again watch the salesman leave, and then (an accident in the filming, according to Duras) a man enters the frame with a dog, who, on nearing the house, suddenly pulls his master away, as if afraid of this house, now in the power of the women.

This technique produces an ambiguous effect in terms of the space within the house and, by extension, the garden also. There is a kind of prison-nest effect (to use Laura Mulvey's term).[22] In a sense, the house is a prison since the women are limited to this space, bound by the confines of house and garden, if they are not to be in the position of Object (controlled), as they must be in the male external realm. On the other hand, the space of the house assumes the security, intimacy, warmth, and safety of the nest; it belongs to the women and to their ways of being; they have control over this space, as far as is possible; it is a space of refuge, possibly even of "cure." The many shots of the rooms and corridors of the house evoke a quiet, peaceful atmosphere; it's almost as if the space of the house, with its solid objects, clean lines, well-worn beauty, has its own, uncanny presence; the uncluttered, open rooms and passages suggest reverie, meditation, the antithesis of the stereotype of domesticity, which is all bustle, noise, mess. And it is the antithesis of the street, which is grey, bleak, stark – a place of movement, work, transactions, noise.

If the shots through the windows suggest that the women are in a sense trapped, those of the garden evoke a sense of freedom, although again this freedom is bounded by the garden walls. But it provides both a release from tensions built up in the house over Nathalie and a way for the women and children to share activities that do not require language and that are productive (burning the fallen twigs and leaves; cleaning up the pond). The fire evokes Freud's symbolism about women's urge to nurture, rather than to destroy, fire.[23] For Duras, perhaps, the women guarding the fire symbolizes their contact with what is essential about human civilization, as against the male order that has lost sight of essentials in a plethora of destructive busyness.

On a deeper level, the camera defines the female space as belonging to Lacan's pre-symbolic, pre-linguistic realm (the imaginary) through the repeated mirror shots of the women. The validation of non-verbal communication reinforces the politics of the film, which advocates silence as a strategy for resistance to patriarchy.

The connection between mirror shots and language as a problem for women in male culture is clear in the scene where a prolonged shot of the women in the mirror is followed immediately by the apparently digressive reference to Moreau's Portuguese maid, Marie. Moreau learns over the telephone that Marie, unable to read the form she was asked to sign, has unwittingly signed her own expulsion from France. This symbolizes women's alienation in male culture through not speaking the same language. As Duras notes in the script for the film: hasn't Isabelle also signed away her right to her child through not knowing how to manipulate male language?[24] The question that the film raises is whether or not women can use the knowledge of their oppression through language positively by *choosing* silence, as against continuing to use "male" language and thereby "signing their own expulsions."

Mirror shots continue to punctuate the film, underscoring the women's space and the narcissism inherent in the pre-symbolic phase. For, as Laura Mulvey has noted, women together often are attracted to each other through an inevitable narcissism – seeing the self reflected in the Other, just as the self is reflected in the mirror.[25] That Duras intends to expose this "reflecting" is clear not only through the many mirror shots that show the women reflected together, but also through the similarity between the women, despite literal physical differences. Their harmony reflects a oneness necessitated by their oppressed position within male culture. An intuitive togetherness is the only possible mode, given that language does not express their position as subject.

The most dramatic way in which Duras reveals the polarity between male and female realms – and the power and significance of the female way of being – is in the device of the salesman's visit. The women have been sitting and sewing Nathalie's clothes, preparing for her departure. A silence as usual prevails, but as always it is heavy with feeling, and with the women's togetherness in the grief over the child. They hear a noise, and a salesman enters. He is immediately disoriented by the women's silence and the power they communicate in this way; his discourse falters in this atmosphere – he stumbles, forgets his lines, repeats himself. The discourse of the male public world is exposed as a meaningless babble in the light of the values the women embody. The more the women sit resisting his discourse (refusing or unable to respond), the more disconcerted he becomes and the more incoherent his speech. Duras has revealed women's power over the male discourse simply through silence: the values that structure his discourse – selling, making money, manipulating, dissecting, etc. – are anathema to their mode; their knowledge and strength, obtained through a deeper level of being, disorient him and expose the superficiality of his project in the world. It is, of course, a direct reversal of what usually happens in discourse, when male words overpower, and silence, women.

The effect of this meeting on the salesman is evident in his return to the house (i.e. to the female space) at the end of the film, as if drawn there against his will; he comes to a place of refuge and calm from the harsh external world whose demands he cannot meet. Once in Isabelle's kitchen, and in the warmth of her presence, the salesman finally breaks down and cries, admitting that he hates his job, that he is really a launderer and wants to return to that work. It is as if the women have shown him the false values on which his current job is based and have helped him return to something a degree more authentic.

In between the two visits by the salesman, the "crisis" with Nathalie comes to a head. It is as if the eruption of the external world into the quiet female space presaged the "violence" that occurs with Nathalie's return in mid-afternoon. Up to this point, we know very little about the child, other than what the principal has said and what we have gleaned from her mother and friend. The friend notes, at one point, that "Nathalie sometimes wants to kill everyone in the world. . . . She wants to be an orphan, a Portuguese, because of all the misery." We know of her mother's suffering over what is happening to her child, and we have sensed a link between Nathalie's violence and that toward women in the outside world. We know of the mother's painful realization that the only way she can break the bond of violence between herself and Nathalie is by separating herself from her child – a separation that she can hardly endure.

But we have so far not seen the child alone: so it is with some interest that we watch her actions in mid-afternoon. Totally isolated from the others in the house (withdrawn into herself), she finds connection only with the pets. We have seen how the cat in some way symbolizes the women, so that it is as if Nathalie tries to reach out to them through the animals. We see her hug and kiss the cat tenderly, revealing an inner need, an inner gentleness none of the "reports" (or their mouthpieces) were able to divine. She tries to be Mother to the pets, putting them in a doll pram and walking with them through the garden. But, frustrated, she throws over the pram suddenly and violently, and walks off, aimlessly now.

Her separation from the others is marked particularly by Moreau's closeness with Nathalie's sister, Laurence, who helps Moreau tidy up the lake, while Nathalie looks on from afar – and her mother looks at her looking.

The music lesson is the moment of high tension, since we know the significance of the lessons to Nathalie's "cure." As Laurence practices with the teacher, Nathalie sits defiantly alongside Moreau, who tries to reach out to her physically, only to be rejected proudly by Nathalie. But finally, to the relief of all, Nathalie agrees to take a lesson, and the music reverberates throughout the house, a quiet, calm signal of her "return" to the family, to what connects her to the other women.

It is only now that Isabelle is willing to express some of the repressed anger at the world she lives in for what it has done to her child. We see her receive a newspaper and letter "from outside" and then tear up the "messages" into small pieces. This is followed by shots of her tearing up Nathalie's school-work books, with the same slow methodical action. All the pieces are then burned, and we hear Isabelle call the boarding school to say that Nathalie will not be attending.

As Duras points out, this is the crucial moment in the film, the climax toward which everything has led. For here Isabelle takes an unprecedented step against the male order in refusing to send her child to any school.[26] No one knows what will happen; the women and the child face an unknown, but it is an unknown arrived at through non-verbal means – not through analysis, dissection, words, but through intuition, silence, passivity, the means Duras had a few years earlier praised the hippies for and was a few years later to advocate as a politics for women faced with impossible dilemmas.

The salesman's return underscores this victory over the repressive male order – and he senses something even more fearful and powerful in the house than earlier. The final shots of him wandering lost through the rooms, not comprehending, not perceiving what is going on, reflect man's alienation in the sphere and modes of woman and parallel those she experiences in his sphere. The salesman looks longingly at the figure of Isabelle, with its black cloak and black hair, weaving in and out of the trees in the garden until finally lost to sight. Suddenly afraid, he leaves the house abruptly, running to his car (we again see him through the window) and departing as if from something that terrifies.

Duras's film raises important questions about the nature of women's oppression and about possible strategies to deal with it. For Duras (as for many other French feminists, as we've seen), the main weapon for oppressing women has long been male-dominated language (and the male-centered culture that followed). Once women understand this oppression, they can choose silence as a strategy for resisting domination. For Duras silence, paradoxically, becomes a means for entering culture; it marks a gap, a fissure through which change can possibly take place.

There are several problems with this politics, however. The first is that of assuming women's essential difference from men. Granted that the domestic sphere, motherhood, and female closeness are spaces not colonized by the male order, and therefore areas where women can resist domination, it is dangerous (as I suggested in chapter 1) to set these spheres up as in some sense belonging to women alone. One must keep insisting that in any new order these would not constitute the realm that would define women (that is the whole point of creating a new order). The second problem is with the concept of a "politics of silence." For Duras, this politics does not leave women in the position of negativity, for she views silence as a positive and liberating stance. Yet it is dangerous to accept women's exclusion from the symbolic realm, since this realm involves large and important areas of life. Obviously, in any new order, women will have to function in the symbolic. The questions that Duras leaves unresolved have to do with *how* women will gain access to the symbolic, the voice, subjectivity, through silence. Silence seems at best a temporary, and desperate, strategy, a defense against domination, a holding operation, rather than a politics that looks toward women's finding a viable place for themselves in culture.

It is by no means clear that language is so monolithically male as to give us a choice only of domination or silence. For obvious practical reasons, language must be our tool for change. If we believe in the symbolic order as fixed, change is impossible for women. However, if language has rather merely been *used* to oppress women, we can begin to change it once we become aware of its oppressive nature. Haunting works like *Nathalie Granger* expose language as the mechanism through which domination functions but leave us with the task of finding ways to enter the symbolic. Von Trotta, whom I will consider next, shows women struggling to find a place for themselves in the symbolic and to avoid suppression in that realm.

8 | Female politics in the symbolic realm: Von Trotta's *Marianne and Juliane* (*The German Sisters*) (1981)

While Marguerite Duras explores the possibility of women remaining within the world of the imaginary, refusing the male symbolic order as far as is possible, Von Trotta analyzes women's political discourses within the symbolic realm. She shows her heroines trying to survive by constructing either a discourse of violence against the dominant order (terrorism) or one that seeks to effect change by working within it (reformist feminism).

Despite their very different relationship to the symbolic realm, the films of both Duras and Von Trotta are important in situating the female spectator very differently than do Hollywood films. In chapter 1, we saw that the repeated masochistic scenarios that characterize the family melodrama effectively immobilize the female viewer. While the male viewer is given idealized screen heroes that return the image of his more perfect self of the mirror phase, the female spectator has only powerless, victimized figures who reinforce an already established sense of worthlessness. It is understandable that some female directors (e.g. Agnes Varda, Claudia Weill) would try to remedy this lack and provide women with new idealized images (i.e. images that show strong, beautiful women while eliminating the male gaze *within* the narrative and the film frame; indeed, Duras herself can be seen as doing just that, since she chooses beautiful female actresses for her films, as in *Nathalie Granger*). But while this may be a dramatic change from the Hollywood construction of the masochistic female spectator, it keeps intact the Hollywood mechanism of fulfilling the need for idealized images. It allows a regression to the realm of the imaginary that is not necessarily progressive just because the figures are female.

In contrast to Duras, Von Trotta refuses to provide idealized images for the female spectator; and while she may be criticized perhaps for offering some masochistic figures, the big difference between her films and Hollywood films is that her female characters are seen as actively engaged in a struggle to define their lives, their identities, and their feminist politics in a situation where the dominant discourse constantly undermines their efforts, or forces them into destructive positions through controlling what choices are available. If her heroines fall into masochism, it is as a result of a choice arising out of a particular political and personal context; Von Trotta reveals how this position has been externally constructed, as against presenting it as "natural" or "inevitable," as in Hollywood films. The female spectator thus sees the masochism as a result of how patriarchy limits and defines the feminine, rather than as something to identify with unproblematically.

Before exploring her film in detail, let me outline briefly the cultural context in which Margarethe Von Trotta was working in making *Marianne and Juliane* and her earlier films, and also her place in the phenomenon known in America as the new German cinema.

When the films of Von Schlöndorff, Fassbinder, Wenders, and Herzog hit the American scene in the early 1970s, American critics praised the new German cinema for its extraordinary power, depth, and complexity. For during the 1950s and 1960s the German cinema had, with good reason, seemed moribund. Bruised for decades by Nazism and the aftermath of the Second World War, German culture faltered as people strove to redefine themselves in a nation, not only split into East and West, but also alienated, first, from its European neighbors (who were slow to forget the horrors of the war), and second, from its own recent past. Into the vacuum thus produced stepped Americanism, in the form not only of Coca-Cola and Burger King houses, but also film, music, clothing. Naturally lacking any positive sense of what it meant to be "German," young people turned to America for inspiration, excitement, identification.

This American influence preoccupied some directors in the first wave of new German films, who at once deplored Americanism and yet were themselves partly seduced by it (e.g. Fassbinder's *American Soldier*, Wenders's *American Friend*, and Herzog's *Strozek*). But it would be wrong to see the works as *only* so preoccupied: in fact, the new German cinema is a far more complex, heterogeneous movement than we are aware of in America, given the highly selective sampling of directors' works that we have been able to see. The "big four" who managed to crash the American art cinema circuit, and who have either made films in America (e.g. Wenders, whose recently completed film on Dashiel Hammett was produced by Coppola) or used English-speaking actors (e.g. Fassbinder with his film *Despair*), themselves differ vastly in style, theme, and mood. A few of the other directors are now beginning to be known, particularly the neglected women filmmakers, giving us a better sense of the variety and extent of the new German film culture.

As we see more of the films, it is clear that they draw on a variety of influences, from the French New Wave (itself linked to Sartre and existentialism), and the Italian New Wave (Bertolucci, Pasolini) to eastern European directors like Andrej Wajda. But if the new German films partly echo the American and European mood of the 1960s in their *angst*, alienation, and preoccupation with the outsider, the reasons underlying this mood are different due to Germany's special postwar political situation.

Many of the recent films have begun to reflect this unique situation in their treatment of both Nazism and 1970s German terrorism (e.g. Fassbinder's *Despair* (Nazism) and *The Third Generation* (terrorism); or the collectively made *Germany in Autumn* (terrorism and Nazism)). The confrontation with Nazism was obviously necessary if young Germans were to free themselves from a heritage with which they had little to do and yet which dominated their cultural reality, preventing a comfortable German identification. Meanwhile, the recent terrorist activity, with its violence and extremism, created a further problem for directors who were often themselves leftists, or at least disillusioned with the Establishment, and supported some of the terrorists' ideas if not their political strategies.

Part of what is new about the recent German cinema is the treatment of politics in connection with personal, psychological problems. The concern of the filmmaker with his own problems of identity lead not to the depersonalized political film of a Godard or to a concern with the politics of representation (which has preoccupied some European filmmakers in the wake of new French theory), but to a unique narrative cinema: this cinema blends anti-Establishment New Wave politics with a bitter critique of German authority (often recalling that of Brecht and some German expressionists in the 1920s), in a style that eschews avant-garde techniques in favor of a distanciation resulting, as Canby notes, from "distilling reality until it looks and sounds quite unreal."[1]

One of the first filmmakers to reflect this intermixing of the personal and the political was Volker Schlöndorff in the films that he made together with his wife, Margarethe Von Trotta. Von Trotta's influence on Schlöndorff is significant in a film movement that was (and continued until recently to be) male dominated. The first two films that Schlöndorff and Von Trotta made together (*A Free Woman* (1973) and *The Lost Honor of Katarina Blum* (1975)) shows a concern with women's positioning and women's issues not evident in the films of the male directors working alone. *A Free Woman* deals with a bourgeois housewife who, influenced by the women's movement, decides to liberate herself without fully anticipating the pain and difficulties. The second film show the vulnerability to ruthless exploitation by the media, and male authorities of all kinds, of a woman who refuses to play the game that is expected of her in patriarchy. In a film movement already interested in combining the personal and the political, Von Trotta's influence rendered that "personal" more intimate, emotional, and less distanced than it had appeared in the films directed by men (Herzog was perhaps an exception here). (It is an intimacy and directness shared by some of the newer female directors now emerging on the German scene, such as Helke Sanders and Ulrike Ottinger.)

When Von Trotta and Volker Schlöndorff decided to work separately, the results were interesting. Von Trotta's influence is sorely missed in Schlöndorff's *Circle of Deceit*, with its inauthentic treatment of the women, while her own series of three films, culminating in that under consideration here, reflect an ever deepening attention to the subtleties and complexities of female relationships, which are always placed in the larger social and political context out of which they emerge.

Marianne and Juliane, like the other films, deals with close relationships between women, all of whom are, in one way or another, doubles. This doubling is not a mere externalization of an inner split (as was the case in the German Romantic *doppelgänger*); nor is it intended simply to show the different possibilities for women struggling to find themselves in an alien, male-dominated realm. It functions rather on an altogether more complex level, revealing, first, the strong attraction that women feel for qualities in other women that they themselves do not possess; second, the difficulty women have in establishing boundaries between self and Other; and finally, the jealousy and competition among women that socialization in patriarchy makes inevitable. Sometimes, the doubling takes place on the imaginary/symbolic axis, one of the pairs functioning smoothly in the public sphere, while the other seems to desire regression to the presymbolic and repetition of the merged phase of early mother–child relating. This produces results very different from the harmonious, close, unconflicted bonding in the presymbolic realm that Duras's figures reflect. Von Trotta's realism is, correspondingly, as harsh and relentless as Duras's is soft and poetic.

The warm, open, liberated heroine of Von Trotta's first film, *The Second Awakening of Christa Klages* (1977), is attracted to the repressed, uptight wife of a military official; while a conventional, bored bank clerk is attracted to Christa, presumably because of her daring, free life. The public sphere in the film attempts to curtail and constrain these female bondings which threaten its order. Von Trotta's second film, *Sisters*, is focused primarily on the intense and destructive relationship between two sisters, one of whom, Maria, has mastered the male domain (she is a successful executive secretary), while the other, Anna, resists entry into the symbolic, yearning for oneness with her sister and wanting to be taken care of. The collusion of these two in their destructive relationship brings about Anna's suicide, since she cannot tolerate the entry of a male lover into their dyad.

Marianne and Juliane brings together aspects of the female relationships shown in the first two films, but carries them to a deeper, more complex level. The theme of sibling rivalry and the debate about left strategies that German terrorism has evoked are treated in the context of the German Nazi and Christian past which shaped the personal, political, and social development of the sisters and accounts for their tortured, conflicted lives.

The early cultural, political, and family environment that molded the sisters is revealed through flashbacks that punctuate the film's present. The past continues to shape the present on two levels: first, that of the sisters' personal, psychoanalytic history, which they continue to live out in their current relating; and second, that of the cultural and political level, where the legacy of Nazism cannot be entirely overcome.

We first meet the sisters in the present (they are in their late thirties, having been born toward the end of the Second World War); Juliane, the elder by a year or so, works on a feminist magazine and campaigns for women's issues, while Marianne has become a dedicated and daring terrorist. The camera begins from Juliane's point of view, placed in her study and showing us a view of bleak houses and bare trees before turning to the bookcases, densely packed with books and files that Juliane needs for her feminist articles. We have a quiet, interior image, a sense (perhaps) of invading Juliane's privacy as she works.

This is soon broken by the intrusion of Juliane's brother-in-law, Werner, who wants her to take care of Marianne's son, Jan, left in his care when Marianne joined the terrorists. At once, the continued love–hate relationship between the sisters is clear, as Juliane expresses her resentment at Marianne for always putting her into the position that she no longer wants. Juliane refuses to keep the child, noting that Marianne deliberately dropped out of Establishment life to spite her at the very moment when Juliane began to live normally.

The flashbacks reveal that indeed the sisters have switched their past positions; for when they were young Juliane was the rebellious one – wearing black jeans to school, smoking cigarettes, disrupting the class and being sent outside, reading Sartre not Rilke. Much of her behavior is seen as deliberately aimed at provoking her upright, religious father, who, while part of the Christian resistance against Nazism, is in every way a traditional, middle-class man, ruling his large family with an authoritarian hand. Juliane's mother, outwardly totally submissive to her husband, is nevertheless secretly in collusion with the rebellious Juliane; this is clear in a comic scene at the school dance, where Juliane, having finally agreed to conform sufficiently to wear a dress, embarks partnerless onto the dance floor, to the horror of the crowd, but to her mother's secret delight in her violation of the codes.

Marianne, on the other hand, is, as a child, the model of obedience and conformity, steeped in traditional German culture and music; she is adored by her father and is a dutifull, well-behaved child. She intercedes for Juliane with her father, and is seen sitting in his lap, having her hair stroked.

While Von Trotta refuses to psychoanalyze the sisters (preferring to let us speculate on why each emerged as she did), it is clear that Marianne's intense identification with her father has resulted in her taking a self-destructive path: Juliane's rebelliousness (if partly due to her father's adoration of the younger

Plate 9 Juliane meets Marianne secretly in a museum. Here Marianne's terrorist image is set off against images of sculptures that reflect Germany's great Christian heritage, in an ironic fashion that calls them into question.

child) has a healthy side to it in her revulsion for the traditional values that her father upholds and that allowed the Nazis to take power. Juliane's cynical existentialism seems healthier than Marianne's intense desire to "serve mankind": "Being useful," Juliane (as a child) notes, "is a form of willing slavery." The remark in part reflects Juliane's subtly suggested identification with her mother's oppressed role in the traditional middle-class family; the film captures this oppression in a beautifully understated way, just as it also exposes the mother's relegation to silence and marginality in a system dominated by the father. (All Von Trotta's mothers are ineffective in helping their daughters; often widowed (as the one in this film becomes), they live out lonely, ineffectual lives, sensing the destruction their daughters are engaged in but feeling powerless to take any action to prevent disaster. The brief scene in the jail, when Juliane brings their mother to visit Marianne, typifies the helplessness Von Trotta's mothers always show.)

Meanwhile, the destructive effects of Marianne's identification with her father suggest that Von Trotta is making a point about the dangers of the patriarchal mode of being. Her excessive obedience as a child reflected perhaps an unhealthy need for her father's approval, an insecure female identity.

With both sisters thus, Von Trotta avoids the simplistic, psychoanalytic account of radicalism as resulting from inadequately resolved Oedipal problems; while these problems are suggested, Von Trotta rather stresses the effect of social and political structures on children's ideological perspectives. In this way, her point is more subtle and devastating. Making a deliberate connection between children raised under traditional values toward Church and family and the new violent generation may not be original,[2] but Von Trotta gives the cliché freshness through her juxtaposition of the two sisters. She suggests that Marianne's blind devotion to her father, as against Juliane's resistance and identification with her mother, has made her susceptible to a new form of fanaticism. The rigidity, intolerance, and idealism of the Nazis is echoed in the implacable, abstract, and detached statement that Marianne utters out of her terrorist ideology. The connection is made explicit when, visiting Marianne in jail, Juliane screams that under Hitler Marianne would have been a Nazi fan.

If the parallel seems ironic, given the opposed ideologies of Nazism and terrorism, Von Trotta sees a similarity in the dangerous, abstract strand in German thinking (identified with the male order) which annihilates ordinary humanist concerns. It is against this annihilation that Juliane (and, to the degree that he is present, her boyfriend Wolfgang) struggle; Juliane strives to keep a sense of balance, an identity of rational choice, in a situation where the intense bonding with her sister – her difficulty in retaining her sense of boundary, of separation – threatens to throw her over the edge of the rational. The sequence in the Youth Retreat Home where the sisters' father projects *Night and Fog* (Alain Resnais's film about concentration camps) to the literal, physical disgust of the two girls, shows how far at least Marianne in the present has hardened.

Yet this is not a completely antiterrorist film, just because of flashback scenes like this one that humanize Marianne. The childhood scenes mitigate the harsh image of Marianne in the present (viz. the scene where Marianne and her friends burst arrogantly into Juliane and Wolfgang's apartment in the dead of night demanding coffee and clothes; or the many prison scenes where she berates her captors). We see that the hostile clichés about terrorists ignore their past selves which may have been stunted by bitterness about the kind of world their fathers had produced. And Marianne's cause is vindicated, first, by Juliane's sharing her critique of western industrial capitalism and her sympathy for the Third World, and second, by the presentation of Marianne as an attractive, intelligent, and brave woman, who, despite her tough, independent stance, craves love and intimacy.

Part of the problem with the figure of Marianne, however, is that she is presented only through Juliane's eyes. This limits considerably what we can know, and leaves unanswered many questions about how exactly Marianne got to be the way she is. On this level, it is tempting to read Marianne as some kind of "double" for Juliane – the repressed self that Juliane partly wanted to be. And such an interpretation would be justified by the second half of the film which shows Juliane's intense identification with her sister after her death in jail. Wanting to know exactly what Marianne went through, and suspecting murder, Juliane absorbs herself totally in re-enacting Marianne's death. Ironically, she becomes as fanatical as was her sister as a terrorist. Through her obsession, she loses her (nearly ideal) lover, Wolfgang, on whom she had hitherto depended for a sort of fatherly love and protection and to support a rather fragile identity. Her immersion in her sister's death paradoxically ends up making Juliane personally stronger, although the precise way in which this happens is unclear.

The presence of Marianne's son, Jan, in the film underscores that Von Trotta is working with some notion of the deeds of the parents falling on the children that follow. Jan's life is drastically affected by the lives of his mother and aunt, as had theirs been by their parents' generation and values. In part responsible for Jan's nearly being burned alive (children in the neighborhood of his foster home set him on fire when they find out that Marianne was his mother),

Plate 10 The camera dwells on Jutta Lampe's anguished face as if trying to penetrate her visage in order to reveal her tortured self-doubts and conflicts. Since the camera itself cannot do this, such unrelenting realism backfires, and becomes over-earnest and humorless.

Juliane finally decides to take him in. The act locates what is important firmly in the realm of the interpersonal. The setting for the act returns us to the start of the film – to Juliane's study and the shots of the buildings opposite through the windows. The circularity suggests that on the one hand nothing has changed, while on the other everything has changed. It seems as if Juliane's brutal encounter with the public sphere, particularly through what happened to Marianne and Jan, has in a sense driven her inside, while preparing her, paradoxically, to shoulder an enormous burden such as taking on Jan must entail. There is thus a loss in the public sphere with a corresponding gain in the private one. But ultimately, the vision is bleak in terms of bringing about change in the public realm.

Von Trotta's relentless realism confirms her bleak vision. The film forces numerous, oppressive close-ups on us; the camera dwells on Jutta Lampe's anguished face, as if trying to do what film really cannot do, namely penetrate her visage to explore the tortured self-doubts and conflicts. The editing forces abrupt changes on us, jarring us deliberately and making us feel as battered as is Von Trotta's heroine. Only brief warm moments with Wolfgang (and their short vacation together) relieve the movement from one painful experience to the next. One is reminded very much of the kind of realism we find in eastern European films by directors like Andrej Wajda, Marta Meszaros, Károly Makk and Pál Gábor. And we see here, perhaps, the limitation of a realism so relentless that Von Trotta has all she can do to prevent herself from being painted into a corner by her own chosen cinematic form. The circularity and repetition threaten to box her heroine in, as the surviving heroine in *Sisters* was boxed in by her compulsion to repeat her obsessive need for control. Only the boy Jan offers a faint hope of movement outward.

In turning to America in the next chapter, we will look first at a non-realist director working in a completely different context from either Duras or Von Trotta in Europe, before turning to American documentary films and a consideration of problems in realism.

9

The American experimental woman's film: Yvonne Rainer's *Lives of Performers* and *Film about a Woman Who . . .* (1972-4)

Yvonne Rainer's first films, made in the early 1970s, are important as representing a bridge between the two main tendencies in the avant-garde as outlined by Wollen (see chapter 6). Rainer's unique positioning as a woman within the various New York avant-gardes from 1962 to 1972 accounts for her fascinating and innovative work. Her justly renowned Judson Dance Performances in the mid-1960s marked her creative use of a whole variety of early-1960s influences, from Merce Cunningham in dance (with his avoidance of story and character), John Cage in music (with his acceptance of noise and accident), and minimalist sculpture (with its reduction of detail) to happenings (with their ash-can expressionism), to Rauschenberg's form of pop art (with its combination of exaggerated focus on ordinary objects with art-historical quotation).[1]

Made in 1972, Rainer's first film, *Lives of Performers*, preceded any coherent feminist film community in New York and any assertion of their voices by the female artists working in the male-dominated avant-gardes. At this time, artists' anti-Establishment politics centered around Vietnam rather than around feminism.

But by the early 1970s women's studies had become an academic discipline and had produced a number of readily available texts which, Rainer says, provided support for the sort of subject matter – sexual conflicts and relationships – she was interested in, and for her desire to deal with emotional life.[2] Yet she did not at that time see herself as a "feminist:" things happened by "osmosis," she notes, rather than by any direct involvement in the women's movement.[3] In this interview with Lucy Lippard (1975), Rainer agreed that in the wake of making her first films, and partly as a result of feminist response to them, she had come to identify, rather reluctantly, with feminism. In the same interview with Lippard, Rainer refuses to admit that there must be a separation between humanist and formalist concerns:

> I'm constantly trying to have the best of both worlds. In fact, that is an underlying theory that I probably will continue to pursue, that the most scabrous confessional Soap Opera kind of verbiage or experience can be transmitted through highly rigorous formal means and have a fresh impact. . . . I accept this dichotomy as a necessity of modern art. I'm not trying to work my way back to a more direct relationship to subject matter.[4]

Thus, Rainer's aims in making her films, if not her formal strategies, are markedly different from those used by the avant-garde-theory-film directors I will discuss in chapter 10; yet, in retaining an interest in "content," a signified (however ambiguous and fluctuating), Rainer also departs from structuralist and minimalist filmmakers.

That Rainer had few consciously feminist or political concerns when she made her films makes particularly fascinating the interest of feminist film critics in her work. In their introduction to an interview with Rainer in 1976, the editors of *Camera Obscura* say they found Rainer's films "an exemplary filmmaking practice which in its modernist self-reflexiveness and formal rigor made a decisive break with illusionist practice, and, at the same level of priority, explored problems of feminism."[5] The editors praise Rainer's departure from a realist film practice which they had come to question because they saw emotional identification with characters as politically ineffective: it left no room for analysis of women's situation as *women*.[6] The editors saw a need for "situations in which we could imagine ourselves, within a structure of distanciation which insures room for critical analysis."[7] Rainer offers this in her films without, however, leaving her own experience behind in the manner of the advocates of minimalist and structural film. As the *Camera Obscura* editors note, she manages to combine examination of her own experience with exploring the material and temporal qualities of film.[8]

In their introduction, the editors refer to the fact that Rainer resisted (or did not agree with) their reading of the larger political implications of her formal strategies. This difference between a filmmaker and her theoretical critics is interesting in that directors and critics are differently positioned and thus "see" differently; but the interview reveals the productive effects of such a confrontation: one can see that both sides were led to question their assumptions in meeting the challenge of the Other. It is not a matter of discovering the "truth," but of recognizing the different place from which each is looking.

Rainer was evidently going along a trajectory that arose out of the artistic world in which she moved and her own inner "voices." Her formal and emotional concerns are what led her to make *Lives of Performers* and *Film about A Woman Who . . .*, and were responsible for the shape the films took, rather than any application of an *a priori* theory. The feminist film critics, on the other hand, had been analyzing dominant and independent film practice with a view to discovering what was limiting about dominant strategies and what could be liberating about feminist ones. (The differences on this matter between Rainer and her critics are most clear in the lengthy interchange over Eustache's *The Mother and the Whore*.⁹)

Another fascinating discussion takes place about identification. Perhaps surprisingly, both the critics and Rainer see her films as easy to identify with although in totally different ways. The *Camera Obscura* editors find that, as against the emotional identification that a realist film like *Janie's Janie* demands (and relies on), Rainer's films allow for "substitution on the basis of conscious, recognized sameness."¹⁰ Rainer, on the other hand, evidently saw herself as going back to emotional identification in making *Film about a Woman Who . . .*: "I was interested," she says, "in the plain old Aristotelian catharsis. I wanted the audience to be swept away with pity, and if not terror, then a strong empathetic unease."¹¹ In other words, Rainer thought that she was, indeed, making a film geared to provide direct emotional identification of the kind realist and Hollywood films rely on.

This difference between Rainer and the *Camera Obscura* editors is, like the previous one, thought-provoking. To begin with, an exploration of the essential differences between what Rainer calls "identification" and the editors "substitution" is needed. How precisely is "substitution" different? Substitution involves more distance, more "room for analysis," at least theoretically, but still involves some kind of "placing oneself in the position of" the screen figures. Is it simply less personal because the figures are less personalized?

Further, there is the vexed problem of who can and cannot identify with, or substitute themselves for, which screen figures. The *Camera Obscura* editors claim that they would find it difficult to "identify" with Janie, as the film demands. But many women would also not be able to "situate" themselves alongside the figures in Rainer's film. This ability to identify, substitute, is connected to the sociological positioning of the spectator and her experiences with signification as much as to formal strategies *per se*.¹² The whole matter seems more open and more complex than the rigorous application of the theory would allow for. And we do not have sufficient information upon which to base such theory.¹³ Rainer herself is interestingly skeptical about the possibility of having an effect on a large number of people and is resigned to speaking to "an audience already disposed to share my point of view and appreciate the manner in which it is conveyed."¹⁴

That there is some justice in her position is evident in the editorial comments comparing Rothschild and Rainer which preface the interview by Lippard in the *Feminist Art Journal*. Cindy Nemser, while being careful to thoroughly *respect* Rainer's film, clearly prefers the transparent realism of Amalie Rothschild (an American documentary filmmaker) who, Nemser argues, "has pulled the barriers down, thrown away the old rules of what is acceptably 'avant-garde' and is delving wholeheartedly into herself by investigating and validating her own roots."[15] She sees Rainer, on the other hand, as striving for effect, and only inadvertently allowing her "artists' feeling, her anger and fear," to come through in some "authentic fragments." (According to Nemser, "Rainer is indeed the epitome of the alienated artist tormenting herself with her own intellectual pretensions, unable to get back to her living source and as a result producing endless, zombie-like avatars of her ongoing, unresolved state."[16])

These different responses to Rainer's films look toward the debate about realism that I will explore in chapter 10. Here I want to examine Rainer's films as an example of a unique way of using the cinema for feminist ends. Hers is not so much an anti-illusionist cinema as an anti-narrative cinema. Rainer herself questions the degree to which she departs from illusionism as we saw in her desire to produce the emotional effects of a conventional realism through her cinematic strategies.[17]

Perhaps we can begin to find a way out of this dilemma of how Rainer's films *ought* to be read by looking briefly at *Lives of Performers*. For in that film Rainer, first, allows us to see how she constructs her film, and second, she teaches us how to read *Film about a Woman Who . . .* through the device of the audience within the film. There are two aspects that I want to focus on: first, the way Rainer foregrounds narrative processes, making us aware that narratives are constructed – she reveals the need for narrative at the same time as showing how narrative limits, defines, homogenizes; second, Rainer's interest in emotional struggles, particularly the emotions around love relationships – here she shows her awareness that love relationships so easily fall into the clichés of dominant narratives (Hollywood melodrama, soap opera), which is partly why she tries to avoid narrative, not knowing how to make a story outside of the stereotypes of dominant forms. But she wants to retain the validity of the *emotions*; in fact, she frees emotions from the trappings of dominant narrative forms, representing emotions through narrative words. She thus tries to work her way out of the dilemma: simulation = clichés of dominant narrative forms → need to avoid emotions → structuralist or minimalist cinema. Even though Rainer herself believes she is not concerned with the politics of representation that the *Camera Obscura* editors exposed, but rather with a politics of content, she is concerned to portray emotional issues or conflicts without falling into the ideology that structures these struggles in bourgeois capitalism.

One of her strategies is to ask her actors to affect an outer "neutrality," reflected in both the affectless, immobile faces of the characters and the flat, expressionless voices of the actors reading thoughts and feelings. This deliberate depersonalization is one of the ways in which Rainer deconstructs traditional narrative, which relies on presenting the unique individual through body gesture, facial expression, elaborated and characteristic voice-patterns, and "individual" speech. The disjunction between depersonalized presentation and the intensely personal thoughts and feelings is what gives Rainer's films their special power and effect.

In depersonalizing, Rainer situates herself squarely within modernism, but keeps herself to the historically earlier period, as we have seen, rather than taking on the full-fledged rejection of meaning and reference that minimalism and structuralist film represent. Jameson's discussion of the differences between Flaubert and Balzac are relevant here in defining precisely where Rainer is located. Taking a neo-Freudian, Lacanian position vis-à-vis narrative, Jameson sees texts in terms of Lacan's imaginary-symbolic distinction. For Jameson, all narrative texts are in some sense wish-fulfilments arising out of an original family situation which he calls the "fantasy master narrative." He goes on:

> This unconscious master narrative – which we will call . . . a *fantasm* in order to distinguish it from the connotations of daydream and wish-fulfilment unavoidable in the English term "fantasy" – is an unstable or contradictory structure, whose persistent actantial functions and events (which are in life restaged again and again with different actors and on different levels) demand repetition, permutation, and the ceaseless generation of various structural "resolutions" which are never satisfactory, and whose initial, unreworked form is that of the Imaginary, or, in other words, those waking fantasies, daydreams and wish-fulfilments of which we have already spoken.[18]

This imaginary text has to undergo some modification when it is used in representation; for then the author enters the world of the symbolic, of signifying systems, which set up obstacles for the resolution of imaginary wish-fulfilments. Nevertheless, some texts, like Hollywood films and popular culture generally, leave traces of the wish-fulfilment in the narrative surface; while others, texts of "high realism," Jameson says,

> entertain a far more difficult and implacable conception of the fully realized fantasy: one which is not to be satisfied by the easy solutions of an "unrealistic" omnipotence or the immediacy of a gratification that needs no narrative trajectory in the first place, but which on the contrary seeks to endow itself with the utmost representable density and to posit the most elaborate and systematic difficulties and obstacles.[19]

Jameson sees precisely here a big difference between Balzac and Flaubert – Balzac retaining the presence of the psychic mechanism of wish-fulfilment and Flaubert doing all he can to remove traces of wish-fulfilment from the narrative surface through the depersonalization of the literary text. This "program of depersonalization," Jameson suggests, in some sense answers Freud's recognition of the fundamental problem of aesthetic creation, namely that it must "somehow universalize, displace, and conceal the private wish-fulfilling elements of its content if it wants to make the latter receivable as art by other subjects who are 'repelled' by the poet's own private wish-fulfilments." [20]

One feels that the project of depersonalization as undertaken by Rainer is carried out for reasons very similar to those of Flaubert as outlined by Jameson. She was able to displace and generalize her private experiences through her distancing devices, but nevertheless held on to the notion of the importance of the emotional life. A voice-over comment in *Lives of Performers* outlines what must have been Rainer's own aims in both this film and *Woman Who . . .*: "The face of this character is a fixed mask. . . . She must function with a face of stone, and yet reveal her characteristic dissembling." [21] In Lacanian terms, Rainer wants to give us more than an imaginary, wish-fulfilment text. In Jameson's framework, she is giving us a "high-realism" text, in the sense of aiming to use the symbolic to raise obstacles in relation to the Imaginary. Her films analyze the problem of desire from the perspective of the Real, of what is available. And this analysis is possible only within the signifying practices of language and the cinematic apparatus, within the level of the symbolic. She strives, however, to *use* these signifying practices in new ways so as to accommodate her "new" meanings and to subvert the old "bourgeois" ideology.

In *Lives of Performers*, Rainer decided there were two ways of avoiding the old ideology: first, by the device of deconstructing the soap-opera-like "script" through foregrounding its "performance;" second, by the further device of introducing unexpected elements into the "script," such as having the two women (who are being made love to by the same man) come together and sympathize with one another (one finally renounces the man voluntarily, finding the situation ridiculous), and of having "comments" on the drama.

The performance is foregrounded in two ways, making a double distanciation: first, there is the device of a script, read off screen by some actors, over their silent performance; second, there is the sound of a real audience, viewing a performance of some of the material included in the film. But balancing this anti-illusionism, this deconstruction of narrative, is the fact that the people doing the performance have their real-life names (so there is a sort of "documentary" level); and also one senses a real-life (autobiographical/documentary) situation that originally gave rise to this "performance."

Thus, Rainer manages to deconstruct melodrama while at the same time conveying a recognizable relationship struggle. Letting us in on the "construction" of the melodrama prevents our identifying in the usual way with the characters (as against Hollywood strategies that force such an identification), but at the same time we are moved by the poignancy of the situation itself. However, having got us involved in the poignancy, the voice-over descriptions and comments make us ponder on what we see. At one point, the narrator asks: "How did she get herself in such a fix?" The "script" also contains questions about it, posed to one another by those reading it. And there are (occasional) comments addressed to "Rainer" as director (within the film). (For example, at one point a woman says: "Yvonne, were you reading that? I just wanted to know." At another, an actor questions a statement, and Rainer says: "We've just gone through that; it's in the text; it's about these two: neither are sure of their feelings.") And there is a debate about a quote from Jung in the script, one reader finding the statement "pompous" and "self-righteous," while "Rainer" admits her weakness for high-flown sentiments by men.

The device of the off-screen audience in *Lives of Performers* is one of the ways in which Rainer "teaches" us how to "read" *Film about a Woman Who . . .*: for this audience takes a sympathetic, but somewhat amused and distanced, stance toward what they are watching; their stance exposes the gentle parody that the film is making of the kind of over-serious, complicated love relationships we all find ourselves in. For instance, when Valda unwraps a present and finding an eyeshade puts it on, the audience laughs; but they are silent as the voice-over commentary explains the symbolic significance of the shade (to revenge her inner pain and outer armory); i.e. the shade, covering half the face and leaving half visible, symbolizes the fact that Valda dare not reveal her inner feelings but meanwhile keeps a "neutral" visible image.

Often in *Lives of Performers* the characters express themselves through the language of their bodies, through dance movement. Two such moments happen toward the end of the film. The first is Valda's solo, representing an extraordinary moment, which, as Ruby Rich notes, moves between "the classicism of the Cunningham style (in whose company she was a dancer) and the exaggerated expressionism of Nazimova in the silent film *Salome*, which, according to Rainer, inspired her choreography here."[22] The solo both highlights woman's position as "spectacle" for the male gaze (her lover is watching and evaluating the performance) and moves beyond that positioning to become an expression of Valda's precarious, vulnerable place in the love triangle. The movements are all about balance, about falling and regaining posture, about extraordinary bodily positions, all of which are analogues to Valda's emotional space (see plate 11, p. 120).

The intertitle for this section, "Emotional relationships are relationships of desire, tainted by coercion and constraint," summarizes the feelings elicited by the solo dance and prepares us for the final group dance which is focused on the dancers placing themselves in turn in the "box" that is at the back of the stage. As Rich notes, this symbol of "coercion and constraint" remains in the background, a warning about the limitations of intimacy as Rainer sees them, and as the film has revealed them to us.[23]

The foregrounding of narrative construction in *Lives* with its concomitant distanciation devices enables one to understand better than one might

Plate 11   Valda's performance foregrounds woman's position as "spectacle" for the male gaze (her lover is watching and evaluating her); but the performance also expresses Valda's precarious and fragile place in the love triangle. The shadow suggests splits, divisions, lack of harmony.

otherwise what Rainer is doing in *Woman Who . . .*, where the construction is more concealed and where more complex distanciation devices are used. *Lives*, as we saw, constructed an audience within its text, who, in a sense, taught the audience in the cinema how to read the text; i.e. we were made to see the humor and the gentle parody of the text being performed through the film audience's laughter; their shuffling, coughing, and occasional comments made us constantly aware of the fact that we were watching a "performance," and in so doing prevented our attempts at identification. The difficulty the actors had in sustaining the roles or in getting them right (they often repeat them) emphasizes the whole nature of narrative as reconstruction, as representation. *Lives* constructed a definite place for the spectator.

Recalling this position may make *Woman Who . . .* less perplexing; for Rainer, I think, wants us to stand in a similar place to that we occupied as spectators in *Lives*, only this time we do not have a responding audience within the film to guide us. Although there is again a visible one, first, it is much smaller, made up only of the four characters (outside of the child) in the film, and second, the audience is not present throughout as in *Lives*. It is there in the beginning when the slides of one couple's struggles are shown; and it reappears from time to time. The members of the audience relinquish their role as the audience to take their position as "characters," and we are left without guidance.

In a way, one misses the lightness and fun that the on-screen audience added to *Lives*; but instead we have a more careful analysis of complicated relationships. The distanciation devices are more complex and they correspond to Rainer's more intense involvement here with the symbolic, as against the imaginative, realm. All Rainer's films, as I mentioned earlier, are preoccupied with words, with language as signifying practice. In this sense, her films remind one of both Godard and of Mulvey and Wollen. But while in *Lives* there was a fairly constant voice-over commentary, there were also quite long silent sections, where we simply watched body movements. In *Woman Who . . .* Rainer uses much more written text, and there is correspondingly much less reliance on dance. In fact, her figures are mainly stationary, as in still photographs; these actually become a theme, a point of reference within the text, a distanciation device at the same time as providing a comment on the cinematic apparatus.

For through her use of still photographs, Rainer seems to be deliberately undercutting the cinematic devices that normally keep the audience locked into the traditional narrative in the classic film; rarely does she use her camera in such a way as to identify with one or another character specifically; and then the actual compositions of the frames are disorienting because so very unusual. For example, the film begins with a series of slides that are still photographs of a beach vacation; the voice-over narration is in the position of the woman, at a moment of disillusionment with the relationship pictured, but recalling the holiday as a happy one. After several slides, we realize that we are now in a moving picture; it takes a while to realize this because the set-up is exactly the same as for the still camera. Suddenly a woman's huge legs enter the frame at the top, while in the far distance we see the man, a tiny figure by the water. The woman first lies down away from us, then, as the voice-over analysis continues, turns to face us; and finally she sits up, huge in front frame, while through her arm the man (joined now by the child) walks along the beach.

It is a stunning and unusual composition, all the more so because of the extraordinary quality of the photography (it reminds one a bit of the Japanese Hiroshi Teshigahara's *Woman of the Dunes*), which is starkly lit to highlight the brightness and which shows, through the clarity of the image, the texture of the sand and the woman's clothes. The surreal qualities are enhanced by the strange, distorting perspective from which we are made to see. Rainer is deliberately refusing us the comfortable positions that we expect from, and are familiar with, in the commercial cinema.

The still photography, the unusual compositions, and the quality of the images thus all function to distance us from the narrative and to prevent the ordinary kind of identification. Three other devices work to the same end. There is, first, the disjunction between word and image which, as in a Godard film, forces us to pay particular attention to each element separately and to notice how each works. For instance, in the scene where the voice in the narration is describing a time when she watched a man dancing with a child, and the effects of this on her, the image shows the man from a high angle, sitting in a room with the child, watching television. This break between text and image gives us pause; the described scene comes alive in our minds, while we watch the actual scene with particular attention because it is *not* the scene in our minds; the woman's discomfort with the dancing scene offers a contrast to this rather cosy scene of man and child sitting quietly. The contrast, however, only emphasizes her feelings of deliberate exclusion by the man; we realize that the man uses his closeness with the child to manipulate the woman, to provoke her and make her feel unwanted.

In another instance, the voice in the narration is talking about having dinner with her lover's male lover, but the image is another high angle one, this time of the man, woman, and child having breakfast. The voice continues to discuss the man, while we see the woman flipping pages of a magazine, the man preparing and giving toast to the child. Again, the disjunction between image and words allows us to concentrate on the *words*, just because they do not fit the image.

Second, Rainer distances us from the narrative flow in *Woman Who . . .* by the use of many more intertitles and frames of written text than she had used in *Lives*. Interestingly enough, Rainer evidently did not intend the device to be as disruptive as it is, cinematically: she was motivated to use it out of a desire to give the words more impact than they have when simply heard:

> When I want to be certain of the strongest impact from a given text, when I want to avoid the possibility that the words merely "wash over" the audience, I present the material in printed form. Four-letter words, erotic, and more emotionally "loaded" materials are dealt with in this manner. The complicity of the audience in being "face-to-face" with such materials is an important factor in the quality of the impact.[24]

But as the *Camera Obscura* editors point out, the "effect is one of calling attention to the intertitle itself rather than to what it says."[25] Held longer than it takes to read, the written text functions as a jarring element in a flow of images, drawing our attention away from the content to the process of cinema itself, since the device is anathema to the cinema as we know it today.

The use of alternating male and female voices to present the characters' thoughts and feelings is yet one more distancing device. We often hear a female figure's thought spoken by a man, and this again draws our attention to the story as "constructed."

Finally, time–space relations in the film are all awry. What we have are

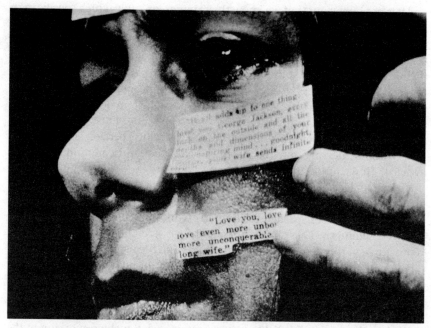

Plate 12   Another distancing device is that of intertitles, used in a variety of ways. Here pieces of text are pasted on the character's face (played by Rainer herself), and the camera moves over each one slowly. The device draws attention to the process of cinema and is anathema to commercial conventions.

snatches of a story, rather than the whole thing. We are given little pieces without really knowing when they happened, or to whom they happened, or in what chronological sequence they happened. Several possible relationship permutations are posited: a woman with a child involved with two men; a woman involved with a man, who has a male lover; a woman involved with a man who is involved with another woman.

We get small parts of all these possible scenarios, but each part remains self-enclosed, not necessarily connected to what came before or to what goes after. While this is disorienting for the Hollywood-shaped filmgoer, and while such a filmgoer may spend a lot of time in a Rainer film trying to piece all the bits together, Rainer's refusal of clarity here does have the purpose, mentioned at the start, of depersonalization and generalization. By refusing to individualize her characters in an ongoing sense, by refusing to connect everything into one tidy package, Rainer leaves her situations open for us to speculate about them. All is not neatly provided for us, as in a Hollywood film; we have to work to construct the film for ourselves, and in so doing we can learn a lot about the way relationships function, especially from the female point of view.

What comes over strongly is the pain that the female characters express, and it is not important that we know their names, or know which specific man hurt them, or who is actually sleeping with whom. What we get is the women's sense of being lost, of not knowing what they want, of anger, disappointment, frustration; we have a sense of the women's powerlessness, their inability to say what they mean at the moment, their lack of certainty as to whether something is wrong with them or with the men they love; a further sense of their not knowing what is actually possible in male–female relationships. As spectators, we begin to ask ourselves questions: Can desire be satisfied? Can there be love without control, restraint, coercion? Can there be love without hurting and being hurt? How can miscommunication be avoided? How can desire flow freely and happily?

If we do indeed arrive at such questions, I believe that Rainer has achieved her end in making the film. And, in having the questions posed through women's experiences specifically, Rainer's work makes an important contribution to feminism. There is, of course, no explicit feminist politics of the kind represented in this book by Marguerite Duras and the avant-garde-theory-film directors; for Rainer takes a very different stance in relation to the symbolic than do these filmmakers, who see signifying practices as capable only of expressing a male positioning. Rainer does not question her tools *per se*: her texts are liberating because she gives her female characters a voice; they speak their thoughts and feelings about their complex relationships, working in the analytic mode; they seek to understand both themselves and their lovers, to discover, as Rainer (we noted) has one character say, how they get into such "fixes."

And in exploring the general problems of closeness, intimacy, loving, Rainer reveals how women get positioned as *victims*, without fully realizing it. As critics have noted, the stills from *Psycho* and the reference to classic movies (viz. the re-enactment of a sequence from *Pandora's Box* in *Lives*) show a concern with woman as victim of male violence.[26] But Rainer is reluctant to build this into a politics of global female oppression. Admitting that she is "obviously involved with victims, and the female as victim," she notes that "my women will probably continue to vacillate between being fools, heroines, and, yes, victims. Victims of their own expectations no less than those of the opposite sex, or of the prevailing social mores."[27]

Rainer thus remains close to personal experience, which while it is generalized, as we've seen, does not yet expand outward to explanations derived from the social and political institutions in which women live. But Rainer was to go on to make such connections in a later film, *Journeys from Berlin*, unfortunately not dealt with here.[28]

10

The realist debate in the feminist film: a historical overview of theories and strategies in realism and the avant-garde theory film (1971–81)

Yvonne Rainer is unusual among American feminist filmmakers in producing feature-length films. As I noted in chapter 7, by and large American women directors have not managed to gain access to feature production in the manner of European women filmmakers like Duras and Von Trotta for reasons that have little to do with American women's capabilities. The few women who have managed to make films in Hollywood in recent years usually turn out to have male connections and do not necessarily make films about women.[1]

By far the largest number of films by American women have taken the cinema vérité documentary form – one of the simplest and cheapest of film forms. While other film styles and modes (e.g. animation, non-narrative abstract films, formalist films, short narrative films) are represented, the vérité style clearly dominates. The precise causes for this, other than economic ones, are unclear; much more experimentation with film form has taken place in Europe, especially in Britain, and this may have to do with the complicated differences between the American and the various European women's movements. (For example, it is frequently noted that the American movement is more activist and pragmatically oriented, more interested in sociological theoretical approaches, than are the European groups which quickly developed Althusser's kind of Marxism and theories based on the thinkers summarized in the Introduction.)

But since, for whatever reasons, the documentary form is so prevalent, and since, further, it has provoked much theoretical debate, this chapter focuses specifically on representative examples of the American women's documentary. In the next chapter, I analyze mainly British examples of (what I call) the avant-garde theory film, which emerged in reaction to perceived inadequacies of the realist film. Here I will, first, discuss two well-known examples of early documentaries by women in order to show that the criticisms have a certain validity, and at the same time I will explore some of the problems with the theory; second, I will define and evaluate the avant-garde strategies mentioned above, in preparation for the analyses of specific films in chapters 11 and 12.

The first independent films by women situated themselves essentially in the realist tradition as it came immediately through the 1960s British free cinema movement and the work of the National Film Board of Canada, in conjunction with influences from the French New Wave. These movements in turn looked back to documentary efforts spurred by the First and Second World Wars. The realism outside of the commercial cinema, stimulated by the wars, whether documentary or fiction, took as its aim the capturing on film of the experiences of ordinary people. Directors saw their closer relationship to lived experience as arising from (1) their use of working-class people and issues for their subjects (i.e. this class, and its concerns, are somehow more "real" than the middle classes, and theirs); (2) basing their films on real-life events as against made-up stories; (3) their use of on-location shooting as against artificial studio sets; and (4) Italian neo-realism and its cinematic techniques, such as the long take, which was assumed to prevent the meddling with actuality assumed in montage, etc.

But particularly important for women's documentaries was the work of the American Newsreel Collective, started in 1962 and largely inspired by Norm Fruchter on his return from working in England at the British Film Institute. The Newsreel group partly modeled themselves on Dziga Vertov, who had established and directed the weekly newsreel *Kinonedielia*, filming events on the Russian warfront, 1918–19. Newsreel's aims were explicitly propagandist in the sense of publicizing the many political events that 1960s radicals were involved in (civil rights, community organizing, black power, the Vietnam movement, the takeover of educational institutions, and finally, the women's movement). They used the by this time familiar vérité techniques (which originated in the French New Wave) of fast film stock (with its gray, grainy tones), hand-held camera, interviews, voice-over track (but not necessarily commentary), editing both for shock effect and to develop a specific interpretation of political events. Made on a very low budget, and in a collective mode, the films are necessarily rough, often sloppy; but this reflected merely the over-riding aim not to produce aesthetic objects but to create powerful organizing tools. It is precisely their validity as organizing tools that the new theory questions. For according to the theory the films draw on codes that cannot change consciousness.

This is expressed most strongly by Eileen McGarry in her article on "Documentary realism and women's cinema." She points out that long before the filmmakers arrive at the scene, reality itself is coded "first in the infrastructure of the social formation (human economic practice) and secondly by the superstructure of politics and ideology."[2] The filmmaker, then, is "not dealing with reality, but with that which has become the pro-filmic event: that which exists and happens in front of the camera."[3] She argues that to ignore the "manner in which the dominant ideology and cinematic traditions encode the pro-filmic event is to hide the fact that reality is selected and altered by the presence of the film workers, and the demands of the equipment."[4]

While this is true to a certain extent (obviously any screen image is the result of a great deal of selection, in terms of what footage to show, what shot to place next to which, angle and distance from subject, what words to use, etc.) as we'll see the documentarist neither has total control over the referent nor is she totally controlled by signifying practices. Paradoxically, what she does have more control over is precisely ideology. For I cannot even begin a discourse about the films without differentiating them according to ideological perspective – i.e. their feminist politics – and this is a distinction that the theory does not allow for, given its high level of abstraction. All the early films used the same cinematic strategies, but the ends to which these strategies were directed fell into two broad camps: there were, first, films like the pioneering Newsreel's *The Woman's Film* (1970), which exhibited a clear leftist-activist politics; and second, films like Reichert/Klein's *Growing Up Female* (1969), which reflected a more liberal-bourgeois stance, showing how sex roles in our society are clearly demarcated so as to privilege men but not analyzing the underlying reasons for gender-typing or dealing with class and economic relations.[5] The Newsreel film aimed to raise consciousness explicitly and exclusively about the exploitation of working-class women by a capitalist system geared to support private enterprise and the accumulation of individual wealth; while the second film urged women to try to free themselves from the sex roles that limited their opportunities for a rich, fulfilling, challenging, individual life. Yet, the cinematic devices in the two films were identical.

Let us now look at two early films, *Joyce at 34* (1972) and *Janie's Janie* (1971) (made shortly after the ones already mentioned), in order to assess the degree to which some of the semiological theoretical criticisms are indeed valid, and the degree to which they are clearly inadequate to explain concrete differences between the films in terms of (1) their ideology; (2) their conception of the cinematic apparatus (fiction and documentary are seen as essentially the same); and (3) their conception of the spectator as "fixed" by the codes of the signifying practices.

To begin with, let me summarize the degree to which the structuralist, semiological criticism of realism is valid for aspects of both *Joyce at 34* and *Janie's Janie*. First, the cinematic strategies of both films are indeed such as to establish an unwelcome imbalance between author and spectator; the authors in each case assume the position of the ones with knowledge, while the spectators are forced into the position of passive consumers of this knowledge. The filmic processes leave us with no work to do, so that we sit passively and receive the message, in the first film, about how marriage, family, and career can all function harmoniously, and in the second, about how, with some determination, a woman on welfare can organize her community for needed changes. There is classic resolution in each case, since both heroines arrive somewhere, leaving us with a sense that we do not have to do anything.

Second, the sort of direct mode of address in both films encourages us to relate to the images of Joyce and Janie as to "real" women, as if we could know them. Yet, in fact, both figures are constructed in the film by the processes of camera, lighting, sound, editing. They can have no other ontological existence for the spectator than that of representation.

Third, the reason we do not realize that each female figure is merely a representation is that neither film draws attention to itself *as* film, nor makes us aware that we are watching a film. Neither film, therefore, breaks our usual habits in the commercial cinema of passive viewing.

Fourth, underlying all of the above is the key notion of the unified self which characterizes pre-semiological thought. Both Joyce and Janie, as subjects, are seen in the autobiographical mode, as having essences that have persisted through time and that reveal growth through individual change outside of influence from social structures, economic relations, or psychoanalytic laws. The use of both home movies and old photographs is crucial as a device that establishes continuity through time and that reflects the fiction-making urge that, as Metz and Heath have shown, pervades even the documentary. Used as unproblematic representations, the past images function to seal individual change instead of their being evidence of the way women and their bodies are constructed by the signifying practices of both the social and psychological institutions in which they are embedded. (Interestingly enough, this construction is something that Michelle Citron makes a main theme in her film *Daughter-Rite* (1978), where the slowing down of home movies enables us to see that the representations are far from being any "innocent recording," the process of making the movies in itself functioning as construction of the place for the female children.)

But this is as far as the similarities in the realist mode go; the differences that follow arise out of the different relationship to class issues on the part of the filmmakers. In *Joyce at 34*, all mention of class and economic relations is suppressed, so that we are never made aware of the privileged situation that Joyce enjoys with her freelancing writer husband (he can be at home a lot of the time) and the support of her comfortably middle-class parents. The cinematic strategies here work to suture over conflicts and contradictions as in a Hollywood film. Joyce's voice-over, with its "metaphysic of presence," keeps the spectator believing in Joyce as a person guiding us and making coherent what would otherwise be a disoriented, disconnected, chaotic world – a series of shots with no necessary relationship. Her voice alone makes a comfortably reassuring world where the signifiers respond to an apparently solid signified. And as representation, Joyce does not in herself threaten accepted norms, while her unusually handsome husband adds a gloss to Joyce's environment,

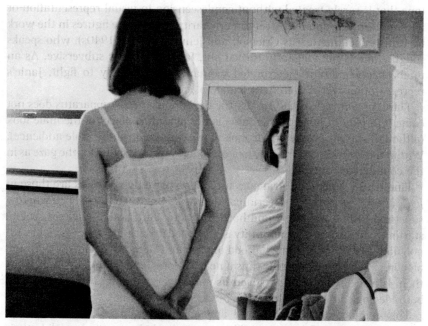

Plate 13 Joyce (in *Joyce at 34* by Choppra and Weill) is seen in the autobiographical mode, as the film's title emphasizes. She is assumed to have an essence that has persisted through time separate from social structures, economic relations, or psychoanalytic laws. This shot shows Joyce catching her pregnant reflection in a mirror, and it supports a voice-over narration by Joyce, telling of the dreariness of the waiting. The film's strategies limit possible exploration of other implications of the shot as a comment on female representation and on the way the mother is positioned in patriarchy.

which in any case fits the bourgeois model central in commercial representations.

The structure of *Joyce at 34* thus perpetuates the bourgeois illusion, first, of the possibility of the individual to effect change, and second, that the individual is somehow outside of the symbolic and other social institutions in which s/he lives. In fact, reading the film against the grain, one can see how Joyce is very much at the mercy of the structures that shaped her! *Janie's Janie*, on the other hand, shows a woman aware of the economic and class structures that formed her and who has made a deliberate, and decisive, break with those structures. First, she speaks her awareness of her position as Other to the two men in her life – father and husband – without blaming them personally for the oppression she suffered at their hands. They are also victims of the symbolic organization of things.

Second, Janie's image itself violates normal codes. As a working-class figure (one that is rarely treated without condescension in visual representation or without being co-optable by reform or charity – as are the figures in the work by British documentarists Grierson and Jennings in the 1940s), who speaks roughly and is not elegantly turned out, Janie's image is subversive. As an unabashedly militant, determined woman, who is ready to fight, Janie's representation resists dominant female placing.

Third, in contrast to *Joyce at 34*, the traditional "gaze" apparatus does not come into play in *Janie's Janie*. Janie is not placed as object of the male look (although she cannot avoid the look of the camera or of the male audience). Within the diegesis, she is never looked upon by men or set up for the gaze as in the commercial cinema.

Finally, the cinematic strategies are not as boringly realist as are those in *Joyce at 34*. There are soft superimpositions (Janie's face in the kitchen window superimposed on the street and house outside), and Janie's loneliness before starting to organize the community is suggested in dark-lit shots, overlaid with poignant music track, filmed at odd angles, and suggestive shots of washing blowing in the wind. There is thus a neat "before" and "after" division. This, then, is a realist film which, given its parameters, manages to achieve a lot both ideologically and visually.

This comparison of *Joyce at 34* and *Janie's Janie* has shown that while criticisms of the realist vérité film are to a degree entirely valid, their monolithic, abstract formulation is a problem. When one looks closely at individual realist films, one realizes the weakness of the large generalizations. Realist films, that is, are far more heterogeneous and complex in their strategies than the theoretical critique can allow for.[6] We need a theory that will permit and accept different positionings toward class and economic issues in the realist mode and that, while not mitigating any of the semiological problems, especially around the overall positioning of the spectator as passive recipient of knowledge, at least grants a limited area of resistance to hegemonic codes in certain examples of the form.

It is at this point important to explore the implications of the position from which the critique of realism emerged, particularly in relation, first, to the concept of the human subject in society as well as in film (i.e. is the theory of knowledge underlying the objection to realism valid?); and second, in relation to the theory of the cinematic apparatus and the way that it functions.

The stress on signifying practices followed logically from the theory that, given their hegemonic shaping function, these practices are in fact all we can ever "know." Yet, as Derrida has noted, people cling to the belief that there is "some final, objective, unmediated 'real world' . . . about which we can have knowledge."[7] The conventions of traditional art commit us to the voice as the primary means of communication, and this involves what Derrida calls "a falsifying 'metaphysics of presence' based on the illusion that we are ultimately able to 'come face to face' with objects." There will always be kinds of art that "appear to involve an apparently straightforward and stable commitment to an unchanging world 'beyond' themselves."[8]

Realism as an artistic style is designed to perpetuate this illusion of a stable world; and within realism it is of course the vérité documentary that seems most confidently "a window through which . . . the world is clearly visible" and "where the signifiers appear to point directly and confidently to the signified."[9] The realist theory semiologists object to was developed in the postwar period, stimulated in part by the Italian neo-realist movement; the theorists Kracauer and Bazin argued for the cinema "as the redemption of physical reality," and for the assumption that realist techniques allowed us to perceive actuality for ourselves, unmediated by the distortions produced through other cinematic techniques.[10]

It is precisely here that semiologists have taken issue with realist theory, since for them there is no knowable "reality" outside of signifying practices. The first clear statement of the objection to realism was a by now famous essay by Claire Johnston; Johnston argued that cinema vérité or the "cinema of non-intervention" was dangerous for feminists since it used a realist aesthetic embedded specifically in capitalist representations of reality. Vérité films do not break the illusion of realism. Since the "truth" of our oppression cannot be captured on celluloid with the "innocence" of the camera, she argued that for feminist cinema to be effective it must be a counter-cinema:

> Any revolutionary must challenge the depiction of reality; it is not enough to discuss the oppression of women within the text of the film: the language of the cinema/depiction of reality must also be interrogated, so that a break between ideology and text is affected.[11]

Feminist filmmakers, that is, must confront within their films the accepted representations of reality so as to expose their falseness. Realism as a style is unable to change consciousness because it does not depart from the forms that embody the old consciousness. Thus, prevailing realist codes – of camera, lighting, sound, editing, mise-en-scène – must be abandoned and the cinematic apparatus used in a new way so as to challenge audiences' expectations and assumptions about life.

Noel King argues something very similar in a *Screen* article on two political feminist documentaries – *Union Maids* (1976) and *Harlan County, U.S.A.* (1976) (which belong in the category of historical/retrospective films). He elaborates on points that Johnston, given the briefness of her essay, was unable to develop, and attempts to "read these documentaries against the grain, to refuse the reading it is the work of their textual systems to secure."[12] In doing this, he is applying the same critical categories that have been used to decode Hollywood films, making essentially no distinction between the realist techniques used in the classical Hollywood tradition and those being used in the new feminist documentary. (He is here building on work done by Stephen Neale on the 1930s populist and Nazi propaganda films.[13])

King points, for example, to the way the films' strategies work to suppress any discourse on the social construction of the subjects being interviewed, in the interests of asserting the individual's responsibility for bringing about change through a moral insight into injustice:

> In this sense, the politics in Union Maids might be termed a "redemptive politics"; that is to say . . . a system where questions of individual responsibility are paramount. It is a politics articulated by textual mechanisms which fix the individual subject as responsible, as either fulfilling, or not fulfilling a morally given imperative and this in turn results in a notion of triumph or guilt.[14]

He then talks of the films' strategies as essentially narrative ones; they use, he says "a series of sub-forms of narratives: biography, autobiography and popular narrative history." These, King shows, all follow a cause–effect relationship, the origin always containing the end. Through the linking of archival footage, the anecdotal reminiscences constructed in the interviews, and the bridging voice-over narration (spoken by the three women) talking about America in the 1930s, Union Maids produces a "'discourse of continuity' which results not in 'the past' but in the effect of the past."[15] What King is ultimately objecting to is the way the narrative in Union Maids and Harlan County, U.S.A. produces a "syntagmatic flow of events, an easy diachronic progression which ensures a working out of all problems, guarantees an increase in knowledge on the reader's part, promises containment and completion."[16] This kind of suturing is, of course, the traditional device of the classic Hollywood film in its aim to smooth over possible contradictions, incoherences, and eruptions that might reflect a reality far less ordered, coherent, or continuous than Hollywood wants to admit or to know. Like Claire Johnston, King concludes by asserting the necessity for creating a different type of text, one that resists the rhetorical conventions of populist cultural history, that "depicts its own strategies and practices, and which does not provide a complete, unified representation of class and collectivity."[17]

While this is in many ways a logical conclusion to reach, it may be too monolithic a position to sustain the kind of detailed analysis of specific films like Janie's Janie and Joyce at 34 undertaken above. If the eighteenth-century neo-classical critics went wrong in demanding that the discrepancy between poetry and reality be eliminated (i.e. in asking that poetry imitate the external world as it is, keeping to "the kinds of objects that we know to exist, and the kinds of events that we know to be possible, on the basis of an empirical knowledge of nature and nature's laws");[18] and if the Romantic critics who followed went wrong in asserting a privileged poetic discourse that now

Plate 14 Through the linking of archival footage, anecdotal reminiscences, and bridging voice-over narration, *Union Maids*, according to Noel King, produces "'a discourse of continuity' which results not in 'the past' but in the effect of the past." Here Reichert/Klein insert an archival shot of a laundry strike in *Union Maids*.

reflected not external reality but the spontaneous overflow of feelings (i.e. the poet's mind has already transformed external nature and now puts forth images, produced by intense emotional excitement, that correspond to nothing outside of the poet);[19] then semiology goes wrong (in some applications) in conceiving of art and life as both equally "constructed" by the signifying practices that define and limit each sphere.

The documentary filmmakers were misguided in returning to the eighteenth-century notion of art as one able simply to imitate life, as if through a transparent glass, and in believing that representation could affect behavior directly (i.e. an image of a poor woman would immediately bring political awareness of the need to distribute wealth more fairly); but there are problems also in making the signifier material in the sense that it is all there is to know. Discussing semiology in relation to Marxism, Terry Eagleton points out the dangers of this way of seeing for a Marxist view of history. History evaporates in the new scheme; since the signified can never be grasped, we cannot talk about our reality as human subjects. But, as he goes on to show, more than the signified is at stake: "It is also," he says, "a question of the referent (i.e. social actuality), which we all long ago bracketed out of being. In re-materializing the sign, we are in imminent danger of dematerializing its referent; a linguistic materialism gradually reverts itself into a linguistic idealism."[20]

Eagleton no doubt overstates the case when he talks about "sliding away from the referent," since neither Saussure nor Althusser denied that there *was* a referent. But it is true that while semiologists talk about the eruption of "the real" (i.e. accidents, death, revolution), on a daily basis they see life as dominated by the prevailing signifying practices of a culture, i.e. as refracted through those discourses which define "reality" for people. While I have no quarrel with this concern with the discourses that define and limit our notions of "reality," and agree that these discourses are essentially controlled by the classes that are in power, it seems important to allow for a level of experience that differs from discourse, or that is not *only* discourse. Where semiology and poststructuralism are very important is in finally getting rid of the notion of a privileged aesthetic discourse – a notion that has only perpetuated a hampering dualism between art and science (broadly conceived). But if we want to create art that will bring about change in the quality of people's daily lives in the social formation, we need a theory that takes account of the level now usually referred to scornfully as "naïvely materialistic."[21]

But before leaving the attack on realism as a cinematic strategy, I want to deal briefly with two assumptions about the cinematic apparatus that appear in the theory. First, how valid is it to apply the same criticism to realist practices used in the commercial, narrative cinema and in the independent documentary form? I would rather loosen up the theory and argue that the same realist signifying practices can indeed be used for different ends, as we have already seen in comparing *Janie's Janie* and *Joyce at 34*. Realism in the commercial cinema may indeed be a form analogous to the nineteenth-century novel, in which a class-bound, bourgeois notion of the world is made to seem "natural" and "unproblematic." But *Janie's Janie* is not *An Unmarried Woman*; while *Joyce at 34* does come close to the way the form is used in Mazursky's work.

Johnston's and King's attacks on realism are confused by their assumption that the realist cinematic mode in *itself* raises problems about the relation of representation to lived experience. The problems reside rather either in the assumptions of the filmmakers about this relation or in the audience's assumptions about the relation. But taken simply as a cinematic style, which can be used in different genres (i.e. documentary or fictional), realism does not insist on any special relation to the social formation.[22] As Metz has noted, it is "the *impression of reality* experienced by the spectator . . . the feeling that we are witnessing an almost real spectacle" that causes the problems.[23] It is, Metz continues, the fact "that films have the *appeal* of presence and of a proximity that strikes the masses and fills the movie theaters."[24]

In fact, as Metz goes on to show, the crucial difference is not between cinematic modes (illusion of realism versus anti-illusionism), but between an event in the here and now and a *narrated* event. As soon as we have the process of telling, the real is unrealized (or the unreal is realized, as he sometimes puts it).[25] Thus, even the documentary or the live television coverage, in *narrating* the event, creates the distance that causes unrealization. "Realism," Metz notes, "is not reality. . . . Realism affects the organization of the contents, not narration as a status." [26]

Thus, despite the fact that documentary and fiction films begin with different material (the one, actors in a studio, the other, actual people in their environment), once this material becomes a strip of film to be constructed in whatever way the author wishes, the difference almost evaporates. Both fiction and non-fiction tend to create fiction, as we've seen – often in the family romance mode. And indeed, if we go along with McGarry, we have seen that even before the filming starts, the pro-filmic event is heavily coded by the cultural assumptions people bring to the process of making a film.[27] Thus the documentary ends up as much a "narrative" in a certain sense as an explicitly fiction film. Working from the other side, in addition, one can argue (as has Michael Ryan) that all fiction films are really "documentaries" in that all of us watching know, on one level, that everything has been enacted, that we are watching a star playing at being someone, at actions manipulated in a studio to look like real events.[28]

Yet, on two fundamental levels, one that affects the filmmakers and one that involves the spectator, documentary and fiction *are* different. As regards the filmmakers: there is clearly a degree more control in the fiction film than in the documentary. It is true that documentary filmmaking may permit more or less control depending on the project (i.e. a retrospective film, relying on real footage, allows more re-construction of actual events through montage, in the manner of narrative films, than, say, does a documentary about a demonst-ration, when the filmmakers on the scene have little idea as to how things will work out). But what happens in fiction is only controlled if one is working within certain genres, or within institutions, like Hollywood, that only permit certain things to happen. Otherwise, fiction has the potential for representing imaginative possibility – (e.g. models for change) – once the Oedipal mode is broken.

My aim in asserting a difference between fiction and documentary from the perspective of the filmmakers is to avoid the unsatisfactory alternatives of a fixed, binary opposition between fiction and documentary or annihilating *all* difference through the assertion that all cinematic discourse is controlled by the same signifying practices that define and limit what can be represented. While Metz's broad distinction between an event and a *narrated* event obviously holds, it works only on a very abstract and general level. In fact, we need to make distinctions between different genres in the "narrated" category, recognizing that there is a broad spectrum of film types, from narrations limited by their reliance (to a degree) on the physical world to those that use everyday logic but construct their environments to those that use the supernatural (what Metz calls a "non-human logic"). The problems that the filmmakers face in each case will be different, and each film type will have certain dangers, certain advantages.

As regards the spectator: audiences are clearly positioned differently in fictional and in documentary films, as may be seen from the betrayal spectators experience in films like Mitchell Block's *No Lies* (1973) or Michelle Citron's more recent *Daughter-Rite*. In both cases, the directors use vérité techniques, deluding us into thinking we are watching non-actors when in fact at the end we learn that everything was scripted, with actors playing the roles. The anger that audiences experience must mean that a different identification process takes place in the two situations, and this may well have implications for the ultimate effect on the spectator.

Any discussion of these effects must, unfortunately, be entirely speculative, given the lack of reliable research into this area. If I may descend to totally non-scientific evidence for a moment, some responses by students lead me to believe that it's true (as Mulvey has argued) that the identification with stars in a fiction film involves a return to the world of the imaginary (i.e. some evocation of an ego-ideal that, in Lacan's system, predated the entry into the symbolic); whereas the documentary involves a relating to images that is *analogous* to, i.e. *not* the same as (this was the error of the neo-classical movement), the way we respond to people in our daily lives. Although on one level the documentary realist strategies do indeed construct the spectator as passive recipient of the "knowledge" the authors hold, on another level, the spectator may be making judgements about the screen-image woman that indeed have to do with the codes of signifying practice, but that result from the sociological and political positioning of the spectator, i.e. his/her class, race, gender, educational background, as this affects experiences with signification. For instance, some students react in quite a hostile way to Janie, criticizing the way she treats her children (she is too rough on them, she does not dress them well, she does not love them enough, she does not educate them properly); some may object to the way she looks, to the fact that she wears a wig or dyes her hair different colors, etc.

Two things may be happening here: a Barthesian answer is that the spectator is applying to the screen image the codes through which we learn to perceive reality in the outside world; but, on the other hand, the spectator may be resisting being presented with an unconventional image, one which violates his/her expectations, given commercial representations. In other words, much more may be taking place as people watch such documentaries than we know about (the representations may bore, shock, please, or inform, depending on the class, race, and background of the spectator), but an *active* response is being evoked, one that has potential for challenging assumptions about what we expect from cinema and adding to what we know about the world.

However, as organizing strategies specifically, the films may well not work. If semiologists were wrong in denying that realism can ever produce any effect leading to change, then leftist activists were wrong in assuming that merely *showing* something is an argument in its own right. The authors of *Janie's Janie* evidently assumed that any spectator would automatically side with Janie because they had set her up as a figure to be admired, her change as an exemplary one. They did not seem aware of the possibility that Janie as *image* and Janie as the real woman they knew would appear in different lights, and thus would be shocked by the kinds of readings my students gave.

The attack on realism outlined above arose precisely out of the perception that the realist women's documentaries, in the prevailing forms, did not work strategically.[29] One possibility would have been to attempt to modify the dominant realist form, but instead the critics posited the need for a counter-cinema. The very women (like Claire Johnston) active in the critique of realism took it upon themselves to make some of the first avant-garde theory films. In the mid-1970s Johnston, Cook, Mulvey, and Wollen in Britain began to

Plate 15   When one looks closely at individual realist films, one realizes the weakness of large generalizations. Even if the spectator is always passive recipient of assumed authorial knowledge, realist films reflect different positions toward class and economics. Here Barbara Kopple exposes the brutality of the management in the Kentucky mine in *Harlan County, U.S.A.* The realist error lies in assuming that *showing* oppression is sufficient argument in itself.

develop a new feminist avant-garde which, while it drew on earlier avant-gardes (Russian formalism, Brecht, surrealism (Dulac), and the recent counter-cinema directors like Godard, Akerman, and Duras), was new in its particular combination of semiology, structuralism, Marxism, and psychoanalysis. Given their complex cinematic strategies and dense theoretical underpinning, the films require individual and in-depth analysis. Here, I can only sketch in some of the alternative film practices that various directors employed in a deliberate attempt to avoid the theoretical problems that they believed afflicted realism.

These theory films do not reflect the danger outlined by Terry Eagleton, where the referent has been "bracketed out of existence." They stand rather in a relation of tension to the links between the social formation, subjectivity, and representation. All break with the notion of a simple connection between any two of the three areas, and show the complexity of establishing relationships. The directors are concerned with demystifying representation so as to make women aware that texts are producers of ideology, and that we live in a world of constructions rather than of solid essences.

The films have the following aspects in common:

(1) They focus on the cinematic apparatus as a signifying practice, on cinema, that is, as an illusion-making machine; they draw attention to the cinematic process and use techniques to break the illusion that we are not watching a film, but "reality."

(2) They refuse to construct a fixed spectator, but position the spectator so that s/he has to be involved in the processes of the film, rather than passively being captured by it. Distanciation techniques insure the divorce of spectator from text.

(3) They rather deliberately refuse the pleasure that usually comes from the manipulation of our emotions (particularly around the Oedipus complex in the case of the commercial cinema – the reliance of narratives on Freud's family romance). They try to replace pleasure in recognition with pleasure in learning – with cognitive processes, as against emotional ones.

(4) All mix documentary and fiction either (a) as part of the belief that the two cannot ultimately be distinguished as filmic models or (b) to create a certain tension between the social formation, subjectivity, and representation.

There are roughly three broad types of theory film:

(1) Films (like those by Mulvey and Wollen which have had a lot of influence) that deal with the problem of female subjectivity, the problem of woman finding a voice, and a position from which to speak. Using Lacanian psychoanalysis, these films reveal women's position as silent, absent, or marginal in a phallocentric language system.

(2) Films linked to the first in relying on Lacan and which take as their aim the deconstruction of classical patriarchal texts, exposing how woman has been "spoken" rather than asserted as speaking subject, functioning as an empty signifier to satisfy something for the male hero. Sally Potter's *Thriller* and the McCall/Tindall/Pajaczkowska/Weinstock *Sigmund Freud's Dora* are good examples here.

(3) Films concerned with women's history, and with the whole problem of writing history. Filmmakers in this category would agree with Noel King's criticism of *Union Maids* and *Harlan County, U.S.A.* for not presenting any problem about history; following Foucault, directors of the historical theory films show that no history is possible outside of a shaping, distorting point of view, usually that of the ruling classes. Clayton/Curling's *Song of a Shirt* (1980) (about nineteenth-century sempstresses) is perhaps the best example of this kind of film. As Sylvia Harvey has shown, the directors reveal that history is a series of interlocking discourses which involve very specific constructions.[30] The film plays off against one another a variety of documents, including different accounts of the position of sewing women and of their historical context. In addition, as Harvey notes, the *Song of a Shirt* draws attention to the means of representation within the film itself by having the camera move across various blackboards and television monitors, showing the filmed reconstruction of history scenes but also presenting prints, documents, etc.[31] The alternation between documentary footage, documentary "reconstructions," fictional enactments of real events, dramatizations of fictional accounts, and so on, makes us realize that images are reproductions of reality, not reality itself. The constantly interrupted narrations provide a frustration that forces us to understand the seductive power of narrative; this point is underscored in the brilliant sound track, where a lyrical classical tune is repeatedly drowned out by atonal, concrete music representing the dissonances and contradictions of historical discourses which the Establishment continually strives to smooth over. The effect of all these mediations, Harvey concludes, is to make us ask the important political question: "Who is representing? And for whom?"[32]

I will leave for chapter 11 a discussion of problems that emerge from these theory films in terms of audience response, accessibility, and relativism. In concluding my discussion of the attack on realism, I want to evaluate the social and political implications of the change from what I have called the essentially didactic and "propagandistic" strategies of left-activist and bourgeois-liberal women's films to the strategies of the new feminist theory films (still identified with leftism), which focus on signifying practices, on the problems of female subjectivity, and on representation itself.

I have tried to show that the debate about realism is in some sense a false debate, premised first on an unnecessarily rigid theory about the relationship between form and content; and second on a theory of knowledge which, while it illuminates our contemporary system of relationships (particularly the relationship between the individual, language, and the social structures in which we live), is nevertheless inadequate when applied to practice in the sense of bringing about concrete change in the daily lives of women.[33]

Let me say a little more about the inadequacy of the theory of knowledge from which the critique of realism emerged, and which has also conditioned the shape of anti-illusionist films. The danger of semiology has been the "sliding away from the referent" which I quoted above; this is problematic because if all "reality," all external, lived experience is mediated through signifying practice, we can never "know" outside of whatever signifying system we are in. In attempting to get rid of an unwelcome dualism, inherent in western thought at least since Plato, and re-articulated by Kant on the brink of the modern period, some semiologists run the danger of collapsing levels that need to remain distinct if we are to work effectively in the political arena to bring about change.

As I noted, the best theory films do not abandon the referent, and exist in a deliberate tension (created through the combining of documentary and fictional modes) with the social formation; but the problem with the new theories is that they lead, paradoxically, to a focus on the subject in their very attempt to counter notions of bourgeois individualism. As Christine Gledhill points out, the linking of Althusser's and Lacan's theories has explained both the way that individuals have become detached from their consciousness and the different positioning of the sexes within the symbolic order. But the theories do not accommodate the categories of either class or race: economic language as the primary shaping force replaces socioeconomic relations and institutions as the dominant influence. Sexual difference becomes the driving force of history in place of the Marxist one of class contradictions. Thus, we learn about the construction of the subject as individual, but learn nothing about individuals in social groups.[34]

The exposing of the decentered, problematic self through semiology and psychoanalysis (I am not now denying the validity of the analysis) has not been followed by sufficient study of its political and social implications. So much concern has been given to undermining bourgeois modes of thought and perception that we have failed to consider the problem of where this leaves us. Women critics and filmmakers have been positioned in negativity – in subverting rather than positing. The dangers of undermining the notion of the unified self and of a world of essences are relativism and despair.

At this point, then, we must use what we have learned in the past ten years to move theoretically beyond deconstruction to reconstruction. While it is essential for feminist film critics to examine signifying processes carefully in order to understand the way in which women have been constructed in language and in film, it is equally important not to lose sight of the material world in which we live, and in which our oppression takes concrete, often painful, forms. We need films that will show us, once we have mastered (i.e. understood fully) the existing discourses that oppress us, how we stand in a different position in relation to those discourses. Knowledge is, in that sense, power. We need to know how to manipulate the recognized, dominating discourses so as to begin to free ourselves *through* rather than beyond them (for what is there "beyond"?).

It should be clear that I am far from advocating a return to realism as the best or only viable cinematic strategy for bringing about change, and it should also be clear that I am excited by (and have in fact been one of the main promoters of) the new theory films. On the level of theory, I am arguing for a less dogmatic approach to cinematic practice, such that directors can see realism as a possible mode, given that we now know what it is, are aware of its limitations, and know its status as representation not "truth." Meanwhile theorists should continue to push the limits of cinematic practice, to see what different techniques can yield.

We will now turn, in chapters 11 and 12, to consider the results of precisely such "pushing of the limits of cinematic practice" that is an essential part of discovering what a feminist cinema might be outside of the realist mode.

| 11 | The avant-garde theory film: three case studies from Britain and the USA: *Sigmund Freud's Dora* (1979), *Thriller* (1979), Mulvey/Wollen's *Amy!* (1980) |

In chapter 10 I outlined the characteristics of the avant-garde theory film as it has evolved particularly in Britain. Here I want to explore three representative examples of such films so as to demonstrate the differing strategies that are employed to similar ends, and the way that theory is worked into the text as an integral part of its form. Demanding, sometimes difficult films, they represent important advances in film practice. We will look first at Tyndall, McCall, Pajaczkowska, and Weinstock's *Sigmund Freud's Dora*; second at Sally Potter's *Thriller*; and finally at Mulvey and Wollen's *Amy!* In chapter 12, I will discuss an earlier Mulvey/Wollen film, *Riddles of the Sphinx*, and Michelle Citron's *Daughter-Rite*, both of which deal with theoretical and formal issues but which I have grouped together separately so as to focus on feminist responses to the conventional representations of the mother and of mother–daughter relationships.

The three films to be considered in this chapter all address and develop issues raised in the analysis of the Hollywood films. (This is not surprising since that analysis was itself shaped by the theoretical issues foregrounded in the avant-garde theory films.) In fact two of the films (*Dora* and *Thriller*) present ways of reading classic texts (in the first a famous Freudian case history, in the second a famous opera) which, in being "melodramas," have direct bearing on the Hollywood form that we have been exploring. The new films, that is, "deconstruct" the classic melodrama to reveal, first, how it is that the heroine is "spoken" rather than having the voice and controlling her destiny, and second (in *Thriller* successfully, in *Dora* less so), how patriarchy attempts to sacrifice the heroine for patriarchal ends. In highlighting the absence/repression of the mother in patriarchy, *Dora* looks back to the analysis of *Blonde Venus* (as does also Mulvey/Wollen's *Riddles of the Sphinx*, discussed in the next chapter); while *Thriller*, in foregrounding the necessity for the heroine to die in order for the hero to fulfil narrative and patriarchal requirements, looks back, as we'll see, to the discussion of *Camille*. Mulvey/Wollen's *Amy!*, meanwhile, shows the ways in which a historical heroine (the pilot Amy Johnson) is appropriated by patriarchy and structured so as to lessen the threat that her real deeds occasion. She also must be "sacrificed" to patriarchal ends, made into a narrative figure paralleling those in melodrama. Patriarchy, in other words, cannot tolerate violations of its representations, its constructs.

Further, all three films raise issues about the links between psychoanalysis and history. Besides offering a placing of the Freud–Dora dialogue in the context of bourgeois capitalism, *Dora* also questions the very concept of traditional history as it relates to women, who have been placed outside of culture. *Thriller* and *Amy!* show the necessity of looking at women in both a psychoanalytic and an economic/social/political dimension, if we are to understand their positionings.

Finally, all three films mark their status as avant-garde theory films by drawing attention to their own cinematic processes, making us aware of their construction and of the fact that we are watching a film. They are thus able to illustrate the role that cinema itself (in its dominant, commercial forms, which were analyzed in the opening chapters) has played in perpetuating women's oppression.

"Sigmund Freud's Dora": feminist approaches to history, psychoanalysis, and cinema

Sigmund Freud's Dora is an important film in several ways: first, as an intervention in the ongoing theoretical debate about redefining psychoanalysis and history which we have been tracing in feminist film theory; second, as foregrounding issues about the place of women in narrative and in representation that emerged from the analyses of the Hollywood films in part I of this book; and finally, as an example of the type of avant-garde film discussed in chapter 10 which builds on the work of feminist and independent filmmakers in France and Britain, particularly Godard, Mulvey and Wollen, and women in the London Women Filmmakers' Collective.

Let me add briefly to what I said in chapter 10 about the context out of which these avant-garde theory films emerged. All the above-mentioned filmmakers, who were to influence the shape of films building theory into their forms, are unusual in having also been film critics and/or theorists – a combination which results in a type of film very different from that made by other independent directors. Defining themselves as leftists and (except Godard) as feminists, all were involved with a theoretical critique of bourgeois cinematic strategies, particularly realism, and with the debate about the relation between the cinematic apparatus and ideological content. When they turned to filmmaking, all attempted to put their theories into practice, experimenting with forms of cinema that would avoid the mystifications and manipulations of commercial conventions and that would foreground their theoretical concerns. The films explore and expose the codes through which meaning is signified and represented within culture, especially as these affect images of women.[1]

Sigmund Freud's Dora was made in a context similar to that of these films. All the filmmakers had been involved in theory – two in a Freud-reading group, two in relation to the avant-garde film; the work arose out of theoretical issues emerging from an earlier project, the film *Argument*, made by Tyndall and McCall,[2] and out of interest generated particularly by the work of Mulvey and Wollen. Mulvey's "Visual pleasure and narrative cinema" (see especially her contention that "Unchallenged, mainstream film coded the erotic into the language of the dominant patriarchal order"[3]) and Mulvey/Wollen's *Riddles of the Sphinx* (embodying the notions that "Women within patriarchy are faced with a never ending series of threats and riddles – dilemmas which are hard for women to solve because the culture within which they must think is not theirs" and "We live in a society ruled by the father, in which the place of the mother is suppressed") provide the context for many of the questions raised in *Sigmund Freud's Dora* about discourse, phallocentric culture, and voyeurism. I will deal first with these aspects of the film and then talk about the important, but provocative, notions about history and narrative that underpin the entire film.

The opening section of the film immediately foregrounds the problem of discourse. While a list of historical "facts" appears on the left of the screen (of which more later), the image of a woman on the right (whose lips only we see, in extreme close-up) recounts a debate she had with her sophisticated boyfriend about the kind of discourse psychoanalysis is. The Talking Lips argue against their lover's belief that psychoanalysis is a discourse that offers reality; for the woman, it is rather a discourse shot through with bourgeois, capitalist ideology that looks at the individual outside of real history and of real struggle, and is ultimately more like a sophisticated language game which was never innocent. While the man significantly thinks that it is at the level of *desire* that women will find *answers* to the questions about discourse (a belief that comes out of the psychoanalytic way of seeing), the woman argues that it is rather at the level of the *history* they make that women will find the right *questions*.

These two views of discourse reflect the sex of each speaker and prepare for the interchange between Freud and Dora. The man is confident in having access to a discourse that "explains" reality and his relations with others, while the woman feels alienated from that discourse, finding that it is unable to approach/illuminate *her* reality as a woman. She realizes that women have been closed from history so far because the discourse was not theirs; and that women can only begin to forge their own history, and thus own discourse, as they start to ask *questions*.

After this preface, the filmmakers proceed, in the second section of the film,

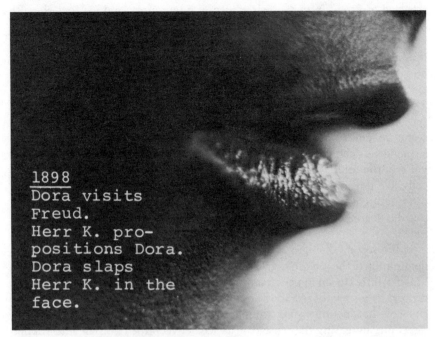

1898
Dora visits
Freud.
Herr K. pro-
positions Dora.
Dora slaps
Herr K. in the
face.

Plate 16   The image of Talking Lips in huge blow-up at the start of *Sigmund Freud's Dora*. The speaker reconstructs a debate about the kind of discourse psychoanalysis is, while at the left of the frame, titles show relevant historical events and people.

to give us an example of psychoanalytic discourse through the partial dramatization of Freud's interchange with his patient Dora as recounted in his case history. On one level, the interchange supports the view that psychoanalysis is a sophisticated language game which excludes the subjectivity of women. While Freud speaks out of himself, in the first person, Dora is for the most part "spoken;" her apparently first-person responses are undercut by her adding "she replied" or "she confirmed" to show the controlling hand of Freud over the retelling of her discourse. She has no easy access to her own voice in a discourse that is clearly phallocentric; but within the terms of this discourse we nevertheless see Dora's struggle for control of signification, meaning, and ultimately her own sexuality.

Viewing reality through psychoanalysis, Freud's aim in the series of dialogues (there are four altogether) is to place Dora's sexuality in phallocentric culture; he wants Dora to admit (1) her attraction to her father, which, repressed, emerged as attraction to Herr K.; (2) that this second attraction had to be repressed because of its origins in forbidden sexual interest in her father; (3) that her sexual wishes, frustrated, are displaced by somatic symptoms – the cough, lack of interest in food, suicidal impulses; (4) that her masturbating reflected a retreat from the feared idea of intercourse; and (5) that she also harbored sexual desires in relation to Freud himself.

Freud wins Dora's assent to the first three of these propositions in the opening dialogue between them, when Dora appears at her most submissive and vulnerable. She is here dressed in a dull gray dress and filmed in close-up, staring directly into the camera and placed against a plain, white background. The lighting is harsh and cold, complementing the anonymous, monotonous speech of the actors. Freud is shot in a manner similar to Dora, although he seems in control, not vulnerable because directing the interchange. The sequence is deliberately cut so that we often see one speaker listening to the voice of the other, and, to highlight the distance between them psychologically, we never see a shot of them together. Freud is aggressive with Dora, interpreting what she says for her, telling her what she felt and why, ferreting out the degree of Dora's sexual knowledge, and suggesting that she tried to hide it.

In the second dialogue, however, Dora begins to struggle against Freud's domination of the interchange, and it is as a result of this that a flaw emerges in Freud's hitherto compact, seamless discourse. Dora is now, significantly, dressed in a striking red shirt and is shot facing center frame. Breaking the rules of shot, counter-shot, the filmmakers have Freud facing in the same direction, increasing the sense of distance between the two. The interruption in the smooth flow of the analysis occurs when Dora asserts her resentment for being handed over to Herr K. by her father as the price of Herr K.'s toleration of relations between his wife, Frau K., and Dora's father. This insight momentarily stuns Freud – he admits that he "does not know what to say;" then, recovering, decides that such a brilliant perception must cloak something significant that Dora is hiding; he proceeds to question her about her closeness with Frau K. and the sexual knowledge she gained through reading books with her friend. He concludes triumphantly that Dora is hiding a deep-rooted homosexual love for Frau K.

But the triumph is only superficial, for in fact this suggestion inserts a difficulty in the analysis that Freud was unable to deal with; namely, that if Dora loved Frau K., she could not also have wanted Herr K. Freud's carefully laid-out hypotheses collapse into the possibility that Dora's aversion to Herr K. was motivated by distaste for heterosexual relating and by awkwardness resulting from his being Frau K.'s husband.[4]

All the intriguing questions about this homosexual love (e.g. that it possibly provides a way out of phallocentric discourse, unless of course the love arrives by way of masculine identification) are left until the final section of the film, since Freud was himself unable to deal adequately with homosexuality at the time he was treating Dora. Thus, the next dialogue continues as if the momentous discovery had not taken place; or perhaps what we see is a supreme effort by Freud, in the light of the "discovery," to incorporate Dora in the heterosexual mode of relating by effectively seducing her himself. The form of the dialogue and the cinematic strategies suggest the symbolic sexual union of Freud and Dora: we now see both Freud and Dora only from chest to thighs; Dora's hands hover around her pelvis and she is holding a maroon bag (her vagina?), while Freud is holding out into the frame a phallic cigar. The dialogue diverges from the previous pattern, by which each spoke in turn, and now the two finish each other's sentences in a kind of merging. Freud's triumphant conclusion is that Dora had masturbated in childhood and wanted a kiss from him.

At this point, Freud appears to have dominated Dora completely; his psychoanalytic discourse seems to have accounted for everything. But the final dialogue shows that this is not so. Although unable to intervene in the discourse verbally (she does not have a language in which to speak), Dora takes the only action available to her – she removes herself from the context of the discourse by walking out of the therapy. Dora's new independence is signified iconographically by her placement in front of a shelf of books on Marxism, psychoanalysis, and film theory. Her black dress signifies a kind of strength, and the books suggest that she has won entry into the symbolic through theory. Freud, meanwhile, is shot in an outside location (this, of course, violating cinematic conventions and highlighting the distance be-tween the two even more), with the Statue of Liberty (representing capitalism, the status quo, the discourse signified by psychoanalysis) in the background. Freud of course can only interpret Dora's departure as her taking revenge on him for failing to love her enough, analogous to her revengeful behavior to Herr K. for seeming only to play with her as he had played with her governess. Freud concludes that the therapy failed because Dora was unable to deal with her erotic feelings for him.[5]

The fact that the case history is incomplete, the analysis not concluded, makes it particularly interesting for discussion from a feminist point of view. The gaps in Freud's theory (i.e. he had not developed a coherent position on homosexuality, particularly in relation to women, and had not yet fully understood transference) leave "spaces" in the discourse that permit the raising of questions crucial for women. The third and final section of the film allows for a revisit to the text of the film so far, for a going over to foreground all the issues it leaves unsolved and which point the way forward for women.

But before going into the final section, it is important to discuss the second theme of the film, i.e. the comment on media representations of women and on the place of woman in narrative. Woman as site of multiple and often contradictory representations is emphasized throughout the second section of *Dora*, in the television advertisements and porn clips that preface each dialogue and that are linked thematically to it. On the surface, these present polarized images – the television advertisements representing the "normal," healthy American woman in her roles as housewife, glamour girl, and business executive; the porn clips showing the secret, "unhealthy," sexual woman at the other extreme. But the thematic link with the Dora–Freud dialogue, in addition to the similarity in the cinematic apparatus that produces all the images, highlights the commonalities in the images, i.e. first, that woman is object of the gaze of the spectator, the camera directing the view, in each case; and second, that her role is defined by phallocentric discourse. Thus, in the first sequence, the TV advertisement showing a rather giddy woman, in awe of her male interviewer and delighted with how easy liquid Tylenol is to swallow, and the porn clip presenting a woman in ecstasy over a blow job, are linked to each other and then to the Freud–Dora dialogue, in which Freud insists that Dora's cough reflects her repressed wish for oral intercourse with her father – a mode of intercourse she suspects Frau K. is enjoying with him. In each case, the woman is represented as anxious to please the man, to serve the phallus, as it were, and, from a male point of view, as correct in so doing.

Although these linkings are theoretically serious, there is a comic, playful aspect to them. The advertisements showing deodorants become hilariously phallic in the context of the film, as do the porn clips (at least on repeated viewings); the bondage clip that precedes the final Freud–Dora dialogue seems to me a comic reflection of the way that Dora is finally tying Freud up in knots by introducing the lesbian interest and leaving therapy.

The contradictory notions of woman as she is constituted in representation are further stressed in what the film shows about the place of woman in narrative. As Tyndall recently noted,[6] three parts of the film could be viewed as illustrating the three aspects basic to any narrative. The introduction foregrounds the way every story is a series of events and a particular kind of discourse. The second Freud–Dora, section represents the inevitable "romance" which begins with the reluctant woman, hiding her sexuality and afraid of, or unwilling to succumb to, the man; continues with the man's pursuit of the woman and his determination to win her sexually; and ends with the successful submission of the woman to the man which re-establishes the patriarchal dominance momentarily threatened by the woman's resistance. The third instance of the narrative is the text as "read," the use that is made of it once it has been written.

The fact that in this particular case the "romance" is not completed, i.e. the analysis not finished, makes the Dora text particularly interesting as a topic for discussion. Dora does not "succumb" to Freud's "seduction" but rather takes the only course of resistance available and suddenly leaves him. The narrative is truncated, unresolved, because the woman refuses the place that would enable the narrative to end. What the filmmakers here pinpoint is the necessary connection between traditional narrative and patriarchy: our concept of "resolution" is premised on the basic structure of narrative as a quest, with woman as the object to be sought and finally possessed. If she refuses, the narrative is left hanging.

The third part of the film thus becomes a reflection upon all the issues of representation, narrative history, psychoanalysis, and feminism raised in the first two instances of the narrative. In an article on Freud's "Dora," Jaqueline Rose raises the question which becomes a main focus in the final part of the film: namely, "What does the little girl want of her mother?"[7] This question is foregrounded in *Dora* by the device of a series of letters, some written by Dora, to a mother (who is sometimes Dora's mother, sometimes any mother). The letters are read from postcards that depict, first, various scenes from the film itself (cards showing the porn clips or Dora in the dialogues with Freud); second, various portions of Leonardo da Vinci's painting of the Virgin and St Anne; or finally, a series of male heroes.

One of the main objectives here is to show that in traditional narrative, as in Freud's model, the mother has been omitted – repressed, forgotten – a fact that Mulvey/Wollen first drew attention to in *Riddles of the Sphinx* and that Rose emphasizes. In the Freudian model, the girl is only connected to the mother pre-Oedipally; after that, she has to renounce her mother and focus on her relationship to her father. The mother has importance only as an element – and a negative one at that – in the father–daughter relationship. The daughter competes with her mother for the father – and sees herself as her mother's rival. The Lacanian revision of Freud does not deal much better with the mother: now the pre-Oedipal period is defined as the imaginary, and for the girl to enter into the symbolic she must recognize castration, renounce her mother as object of desire and then find her place in the order of language and culture as subordinate to the Law of the Father.

By centering this section on a mother, the filmmakers foreground her omission in the earlier sections of the film which followed the pattern of the traditional narrative. This matter of the mother's place is gradually built up in the series of letters. In her first letter, Dora speaks to her mother about her therapy with Freud, referring to Freud's analysis of a dream in which Dora looked at Raphael's *Sistine Madonna*. The *Madonna*, Freud says, is a counter-idea used by Dora to avoid her repressed sexual fantasies. Women, that is, turn to the Mother image as a relief from sexuality, not for what it is in itself. The cards the mother reads from fittingly reproduce sections from each of the porn clips, showing women in all varieties of sexuality – from masturbation to bondage. But Dora proceeds to question Freud's interpretation by asking a series of important questions – questions that feminist theory has been raising and to which as yet we have no answers. In relation to Freud's analysis of her interest in the *Madonna*, i.e. that Dora is engaged in a masculine process in the act of looking, Dora asks in a letter read from a card of the Leonardo painting: "If this active looking is a masculine drive . . . is this position of being a spectator any more masculine when the picture is of a woman?" A second question, read from a card with a porn image of a woman masturbating, asks: "Is this voyeuristic drive, which Freud insists is sexual, any more sexual when the image is of a sexual act?" In a final question about pornography, Dora asks how images of sexual relations between women constructed for a masculine viewer inform her actual physical relations with other women.

The second letter consists of a series of theoretical questions for which the mother is simply the vehicle. The questions have to do with Charcot's scientific discourse on hysteria in relation to his scientific photography – both reveal woman as object. The postcard significantly shows a picture of Dora in the dialogue with Freud in which he symbolically seduced her.

The third letter, written by any daughter to her mother, is the clearest example of what happens to a text once read. The daughter talks of a debate over Freud's "Dora" that took place in her women's group: some women saw the text as offering two equally repressive alternatives – i.e. Dora could be exchanged as female *object* of desire or become a masculine *subject* of desire; others viewed Dora's departure from therapy as heroic, a refusal to submit to the place Freud designed for her in phallocentric culture. The daughter rejects both readings, saying that she doesn't want a heroine and that "Dora" is interesting because of the questions it raises rather than because of the *answers* it offers. Fittingly, the series of cards for this letter show various images of male heroes – Che Guevara, Christ, Elvis Presley, Mohammed Ali, and Freud, underscoring the fact that there are no female heroes and revealing how male heroes are constructed. The image for the daughter's last statement is the bookshelf of theoretical texts, suggesting that through theory she will find the questions that need asking.

A fourth letter (analogous to the second letter in being a series of theoretical questions for which the mother is merely the mouthpiece) raises the crucial issue of how, given a phallocentric language, women can articulate resistance to their representation.

The final letter looks back to the first one: it is again by Dora, and deals with Freud's analysis of her, only now the focus is on the place of the mother in psychoanalysis. Dora complains about Freud's easy dismissal of her mother as merely "a foolish woman, suffering from 'housewife's psychosis.'" She argues that Freud ought to have talked about the mother as the site of many representations, of which the real person is only one. After listing the various roles her mother fills, Dora notes how she is left with the tension between her symbolic mother, who is always absent and toward whom Dora thus has hostility, and the real person, with whom Dora longs to share things, particularly their lives as women.

This last letter is important in foregrounding the way both Freudian and Lacanian theory omit the place of the mother. This is one of the gaps that the filmmakers see feminists as being able to remedy, despite the dominance of phallocentric language. The tension between symbolic and real mothers that *Dora* ends with is played out in people's reactions to the final part of the film. For some people, the figure of the mother evokes feelings about their actual mothers in the form of longings for nurturance; for these, the mother is a tragic figure because, although crucial to the family as we know it, she goes unrecognized, unclaimed, and has the task of holding the family together in spite of the tensions that exist. For others, she is important theoretically in the light of the "Dora" texts which omitted her: she is inserted forcefully into the film, asserting a symbolic significance as crucial as that of the father – Freud whom we have just seen attempting to dominate Dora.[8]

The filmmakers, however, still deny the mother her own voice, as Dora has been denied direct speech throughout the film. The mother only reads Dora's thoughts, or those of another daughter, or impersonal questions on the level of theory. Although the film as a whole seems to offer the possibility of finding gaps in phallocentric language and structures through which women can begin to find their own voices and realities, the film itself does not show women theoretically other than as defined by patriarchal language. Dora does struggle against Freud's definition of her sexuality; we see her exercise her right to leave him and his analysis, and we assume that her "retreat into theory" really is more than a result of her need "to maintain [her mother] as blameless,"[9] i.e. that she will discover the questions that will lead to the answers women have to find. The mother's effect, regardless of the lack of her own discourse, is strikingly powerful and suggests precisely a level of communication and influence that is lacking in the abstract, theoretical formulations that the film depends on.

The problem with the film is that while it opens up hitherto closed areas in the Lacanian framework, thus avoiding much of the fatalism of that framework, it is still limited by its own system. It would be interesting, for instance, to engage in a debate *between* systems, e.g. between the Lacanian one and those like Dinnerstein's and Chodorow's which also rely heavily on Freudian psychoanalysis. The virtue of these latter systems is their closeness to problems as they emerge in the clinical context. One of the things that has always been problematic for me in Lacanian systems as used by feminist filmmakers and critics is the omission of the perspective that comes from the experience of therapy, i.e. a closeness to the daily problems of anxiety, separation, and projection of early childhood experiences onto adult situations.

Perhaps, as Jane Weinstock noted,[10] the theoretical universes of Lacan, say, and Chodorow are too far apart to be entertained at the same time: for me, reconciliation is less important than seeing the usefulness of each theory in particular contexts. While Chodorow may illuminate relations in our daily, interpersonal lives, including the links between our individual psychology and the institutions we were raised in, the Lacanian system, as adapted by feminist film critics, is valuable in illuminating how women have been, and continue to be, constructed in all kinds of media representations. *Dora* is important in summarizing a debate about psychoanalysis and feminism that has enriched and deepened our understanding of female images and of woman's place in phallocentric culture, on the abstract, theoretical level.

But *Dora* interests me because it does more than simply describe how women came to be in the place we find ourselves; Lacanian systems have hitherto disturbed me because of their determinism, ahistoricity, and anti-humanism, and because they seemed to lock us inevitably into a framework that degraded women. I have already noted some of the ways in which the filmmakers suggest working with the gaps in the Lacanian system; but even more important is their attempt to explore a new concept of history that would allow for change in a mode other than that traditionally allowed for by male historians.

The opening section of the film is perhaps intended to show the absurdity of the materialist notion of history – a history instituted by men and that involves looking at male heroes and at the evolution of our present, male-dominated institutions. This kind of history omits women, who, as housewives, i.e. invisible laborers, lie beyond its parameters. For Pajaczkowska, it is wrong to mythologize the few female heroes we have (and who are mentioned along with the men in the opening list of names and dates that accompany the Talking Lips' words), since this involves denying the contradictions of our daily lives. We must rather fuse a "subjective" history – history as personal memory – with the history of the larger society.

This new conception of history is suggested in the words the Talking Lips speak in the introductory section of the film, when she notes that women are not yet ready for *answers*, that we have first to discover the appropriate *questions*. The film as a whole refuses to offer solutions, since obsession with closure and answers is defined as a male obsession. *Dora* only presents questions, but they are obviously ones the filmmakers see as essential and as providing the means to move forward. For questions give rise to further questions, and although this kind of movement is very different from that assumed by male history, it is seen as the only one possible for women.

I have many problems with this idea of history and am left rather unclear as to how it permits broad political and social change; the category of social class seems entirely missing as does the concept of historical chronology. It's almost as if the filmmakers are involved with some new conception of time as well as of social "reality." It is clear from *Dora* at least that the filmmakers are developing close links between history and fictional narrative – that they do not differentiate the two. Thus, the traditional (male) idea of history as a search for the past, for what is missing, is connected to the traditional notion of narrative (demonstrated in the Freud–Dora section of the film) as starting with a lack and involving the search for the hidden secret, usually linked to women's sexuality. A new kind of story-telling will therefore lead to a new kind of feminist history. It is this new fiction-making, one involving a multiplicity of subjectivities, that the filmmakers try to present in the final section of the film where the mother is the site of many representations and where Freud's Dora speaks in the same time frame as a contemporary "daughter" reading about Dora. Structurally, the section abandons linear development for a series of overlapping shots: we have layers of discourse rather than a single one that progresses logically; the principle for the organization of the content is memory rather than "facts."

Taken as a whole, the entire structure of Dora abandons the linear/logical mode and reflects the new kind of fiction and history the filmmakers consider necessary. Like *Argument*, *Dora* is constructed in a manner closer to music or poetry than to prose narrative. Rhythm is an essential component in both films, and works as a haunting substructure to the words, which are themselves rhythmical and more important than the images *per se*. Tyndall and McCall believe that recent film critics have overvalued image at the expense of sound, and here, as in their attention to rhythmical editing, they look back to Eisenstein. The way the actors speak their words in *Dora* is deliberately unrealistic, since they use a kind of rhythmical blank verse with carefully spaced pauses. The words that appear on the screen are also spaced rhythmically.

The symmetrical organization of the film recalls that of music or poetry: thus the three main parts of the film function like those of a symphony, with themes introduced, left, picked up again, and later developed. Each of the parts within the Freud–Dora section consists of fourteen shots, prefaced by a television and a porn clip linked thematically to the content of the dialogue. Within any section, the editing is made rhythmically expressive of the emotions involved.

The use of color also reflects a deliberate pattern: the main colors are gray, white, red, and black – the last three stark, primary colors. The red of Talking Lips is repeated in Dora's red lips, in the striking red of her blouse, and in the mother's red dress at the end; Dora and Freud are both in gray at first, but as Dora moves away from Freud, so her colors become stronger and bolder, ending in the forceful black of her final scene with Freud, who is now in a pale raincoat.

The film is thus structured so as to reflect the filmmakers' new notions of history and narrative as nonlinear, open-ended, a search for questions not solutions. We are encouraged to *see* in new ways. While the film suffers from some of the same problems of accessibility as other avant-garde films that break new ground, *Dora* is comparatively easy to watch. To be fully appreciated, the film requires some background knowledge, cinematic sophis-tication, and several viewings, but the directors permit a certain amount of pleasure – e.g. in voyeurism, color – while at the same time building in a critique of it. The playful comic tone along with the musical/poetic structure result in a pleasant experience no matter how much is missed on the theoretical level.

The filmmakers are in any case not concerned about general accessibility since they believe that the most useful kind of avant-garde film at this particular historical moment is that geared to a specific situation and group of people. Although *Dora* may appeal to psychotherapists and people interested in film theory, it was intended for a particular kind of feminist audience. Obviously, as the issues the film deals with become more generally known, so the audience for the film will broaden. Despite its theoretical limitations, *Dora* is an intriguing experiment which raises crucial issues and marks a particular moment in feminist film criticism.

Investigating the heroine: Sally Potter's "Thriller"

As I've already noted, Sally Potter's *Thriller* emerges from a theoretical context very similar to that of *Sigmund Freud's Dora*. Once again, we have the feminist deconstruction of a classic melodrama, Puccini's *La Bohème* (1895), only now Potter has gone further back, into the late nineteenth century, for her exemplary text. Like the directors of *Dora*, Potter is interested in how classical narratives position and represent women, but she is also interested in a male conception of creativity as it emerged during the Romantic movement and as it worked specifically to exclude women.

Like *Camille* (when "read against the grain"), *Thriller* exposes the particular hardships that faced women at the turn of the century as the industrial revolution was established and the materialistic, bourgeois class developed. While many "sons" of this bourgeois industrialist class expressed their revolt by becoming Bohemian artists (the type was immortalized, as I noted in chapter 2, in Henri Murger's *La Vie de Bohème*), this was an avenue denied woman because of the rigid sexual and moral codes that hemmed her in. While the wealthy sons could "play" at being poor artists (and the really poor man could at least compete for work as an apprentice or in a factory), the only options available to poor women (outside of marriage) were taking in work (usually sewing) for miserable pay, or becoming a prostitute. Potter explores this contrast between different kinds of "making" as it relates to gender in her feminist deconstruction of Puccini's opera, *La Bohème*, a rewriting of Murger's *La Vie de Bohème*. Puccini, himself an Italian version of the Bohemian artist, drew on his own life in his opera, and his heroine Mimi uncannily foreshadows Puccini's maid, Doria, who committed suicide after Puccini had seduced her and his wife had denounced her publicly.[11]

Since the death of Mimi plays such a large part in Potter's analysis of how classic patriarchal texts exploit the heroine, it is interesting to find Puccini expressing (in letters to his script writer) conflict about how Mimi should die. He demonstrates his concern with creating the effect of sentimental pathos which would add to his hero's stature. That is, he thought of the death solely in terms of the hero, not in terms of the heroine as herself. It is as if she did not exist for him as anything more than a function of his hero's emotions, a catalyst. He writes that he wants her death at once to invoke "proud and gentle emotions" and "to pierce the heart like a knife:" "When this girl, for whom I have worked so hard, dies, I should like her to leave the world less for herself and a little more for him who loved her".[12] Potter uses this blindness to the heroine's existence for herself to expose the repression of female subjectivity in narrative discourse. Her film, thus, looks directly back to the analyses of the Hollywood films in part I, exemplifying the kind of deconstruction of classical texts that is necessary if women are to understand their positioning in culture. Cukor's *Camille* is particularly relevant since the story line is quite similar to that in *La Bohème*, where the heroine again sacrifices herself so that her lover can be free to live his life as he wants.[13]

What makes Potter's film complex is her attempt to link psychoanalytic, feminist, and Marxist discourses with those of narrative. She does this by constructing her speaking subject (Mimi I) outside of the narrative in which she is heroine (Mimi II). She reflects on her place in that classical story, and on the reasons *why* she was so positioned. Mimi I finds that this entails several levels of investigation, and we see her move through a carefully arranged series of stages, from the level of the unconscious to the materialist, historical level, via the level of her place in the narrative. *Thriller* is important in implying a progression from looking at structures as they affect the individual internally (i.e. psychoanalytically) to looking at them as they affect the individual in society. Narrative is seen to occupy a middle ground between the two, exposing the mythic level which drains the sign of its denotative level and fills it with connotative, ideological meanings.

The first investigation takes place on the psychoanalytic level, for, as Mimi I begins to investigate the cause of her death in the opera, recounting the plot for the first time, she encounters a psychoanalytic problem, namely, the status of herself as investigating subject. The male voice, in the conventional thriller has no such problem since, centrally positioned as he is in patriarchy, he owns the gaze and activates desire. Mimi I, as female subject investigating herself as object, understands that before she can begin her task, she has to return to the mirror phase; she needs to understand how her subjectivity was constituted and deal with herself as split subject in a symbolic order dominated by the Father. She learns that the only position she can occupy within male language is that of asking questions. So, she sets up the enigma about her death that is the overall project of the film: "Did I die? Was I murdered? What does it mean?"

The second level of investigation has to do with Mimi II's subordinate place as woman in a classical narrative, while the third takes place on the materialist, didactic level. This last is concerned, first, with Mimi's role as seamstress in a chain of production that is excluded from classical narrative, and second, with her role as mother, also excluded from the classical narrative. The series of investigations enable Potter to open up questions about the links, first, between narrative discourse and psychoanalytic discourse; and second, between narrative discourse and historical discourse.

Before showing how Potter structures these investigations on the verbal, theoretical level, it is important to note how much is communicated visually in the film. The visuals function in a very specific and varying relationship to the sound, which includes, besides the dominant female voice, the repeated laugh (shattering the relationship between conscious and unconscious), the repeated shriek (which evokes the terror of this thriller about subjectivity and objectivity), and the sound of a heartbeat. The very fact that Mimi I is speaking already signals that she has taken a first, necessary step toward making herself subject; and although within the film Mimi I finds herself positioned inside structures that limit and inhibit her investigation, the cinematic devices Potter uses offer us, the spectators, the promise of moving beyond the repressive boundaries. Potter's text, that is, is in itself an intervention in the dominance of classical narrative. As spectators, we have access to a view of Mimi I that she, of course, does not have.

To begin with, Colette Laffont as Mimi I offers an image of a heroine diametrically opposed to the conventional one represented by Mimi II within the opera text. Mimi I's gestures, facial expression, body language, voice quality, dress, hair, body type, all deliberately violate traditional significations. She is dressed plainly, wears no shoes, has short hair, no make-up, does not parade her sexuality, and is for the most part in an uncharacteristic "feminine" mode of meditation (uncharacteristic, of course, in terms of representations); her blackness further sets her in the unspeakable position outside of white culture. Her deep, throaty, accented voice is juxtaposed to the lyrical, smooth, high-voiced singing of Mimi II, and her *questioning* discourse contrasts with Mimi II's *suffering* discourse. The contrast emphasizes the degree to which, in adopting the traditional modes of female discourse and in accepting her prescribed place in patriarchy, Mimi II has indeed cooperated in her oppression.

Underscoring the contrast in heroines (Puccini's and Potter's) is an equally effective contrast in the cinematic spaces each heroine occupies. Mimi II occupies the "frozen" space of the theatrical setting of the opera. This space reflects traditional realist conventions which place figures in the proscenium arch at eye level, in medium-long shot, and create an illusionist/representational mise-en-scène within which actors and objects are harmoniously arranged.

This space is deliberately "frozen" in two senses: first, in that the shots are photographs of photographs of a stage performance ("signifiers of signifiers," as Jane Weinstock puts it[14]), which sets them one stage further from the signified than a cinematic shot would normally be; second, in the literal sense that the figures do not move. Occasionally the camera moves in for a close-up of some detail, e.g. Mimi II's face, or a seamstress's hand, but this only accentuates the silent, passive aspect of the figures. The "frozen" aspect of the stills, echoing Rodolfo's interest in Mimi in the opera *because* her hand is frozen (i.e. because she is poor, weak, and vulnerable), underscores the impossibility of change for women within bourgeois narrative structures.

The space that Mimi I occupies is an attic characterized by its nakedness and unharmonious lines. There is no wallpaper – just bare boards – and no carpets on the floor – that is, again, bare boards; a door to the left is connected to a wall jutting into the space; in the rear are curtainless windows, through which nothing can be seen. The only furniture is a single wooden chair and a mirror with a floral pattern along its frame. This one small sign of decoration emphasizes the mirror's significance in a space that ultimately represents consciousness. The attic is lit so as to be full of shadows – giving it a sinister air befitting the thriller genre and also the heavy implications of the two investigations that are under way. The slightly open door at the left evokes an ominous feeling that someone may enter at any moment, while the blackness beyond both door and windows confirms that the attic is an isolated, inner space.

If this space is the antithesis of the stage space of the opera, which followed bourgeois conventions, then so also are the movements of the figures within the space. Potter virtually choreographs the movements of her actors as they are brought in by Mimi I for the "reconstruction" of her death. Early on in the film, Mimi I, remembering, says: "O Mimi, you were carried from the room, lifted up and taken out of there. Carried away from the attic, yes – in arabesque. Yes, I was, that's important, I was in arabesque. Frozen in arabesque. Your tiny hand." This narration is accompanied by images of Mimi/Musetta (played by Rose English), being lifted up in arabesque by two male actors representing Rodolfo and Marcello. The significance of the arabesque is that it represents the most perfect line that the female form can take, and yet it works only as long as the woman is "frozen," unable to move; she can only come down on one foot and is usually held in the position by her male partner. The physical, bodily movements literalize the psychologically "frozen" position that Mimi II occupies in the opera; she is something beautiful which evokes, and is the object of, male desire, but her position is fixed, defined, permitting no movement of her own. Hers is a position contingent upon the men around her, and at any moment Mimi II can be lifted up and carried away – made silent, absent.

In all the reconstruction scenes, Potter has her actors move in highly stylized, dancelike movements. At one point, the two men pick up Mimi and hold her with her feet in the palms of their hands; at another, they hold Mimi upside down. When Mimi I later on raises the question of being the hero of the narrative, we cut to an image of the male actor in a tutu, held in arabesque. The physical literalization of the psychological placing acts as an ironic underpinning of the issues Mimi I is raising in her narration.

These cinematic devices stress the implications of the investigation; that is, the devices used in the original opera, those of bourgeois realism, assume the dominance of patriarchal discourse and place Mimi II as Other (enigma, mystery). Rodolfo's desire, jealousy, and possessiveness make an object of her and result in her death. The cinematic devices used in Mimi I's attic result from her refusal to accept, passively, the place assigned for her in the original narrative discourse. She turns the original upside down, in her questioning, and thus literally positions herself in totally unconventional ways.

On the materialist level, then, the attic space reflects a deliberate violation of conventional realist codes, but, in terms of the psychoanalytic subtext, the space is a mental rather than a physical one. The repeated mirror shots, while compositionally unconventional, also make literal the mental processes that the mirror phase involves psychoanalytically. As Mimi I searches for a clue to her subjectivity – a necessary first step in her investigation into the meaning of her life and her death – we see her sitting in front of the mirror, her back to the spectator; another disorienting shot shows her head in oblique angle close-up at the far left of the frame, pressed against the mirror that reflects her image in its disquieting angle. These repeated shots symbolize Mimi I's struggle to work her way through the mirror phase. The task here is to move from the level of the imaginary (in which she is fused with the mother) to that of the symbolic, which entails recognizing herself as object, Other, in a discourse controlled by men. Cinematically, Potter represents this by having Mimi/Musetta from the opera move into the mirror space as the camera is positioned behind Mimi I's back. Mimi I, narrating now in the third person to signal her entry into a language structure that tries to deny her subjectivity, says: "When she first looked, she recognized herself as the Other. She saw Mimi there, cold, tired and ill. She saw timidity and vulnerability."

But this recognition of herself as object is followed by her realization that she is also (possibly) subject: she says, "And then, as my image turned away – I saw the other side. Was it me?"

Cinematically, what happens is that as Mimi/Musetta turns away in the mirror, Mimi I's shadow is thrown up on the screen. The shot shows Mimi I now with her back to the mirror, facing the camera, while the shadow is seen at the far left of the frame. The shot is particularly jarring in that instead of Mimi's back, reflected in the mirror, is a series of repetitions of her *face*, suggesting that she is now beyond the mirror phase. That she has in fact moved into recognizing the split subject is represented visually by having Rose English enter the open door at the left (herself a "split" subject symbolized by the light splitting her in two), while Mimi I's shadow is now thrown up against the wall (she is once again facing the mirror) to signal *her* split subjectivity.[15]

The shadow across the screen signals that Mimi I has asserted her own identity rather than letting herself be named, given a character/identity, like Mimi II in the opera. The sound of a heartbeat accompanying these shots signifies the rebirth that is taking place. Mimi I is now in a strong enough position to investigate her role as Mimi II in the (male) narrative and can return to the enigma posited at the start about the meaning of her death. She goes over the plot a second time, the investigation now moving to the feminist-didactic level; Mimi I wonders why Rodolfo found her pain so charming (" and

Plate 17 In this complex shot from *Thriller*, Potter deals visually with the difficult issues of the mirror phase and the split subject. Mimi I now has her back to the mirror, facing the camera, while the shadow seen at the far left of the frame is presumably that of Rose English (representing Mimi II and Musetta from the opera). The jarring effect of the mirror, reflecting not Mimi's back but a series of repetitions of her face and the mirror itself, perhaps signifies that she is moving through the mirror phase into recognition of split subjectivity.

later so alarming''), what the male artists were up to in the attic, how their cold and poverty differed from hers. She realizes that Rodolfo was the hero of the narrative and wonders if she would have preferred to be the hero, saying: "What if I had been the subject of this scenario instead of its object? I am trying to remember." Next she thinks that perhaps she could understand her death if she read *their* (i.e. men's) texts, and we have a shot of Mimi I sitting in her attic, reading a collection of *Tel Quel* articles in French, while in the background Mimi/Musetta watches, listens, and does arabesques against the wall. The narration now again assumes the third person: "She was searching for a theory that would explain her life – that would explain her death. They had written books – by reading she hoped to understand. Meanwhile, that other woman was watching, listening." This third-person narration precedes the next stage in Mimi I's psychological growth which is introduced by the shattering laugh. This laugh represents not so much laughing at male theory *per se* (Potter has her heroine on a trajectory that involves male theorists like Lacan and Marx[16]), but signals a realization that the answers cannot be found in *texts*; one has to discover the answers through one's own *questions*. And the question that now arises has to do with Mimi/Musetta watching and listening. Mimi I suddenly understands that in the opera women were divided into two – Mimi II, the good girl and Musetta, the bad girl, the one who didn't die but who was also not taken seriously by the men. Musetta may have more voice than Mimi II in the opera, but at the cost of being ultimately scorned.

The narration at this point seems to adopt two voices, those of Mimi I and of Mimi/Musetta (Mimi II and Musetta, in the original), and Mimi/Musetta asks Mimi I how she could have let herself be carried away, silent and frozen, from the attic.

Mimi I is now ready for the final look at the narrative of the opera, focusing this time on the roles of seamstress and mother that were excluded from the story. This narration is accompanied not by stills from the opera but by historical photographs of seamstresses, and significantly Mimi I is no longer asking questions but stating conclusions. She goes over the plot for the third time, now understanding that artists "produce stories to disguise how I must produce their goods." This statement is the culmination of earlier ones where Mimi I was interested in the fact that in the attic the artists were making something, but she was not sure that it was *work*. She knew that the hero, Rodolfo, was "searching for inspiration," which he found in singing a song to Mimi II about her frozen hand. She had also realized that while the men were poor and cold, their poverty was different from hers. She now sees that her labor had to be hidden in order for her to be the heroine; the space of her attic had to be excluded from the narrative of the opera because it would make her a subject and not simply the passive object of Rodolfo's desire. Her labor would also raise the question of the difference between her kind of work, inserted in the chain of production, and their work outside of it; it would expose that their work was "romantic," a fit subject for a story, while hers was not.

Furthermore, she finally understands why she had to die; had she lived, she and Rodolfo would have borne children and she would have had to work even harder to feed them. Seen in this light, motherhood is not romantic, and, again, it makes the woman subject; children activate *her* desire, and she is not able simply to be object of male passion. She had to die also because "an old seamstress would not be considered the proper subject of a love story." Old age is anathema to romance.

Mimi II's death enabled the artists to become "heroes in the display of their grief," and Mimi I concludes that it was indeed murder. Mimi I comes to the ultimate understanding that the narrative worked by separating Mimi and Musetta who might have loved each other, and who might have given each other something that they did not get from the men. This is the moment of breakthrough to an integrated subjectivity. Mimi I realizes that she and Musetta are the same; or, put another way, that each is a complete subject in her own right. Neither is split within herself, nor need they necessarily be split subjects narratively. The film ends with the breakthrough symbolized by Mimi I and Mimi/Musetta embracing in the attic, while the men slink silently out of the window.

Sally Potter's film is exciting in several ways. It is, first, an imaginative intervention in the dominance of a certain kind of classical narrative (the sentimental romance and the detective story) making a critique of such narratives into an alternative art form. Potter is in fact doing very much what Laura Mulvey and Claire Johnston have, as we saw in chapter 10, suggested for an alternative cinema, namely, "to challenge the depiction of reality" and interrogate the language of the cinema; and also, "to free the look of the camera into its materiality in time and space, and the look of the audience into dialectics, passionate detachment."[17]

Structured through montage, the film denies us conventional modes of identification, forcing us rather to return constantly to the enigmas about the meaning of Mimi's life and death. The movement of the film is circular rather than linear, repetition being the central mode. But at each return to the basic questions, Mimi I knows more, and can ask more questions, until, finally, she finds an answer.

Second, the film is important in using the new theories creatively. Potter attempts to link the discourses of psychoanalysis and Marxism which are normally considered antithetical or, at best, too theoretically problematic for connection. She shows, first, that the phallocentric language of narrative discourses (with its origins in the unconscious) denies women subjectivity, assigning them to the place of "lack;" but she then goes on to link this psychoanalytic placing to the social and political one that is governed by the same language. Narrative and history, that is, are parallel discourses, and ones that equally exclude women.

We could not expect a short film to work through all the theoretical implications of the connections Potter asserts; her film is art first and theory second. But it is important to see Lacan's theories taken beyond the determinism they apparently imply and to see change achieved at least on the *visual*, if not the theoretical, level (e.g. we *see* the women, formerly split both internally and externally, turn to each other and embrace, recognizing their oneness while the men slink away). In terms of the film's form, the two modes of address – the didactic overt text and psychoanalytic subtext – are cleverly fused, while the film's deliberate formalism guarantees our attention to cinematic practice as ideology.

Appropriating the heroine: an analysis of Mulvey and Wollen's 'Amy!'

Although I am dealing with *Amy!* last, and it is the most recent of the three films being analyzed here, it is important to note the influence of Mulvey and Wollen's theoretical and practical work on the development of the avant-garde theory film. In an unusual way, Mulvey and Wollen have attempted to make films that reflect at least some of their theoretical positions and have, partly because of this, produced works that are not easy cinematic experiences. The aim of their first two films (*Penthesilea* (1974) and *Riddles of the Sphinx* (1976)), to demonstrate certain ideas, may account for the fact that neither film works really well as cinema (although many people, like myself, who are familiar with the theories and with avant-garde strategies enjoy them). Mulvey and Wollen have done all that they could to provide information about their films that might make them more accessible (e.g. they have tried to be present at film viewings to answer questions, have published film scripts and interviews, and have written and lectured about their work).

Mulvey and Wollen's first two films may be seen as initiating a particular analysis of the politics of representation articulated by the French theorists discussed in chapter 1. Surely influenced by Godard's work, Mulvey and Wollen went beyond him in paying particular attention to the problems of female representation. Their work marks a struggle with the question that Christine Gledhill articulated when she asked if we could find a system of representation adequate for a Marxist-feminist analysis of the material, socially constructed world, and for our emerging conception of how that world must change.[18]

As Wollen noted in a lecture, all the stories that he and Mulvey have made involve reworkings of women in struggle. The "raw material," Wollen said, is transformed by placing it within the discourses of psychoanalysis and history.[19] One such discourse, used in all the films, is derived from Lacanian psychoanalysis and establishes women's exclusion from male culture as a result of their positioning in Oedipal processes; but in each of the films the problem is explored from a different perspective and on a different level.

Penthesilea, *Riddles of the Sphinx*, and *Amy!* can be seen to move from an abstract and general exploration of women's exclusion from male culture and language to treatment of a specific form of exclusion, evident in the repression of mothering to, finally, examination of a historical, autonomous "heroine" who was exploited by the media so as to contain her deeds within patriarchal bounds. All three films confront the problem of female representation in their concern to avoid constructing the film for a male spectator (to avoid, that is, making the female body object of the male gaze), but the issue of the appropriation of the female body is foregrounded in *Amy!*, where the heroine's image must be belied and defused so as to contain her autonomy and independence.

In their interview on *Penthesilea*, Mulvey and Wollen explain how they relied in that film on Bachofen's cultural theories in order to show how women have been left out of dominant culture. The first part of the film focused on the Amazons as a final resistance to the establishment of patriarchal law, while the other parts were intended to be a "woman's questioning of language and of the Symbolic Order, the Law," with a view to finding a new speech. As Mulvey noted, the questions they wanted to raise were, first, "how do you change language in order to change your political practice, and then use it to change fantasy as well, in terms of the Symbolic Order?" and, second, "Can a new Symbolic Law be inserted into history?"[20]

The very last section of *Penthesilea* demonstrates the problem of language in relation to politics. The image of an actress reading Jesse Ashley's letters is superimposed on an old comic film about the suffragettes. The two "realities" – that of Jesse trying to convince people of the need to link getting the vote for women to the oppression of the proletariat as a whole, and that of Hollywood images ridiculing suffragettes – are juxtaposed in such a way as to show their total incompatibility. One of Jesse's problems, Mulvey said in the interview on the film, is her inability to be heard:

> She doesn't speak the language of the bourgeoisie, but nevertheless is not heard by the working class. Her language isn't heard by either side. She can't find a language to be heard. She had started off in this very optimistic vein thinking she had only to tell people and people would hear and see the obviousness of the manifest fact that the suffrage movement should align itself with the working class movement.[21]

As will be clear in chapter 12 (where *Riddles of the Sphinx* is analyzed), this second film picks up where *Penthesilea* ended, with the problem of women's discourse not being heard. According to Mulvey, the aim of the film was to see if they could use the avant-garde cinematic form as a new kind of signifying practice, one that breaks with the dominant forms, to open up an area in which women's specific problems and oppressions could be voiced without being dominated by patriarchy.[22] This might represent the start of a new language, a new symbolic Law. Mothering seemed a fruitful area to explore since it has not been colonized by men; *Riddles of the Sphinx* explores how mothering has been repressed in patriarchy but may, for that reason, provide a gap through which women can begin to assert their voices, and find a subjectivity.

In dialectical fashion, *Amy!* synthesizes issues raised in the first two films, and moves outward to examine women's place in popular culture. The previous investigations showed that while women may achieve a degree of autonomy and independence within a circumscribed context, this is only a fragile and private space. *Amy!* moves on to show how dominant culture jealously safeguards its patriarchal mode, not permitting any significant invasion by women. The more successful woman is in the public sphere, the more patriarchy must move in to contain her deeds through representations that reduce the threat that her achievements present.

Classical Hollywood film has been one of the ways in which patriarchy has traditionally sought to use a representational system to "contain" women; with this in mind, *Amy!* offers a perspective on a classical Hollywood film, *Christopher Strong*, made about Amy Johnson's better-known American counterpart, Amelia Earhart. The feminist position of Mulvey and Wollen's work, that is, enables us to read Arzner's film "against the grain." Their analysis of Amy Johnson's challenge to the dominant discourse allows us to see how Cynthia Darington in *Christopher Strong* also causes a "rent in the fabric of family and Law."[23] She challenges the system on two fronts, first, by becoming a successful flyer, and second, in her adulterous relationship with Strong. Her deeds, like Amy's, are "perverse" in that her interest in flying is not a substitute for love. Happy and self-contained before she meets Strong, she continues afterwards to fly, only finally giving it up under pressure from him.

But the film shows the need for Cynthia to be contained, and finally punished, for her transgressions. Significantly, like Marguerite Gautier in Cukor's *Camille*, Darington is not ultimately constrained by outside forces so much as through her internalization of patriarchal values. She makes herself victim by refusing to fight for what she wants, conceding to the rules of the symbolic order that prohibit breaking up the "happy family." Prior to this, she also conceded that being a mother should take precedence over career, this choice again not really being something over which she has control so much as one constructed for her by patriarchy. The film accepts her suicide as the proper thing for a woman to do in her situation and does not challenge the patriarchal discourse that leads to this conclusion.[24]

Amy! exposes the underlying mechanisms whereby a woman like Cynthia Darington may decide to take herself out of a situation that promises to challenge the dominant order. In a sense, the film deals with the problem of female independence at a stage later than those taken up in the earlier films; for here the heroine actually arrives at a degree of autonomy only suggested in the other works. In *Amy!* there is a real sense of possibility, although its fragility is clear in the ending that shows how patriarchy ultimately destroys the woman who creates her own discourse or who aims for subjectivity. What *Amy!* asks is: how can we prevent appropriation of the female discourse by dominant male culture?

Like the previous two films, *Amy!* combines documentary and fiction; the documentary provides the "raw material" Wollen spoke about, and the fictionalized parts allow for raising the historical and psychoanalytic issues without which we cannot understand woman's situation. As Wollen noted, the narrative is thus embedded in a non-narrative discourse so as to suggest the links between narrative and history.

The main body of the film (which itself mixes fiction and documentary) is framed by documentary interviews with teenage girls at Paddington College, London, which establish the theme of investigating the heroine and set up a historical context for Amy's exploits. The girls show sophistication about the need for heroic representations, and also awareness that what was in Amy's day a daring innovation (i.e. a woman doing engineering) is today quite commonplace. The interviews prepare the spectator for a return to the past – to, that is, the events leading up to, and immediately following, Amy Johnson's solo flight around the world in 1930.

These events are told partly through archival footage of the historical Amy's exploits, partly through re-enactments (a feature common to all Mulvey and Wollen's films), and partly through intertitles of episodes in the historical Amy's life, accompanied by voice-over narration using historical information. Used very much in a Godardian manner, these intertitles are more important than they may at first appear, since the images of words establish a kind of metalanguage. As Wollen noted, this written language is separated from other aspects of the film, not for the purposes of providing solutions to the problems raised but in order to establish the terrain on which the answer is to be found.[25] The intertitles, that is, provide yet one more level of discourse within the film, foregrounding issues that arise from the combination of narrative and documentary, establishing yet another space in which to work.

Through the device of repetition, the sequence in Amy's "bedsit" manages to accomplish a lot in a short time. We see Amy twice in the same position, using the same gestures, only in each case everything is directed to completely different ends. The first time around, the room has a warm, romantic glow; the camera is close to Amy, side-view, as she bends over a little brown drawer and pulls out a bundle of letters. Sitting in front of the mirror, beside which there is a photograph of her fiancé, Amy opens the letters, while her voice-over narration describes her momentous decision to end her engagement:

> Now that I am so much older and more experienced, I can look back on those years and see how utterly stupid I have been. I think I am now strong enough to cut it all out and that's what I intend to do. No more looking for letters that come less and less often; no more wondering when you'll come to London again to see me.[26]

And as Amy's voice-over ends, we see her burning the letters and the photograph.

The atonal, disjointed concrete music (played by the Feminist Improvising Group) accompanying this scene neatly undercuts its romantic visual overtones and prepares us for the break with which it ends. A brief shot of Amy's Flying Moth plane[27] signals the start of the repeat, and we pick up Amy at the fireplace where we left her, only now she is making cocoa in the cold, gray light of dawn as she studies engineering. Now when her hand goes to the same brown drawer it is to bring out a tool, not love letters.

Significant here is the reversal of the usual substitution of career for love that psychoanalysis traditionally uncovers; in *Amy!* Johnson's love affair is seen rather as a substitution for her desire to be an airplane pilot. Finally realizing that trying to make love the center of her life simply will not work, she dares to be what she all along wanted to be.

Having shown things from Amy's point of view, Mulvey and Wollen next place her achievements in the context of the dominant culture. The device of recording her solo world flight through the headlines printed by the London *Times* during her journey allows us, first, to perceive the weight given her deeds, and second, to be aware of other historical happenings, such as the rise of fascism, Gandhi's Indian revolt, the escalation of Soviet naval power, labor struggles internationally, the increase of crime in America, events involving the British monarchy. As the longest shot in the film (over 7 minutes), the sequence, tracing Amy's journey along the map she used, underscores her achievement at the same time as the dominant culture is seen to accord it small weight.

Ironically, Amy's triumph is signified by the headline "Message from the King," this message being the highest honor that a heroine can be awarded in patriarchy. But that moment significantly marks the start of Amy's downfall, on both the private and public levels, since patriarchy cannot permit such a triumph to exist in its own right.

The change is signaled by Wollen's voice-over intervention, in the role of authorial persona. With his speech, we move abruptly from the discourse of history to that of psychoanalysis, the contrast between discourses marking the parallel contrast between comprehension and an acknowledgement of the complexity of life. Having looked at the historical importance of Johnson's achievement, the film now turns to its possible private meanings – i.e. as an attempt to overcome "the fear of being abandoned or dropped, as a parent might drop a child."[28] The love of the thrill is viewed in this discourse as a compensation for an unresolved childhood fear; in this way the return becomes truly traumatic, since it means facing the fear which flying temporarily suspended.

But this private fear is seen in the next section to have a social dimension. If the female child has a fear of abandonment by the parents, it is related to the actual social positioning of woman in patriarchy, i.e. as Other, as object, as *dependent*. The placing as dependent cannot help but increase fears of being abandoned or possessed. Women, lacking subjectivity, are particularly vulnerable to expropriation.

It is this expropriation that the film exposes in the following sequence showing Amy's arrival at the airport. That representational systems trap the female body is evident when Mulvey and Wollen position the camera so that it appears to seize Amy as she emerges from Airport House, carrying flask, gloves, and the flowers that symbolize her success. Attempting to resist the camera, Amy at first turns away, but, as if possessing a malevolent power, the camera follows her, forcing her to turn around, to become its object, preventing her from escaping its lure.

A critique of the commercial cinema is implied in the revelation of the camera as an apparatus that forces woman to be spectacle, object of the gaze, reduced to the place of victim. The words of the rock song, describing woman as just a concept, a dream, a symbol or theme, a victim, "reflection of the new regime," [29] underscore the visual meanings of the scene.

Mulvey and Wollen emphasize the appropriation of Amy's identity by the dominant culture in the frightening sequence that follows: here we see how patriarchy forces woman to become a split subject, alienated from herself. While this is an alienation that is basic to the human condition (if we follow Lacan's analysis of the mirror phase), men can recuperate their split selves through the images that surround them, and through their very placing in dominant culture. Mulvey and Wollen expose the alienation that happens to women in the mirror phase in showing Amy making up her face in the mirror, putting on lipstick and eyeliner. She is here creating the representation of femininity that patriarchy desires, namely the pretty object to be displayed for male pleasure. But the psychological impact of taking on the patriarchal image is expressed when Amy draws a face in lipstick on the glass, superimposed on her own image and suggesting a split: by making herself into the desired object, Amy has separated herself from herself (see plate 18, p. 168). Her voice-over tells us that she is trying to lose the identity of Amy Johnson since that person has, as a result of all the publicity and exploitation, now become "a nightmare and an abomination." [30] The problem is that Amy does not have any other identity with which to replace the lost one. The rock song underscores the theme again in talking about "identity as the crisis." Amy is struggling to retain her identity in a situation where patriarchal culture, having ruined her original sense of self, has forced upon her another one that fulfills *its* needs.

The film offers a psychoanalytic reading of what is happening to Amy through the device of Mulvey's words, spoken in her authorial persona role, which balance those of Wollen in the same function earlier. From the patriarchal perspective, Amy's triumphs are "perverse" since they threaten the social order, and they must be contained. In Mulvey's words, the deeds create "a wound in the symbolic flesh of family and law, which has to be stitched up again by the creation of images and myths and legends. The heroine's perverse deeds are translated into exemplary exploits and her symbolic role stabilized for our identification and entertainment." [31]

As an example of the reduction of Amy and her heroism to entertainment, Mulvey and Wollen insert into the film's sound track the 1930s song about Amy; this song trivializes her into a cute object to be "loved." The real threat that her achievements offer has to be contained by the protective, condescending stance of romance. Reduced by the discourse of romance merely to the

Plate 18   Amy here crosses out the image of herself that she had sketched on the glass in an effort to make herself into the desired male object. She does not, however, have any other identity with which to replace the lost one.

feminine, in which she is subject to the Law, Amy's actual achievement becomes simply something that makes her lovable, its real value forgotten:

> There's a little lady who has captured every heart,
> Amy Johnson, it's you . . .
> Amy, wonderful Amy
> I'm proud of the way you flew.
> Believe me Amy
> You cannot blame me, Amy, for falling in love with you.

It is, of course, inconceivable that a parallel male achievement would be minimized in this manner.

But the film, in characteristic Mulvey and Wollen fashion, does not end on this bleak note. Just as in *Riddles of the Sphinx* the images of the female acrobats became a metaphor for liberation, so now Amy's flying, dealt with on the literal level so far, becomes another metaphor for freedom. Following shots taken from a plane, in which, above the earth, one has the sense of being in some other space, away from the constraints of culture, slow-motion shots show a bird gradually extricating itself from surrounding branches and flying freely in the open air. On the sound track, accompanying these shots, Yvonne Rainer's voice-over reads excerpts from writings by other successful women, whether also in flying (Amelia Earhart) or in the arts (Gertrude Stein). The device links Johnson to other achieving women, who struggled on bravely despite the efforts of patriarchy to cancel their voices. The reference to unequal pay for equal work and to the designation of certain menial jobs as "women's work" again sets Amy's struggle in the broader context of women's struggles and suffering throughout history.

The last section of Rainer's monologue, however, leaves us with a moment in which the pain is transcended:

> The clouds form themselves into strange polar patterns, the sun changes. I saw it once bouncing like a scarlet ball from peak to peak. Burning. At that moment I felt I was free. I began to speak more freely, I could even permit myself the luxury of pausing when I felt like it, for I knew that if I didn't want an image to appear, it wouldn't. I felt simply wonderful.[32]

The voice, speaking here for all women, suggests, first, the possibility of moving beyond pain, second, the hope of finding a voice, and finally, the hope of achieving a measure of control.

If this seems somewhat utopian, the framing documentary interviews with the girls at Paddington College bring us back to reality, but still with a sense of possibility. For Beverly notes that "to be a heroine you don't have to be famous," suggesting that the only way to avoid exploitation by the dominant culture is to continue to do great deeds but not to allow oneself to "become famous." While this is no solution, it suggests a place from which to struggle since understanding and resisting the discourses that define and limit women is the first step toward liberation. This kind of understanding immediately puts one in a different position in relation to the dominant, oppressive discourses, and it is through this new placing that change can begin to happen. Indeed, the very framing of Amy's story with the contemporary interviews suggests the advance in positioning of women within dominant discourses, as well as showing how little, on some levels, things have changed. As a result of the women's movement, the young college girls are able to articulate aspects of their positioning in a manner unavailable to Amy Johnson. Yet, they still remain bound by structures similar to those that bound Johnson, especially in relation to representation.

Amy! (although for funding reasons shorter than the previous two films) manages to accomplish a great deal in its span. Its concrete story, based as it is on a historical person, makes it relatively accessible, while the film still works on a complex level. Part of the film's success comes from its symmetry – a symmetry that in itself expresses some of the deeper meanings. For the film falls neatly into two halves, separated by the long shot transversing the map showing Amy's journey around the world. The first half explores Amy's daring transgression of existing codes for women by following her desire to be a pilot; as we saw, her deeds are placed in various discourses, including psychoanalysis and history. After the map sequence, the film explores the effects of her triumph, again through placing it in parallel historical and psychoanalytic discourses. The opening prologue, where issues having to do with being a heroine in the present are raised, is balanced by the epilogue, where historical "heroines" discuss what their achievements actually meant, in terms of pain, suffering, and pleasure.

We thus have a clear and valuable sense of the intermeshing of past and present; we also are made to realize the complexity of events, conveyed through the repetitions, the turning back and starting again, and through the gaps and omissions; views are suggested rather than laid out didactically – they are deliberately left ambiguous.

Thus, in their different ways, these three feminist films reflect a cinema constructed to explore the problems of female representation in the discourses of history and of classical texts. In the next chapter, I will analyze two recent feminist films about mothering, one of which (*Riddles of the Sphinx* by Mulvey and Wollen) is again an avant-garde theory film, while the other (Citron's *Daughter-Rite*) uses vérité realism as a basis for a critique of realism.

12 | Mothers and daughters in two recent women's films: Mulvey/Wollen's *Riddles of the Sphinx* (1976) and Michelle Citron's *Daughter-Rite* (1978)

As we saw in chapter 10, the avant-garde theory films, represented by the three just analyzed, caused a controversy in the feminist film community, particularly in relation to future strategies. Here I want to discuss two films that offer a useful contrast both in terms of cinematic strategies and of treatment of the mother–daughter issue as this concerns patriarchal culture and feminism. Made in 1976, Mulvey/Wollen's *Riddles of the Sphinx* was one of the first British films to apply new feminist film theory to film practice, and it influenced the form taken by the films, like those discussed in chapter 11, that followed. Michelle Citron's *Daughter-Rite* has also been *formally* important as an attempt to bridge realist and avant-garde strategies and reduce the extent of what had become an apparently irresolvable stylistic polarity.

On the narrative level, the films offer an equally interesting contrast: Mulvey/Wollen's film broke new ground in dealing theoretically with the problem of the mother from her point of view (in contrast to the pragmatic level of the realist films *Joyce at 34* and *Janie's Janie*, which we looked at in chapter 10). And Michelle Citron's film is unique in confronting the problem of the daughter's relationship to the mother in a way that combines unconscious fears and fantasies with conscious attitudes and reactions.

In order to underscore the innovative, thematic aspects of these films, let me dwell for a moment on the relative lack of attention accorded mother–daughter issues in feminist filmmaking. This lack is part of a general omission on the part of feminists, and since patriarchy has also left the mother out, historically and culturally, it is important to understand the feminist response and how it differs from that in the larger society. For the purposes of exploration, let me distinguish two distinct levels of discourse: first, the deep, psychoanalytic discourse, by which I mean the level of the unconscious as it translates itself into myth, language, and cultural forms; and second, the discourse of the social formation (i.e. of the social institutions in which mothering occurs).

Since patriarchy is constructed according to the *male* unconscious, feminists grew up in a society that, as Mulvey and Wollen note in *Riddles of the Sphinx*, represses the mother. Although Mulvey and Wollen do not explain precisely how this repression works, I assume that Motherhood cannot be dealt with in terms other than those which arise out of patriarchal needs, based on male Oedipal fears and fantasies. Dorothy Dinnerstein, building on Melanie Klein's and Simone de Beauvoir's work, has shown how the child's ambivalent feelings towards the female parent result in a split between the mother as "good" object and as "bad" object; she further demonstrates how, because of her reproductive function, the mother is linked to non-human natural and supernatural forces.[1] The memory of being mothered, thus, is so threatening that it has to be repressed, and displaced onto myths that vacillate between hypostatization and romanticization (the myth of the nurturing, ever-present, but self-abnegating figure) and disparagement (the myth of the neglectful, sadistic mother). To all intents and purposes, the mother qua *herself* is, in patriarchy, relegated to silence, absence, and marginality. What patriarchy has instead focused on is the status of woman as *castrated*, as lacking a status that confers on males the place of "in possession," which has been used to dominate women.

But while feminists have been sensitive to, and rebellious about, this second construction of themselves as *castrated*, why have they not reacted strongly against the construction of the mother as "outside," as "spectator"? One answer is that, while many patriarchal myths (such as those around women and work) were obvious distortions of capacities women demonstrably owned, women were themselves unable to identify with mothering. Combating the Motherhood myths meant confronting our own unconscious struggles with our mothers. While these struggles are in fact very different from those that confront men, we shared with men the problem of having been merged with a female parent on our first entry into life.[2] Our own complex Oedipal struggles stood in the way of any easy identification with the oppression of the mother, although we were able to identify with female oppression in numerous other areas.

The problem is compounded by the fact that, paradoxically, the very attractiveness of feminism was that it provided an arena for separation from oppressive closeness with the mother; feminism was in part a reaction against our mothers, who had tried to inculcate the patriarchal "feminine" in us. Feminism was an opportunity to find out whom we were and what we wanted. Regardless of whether or not we were mothers in actuality, we came to feminism as *daughters*, and we spoke from that position. It is thus not surprising that we have taken so long to arrive at a position where we can identify with the mother and begin to look from her position.

Unwittingly, we repeated the patriarchal omission of the mother *qua* mother, speaking only from the child's place. Psychoanalytically, we remained locked in ambivalence toward the mother, at once deeply tied to her while striving for an apparently unattainable autonomy. On the unconscious level, we were angry with the mother on two counts: first, because she would not give us the independence we needed, or the wherewithal to discover our identities; second, because she failed to protect us adequately against an alien patriarchal culture by which we were psychologically, culturally, and (sometimes) physically harmed.[3] Paradoxically, our unconscious Oedipal struggles resulted in our assigning the mother, in her heterosexual, familial setting, to an absence and silence analogous to the male relegation of her to absence, although our reasons for doing so were different.

Part of the male relegation of the mother to absence is evident in the omission of the mother in traditional psychoanalysis, except as seen from the child's point of view. Ironically, just because the mother is a central figure in the child's Oedipal development, psychoanalytic theorists, looking from the child within themselves, and anxious to explore the struggle in separating from the mother, put their theoretical energy in that direction, leaving the position of the mother unattended. In a similar way, feminists, not yet properly separated from the mother and having difficulty seeing from her position, have been speaking and theorizing from the child within.

Since psychoanalysis was shunned in the first years of the women's movement, feminists were able to rationalize their anger at the mother and avoid the deep unconscious issues. This is not to say that the analysis on the level of the social formation was wrong, but that it was limited by our inability to link it with psychoanalytic understandings. The analysis of the nuclear family's destructiveness for women resulted in seeing the mother as an agent of the patriarchal Establishment, colluding in our socialization to passivity, inferiority, and marginality. Unable to appreciate the special burdens and sacrifices that go with Motherhood *as constructed in patriarchy* (i.e. that are not inherent to mothering)[4] – that is, the conflicts, contradictions, and self-doubts that the mother has to endure – and unable above all to appreciate the awesome responsibility of total care for another human being (especially if we were not ourselves mothers), we were not interested in analyzing the mother from her position. We were unable to see that the mother was as much a victim of patriarchy as ourselves, constructed as she is by a whole series of discourses, including the psychoanalytic, the political, and the economic.

Mulvey and Wollen's *Riddles of the Sphinx* was theoretically important in providing us with an analysis from the position of the mother; using Lacan's model of the imaginary and the symbolic, the film explores, first, the seductive reversion in mothering to the world of the imaginary, and second, why the voice of the mother has been repressed in patriarchy. The filmmakers show a mother gradually realizing her position in culture and trying to discover a discourse in a symbolic system that has no place for her. Michelle Citron, meanwhile, has given us a film that makes us confront the anger (both unconscious and conscious) that has hitherto blocked our ability to look from the position of the mother. In both films, the cinematic strategies were carefully chosen to express the ideas of the directors.

Taking the films in chronological order, I'll deal first with *Riddles of the Sphinx*.[5] As I noted in chapter 11, Mulvey and Wollen are committed to the avant-garde film, believing that we need new cinematic and linguistic forms if people are to move beyond old ways of seeing, old ideologies, particularly as these affect women. In *Riddles*, Mulvey and Wollen hope to demonstrate that old ways of seeing the mother in fact amount to the repression of her discourse in patriarchal culture. On one level, the film is an attempt to find a new cinematic form and new words through which the mother in the film, Louise, can express her thoughts and feelings about mothering. The experimental form of this film, like that of *Penthesilea*, is a self-conscious attempt by the filmmakers to deny us the "satisfaction, pleasure and privilege of the 'invisible guest,'" and frustrate all our accustomed dependence, in conventional cinema, on "voyeuristic active/passive mechanisms."[6] This is done in the firm belief that there is no other way, given the dominance of the patriarchal symbolic codes that permeate linguistic and aesthetic forms, to present discourses that patriarchy represses.

Some of the ways in which Mulvey and Wollen break with conventional cinematic codes and frustrate our dependence on voyeurism are familiar from experiments that Godard and other New Wave filmmakers have undertaken in the past ten years or so. For instance, the way Louise's narrative is broken into thirteen fragmented sections, introduced by parts of an apparently ongoing written story, recalls Godard's *Vivre sa vie*. Other techniques, such as Laura's direct address to the camera, breaking the illusion of the absent artist and forcing us to become aware of the filmmaking process, recall Godard/Gorin's *Letter to Jane* and Godard's *Comment ça va*. But devices like the telling of Louise's story in a series of single shots, each consisting of a 360° pan, are original and explicitly designed to express Louise's consciousness. While Godard challenges conventional cinematic forms for the sake of deconstructing bourgeois modes of thought, standing outside what he is doing, Mulvey and Wollen seem connected to their film. The formal devices are an integral part of what is being communicated; *Riddles* represents a viable alternative cinema rather than simply calling attention to what is wrong with the kind of cinema we now have.

The film works on two distinct levels, and the formal devices are carefully chosen to differentiate these levels. The three sections on either side of Louise's story told in the thirteen single shots, balance each other and introduce, and then recapitulate, the abstract ideas that form the basis for the film. The film is about women in patriarchy and the difficulties they have "because the culture within which they must think is not theirs." *Riddles* opens with shots of a French book, *Midi-Fantastique*, the pages turning over until they stop at a photograph of Greta Garbo as the sphinx. The point here, perhaps, is to show the presence within contemporary popular mythology of the ancient myth that Mulvey and Wollen are returning to for an understanding of women. Garbo fascinates women because she evokes in us a longing for something other and unknown that we have lost contact with, while she at once allures and threatens men by her mysteriousness.

The next section shows Laura speaking directly to the camera, reading from a text and with a tape-recorder in front of her. The speech, intercut with images of the Greek and Egyptian sphinx, traces briefly the history of the sphinx-Oedipus myth, now focusing on the role of the sphinx rather than on Oedipus, as is usually done. Laura explains that they decided to use the voice of the sphinx for the narrator because it "represents, not the voice of truth, not an answering voice, but its opposite: a questioning voice, a voice asking a riddle." While from the point of view of Oedipus the sphinx is a threat to patriarchy because she resists it and is associated with the mystery (to men) of Motherhood, the sphinx herself symbolizes women's exclusion from patriarchy: "The sphinx is outside the city gates, she challenges the culture of the city, with its order of kinship and its order of knowledge, a culture and a political system which assign women a subordinate place."

Laura's restatement of the Oedipus myth highlights a paradox inherent in it: women, standing outside patriarchy, come to represent the unconscious and thus a threat to the male rational order. Women are here linked to the non-human, the indecipherable. But women, living within patriarchy, feel threatened on their part by male culture, which represents a set of riddles that women cannot solve, since the culture is alien to them: "We live in a society ruled by the father, in which the place of the mother is suppressed. Motherhood, and how to live it, or not to live it, lies at the roots of the dilemma. And meanwhile the Sphinx can only speak with a voice apart, a voice off."

The third section of the film is a montage sequence of photographic images of various sphinx monuments around the world, set to concrete music. The sequence is compelling, if overlong. The music establishes an eerie, far-off mood that suggests the mysteriousness of the sphinx. We have a sense of its place apart from civilization and its links with ways of being that pre-date culture. Women may have forgotten these ways but may yet respond to them. In making the voice of the sphinx the narrator of Louise's story in the main section of the film that follows, Mulvey and Wollen are suggesting that women can perhaps use the myth of the sphinx positively.

The reinterpretation of the myth allows us to see how and why our discourse has been suppressed; if women can't speak with the voice of truth like Oedipus, then we can at least raise the questions relevant to our experience within patriarchy. We can learn to discover the inner thoughts and feelings which lie beneath the superimpositions of male discourse. If we can do this, Mulvey and Wollen seem to be saying, then perhaps we have the beginnings of the way out of our dilemma in male culture. In choosing Motherhood as the specific focus in Louise's story, Mulvey and Wollen are able to accentuate the repression of women's discourse generally.

These first three sections, like the last three which balance them, often cause audiences difficulty. The lack of conventional narrative and drama (for me the ideas are dramatic and involving, however) and the self-consciousness of the cinematic techniques alienate people. Yet it is hard to see how Mulvey and Wollen could have set up the framework for Louise's story without dealing directly with the ideas involved. Louise's story takes on significance and meaning in light of the first three sections. We are prepared for the fact that we will deal (more or less) with her unconscious thoughts, and will view her in terms of her place in male culture.

The fragmented intertitle that introduces the first of the thirteen shots that will make up Louise's story seems to express the male culture's view of Louise, perhaps specifically the voice of her husband. "Perhaps Louise is too close to her child" suggests a criticism of her intense involvement in mothering, as do the next comments about excluding the outside world. But the shots that follow the intertitle attempt, by contrast, to express Louise's inner thoughts which lie beyond male superimpositions in the established symbolic order. The 360° pan of Louise's neat, cheerful kitchen as she prepares a meal for her child, Anna, creates a warm, cosy feeling, while the waist-high placing of the camera suggests that Louise is focused not on herself but on her child. Each apparently ordinary household object that comes slowly into focus takes on significance because of the intense mother–child relationship. As the pan ends, we see a male hand, that of Chris, Louise's husband, picking up discarded bread crusts; his sudden appearance seems a jarring intrusion in the involved mother–daughter closeness.

The words on the sound track during the pan are deliberately scrambled, emerging as word associations and not as coherent, ordered sentences. They present the contradictory feelings of mothering: its burdensome nature, with endless routines, and the warm, cosy feelings of closeness and sheltering that also exist. Presumably, ordered sentences would express only male notions of mothering, and if women are to assert their own discourse, it must take a new form.

The second sequence in Anna's bedroom is closely modeled on the first, only now the voice off focuses specifically on word associations that evoke the close, warm feelings between mother and child when all sense of separation disappears and the mother seems totally satisfied just in caring for the child. The husband is not present, but his demands are resented by the voice narrating and we are not surprised to read in the next intertitle that he is moving out, because "he cannot make her see reason and get more out into the world." The next 360° pan, shot in the hallway, shows Chris packing things into the car; his words and manner seem disconnected, empty, and per-

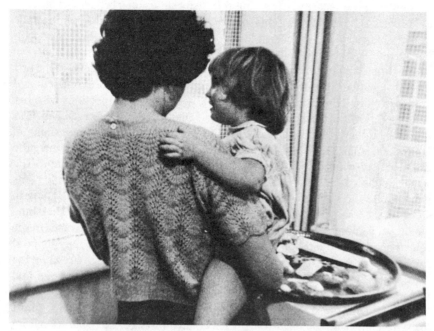

Plate 19   Louise and her child look on while the husband, Chris, carries his luggage to the car. The pain of the separation is compensated for by the closeness of mother and child, shielded as they are from the outside world by the window frames.

functory in contrast to the soft warmth of the voice off. Louise's pain is expressed in the words narrated, but the "cold" of the separation is compensated for by the "warmth" of the connection with the child.

Shots 4 through 9 show Louise's gradual and painful emergence from the womblike closeness with her child into the "male" public world which ignores the problems of working mothers. At the nursery, she befriends Maxine who eases her separation from Anna and her husband. Louise is having difficulty concentrating on her work because of worrying about Anna; Maxine suggests approaching the union about childcare in the work place, but the women are unable to achieve anything. Significant here is the women's lack of confidence, as if they are unsure that their problem is genuine since the union hadn't thought of it. Their voices are low, their tones subdued, and the anger is hidden. Louise painfully discovers that daycare is not a priority since men suppress mothering and what follows from it. Her attempt to reconcile working and being a mother culminates in a series of large questions that she is finally able to articulate. They range from the practical, political ones about how to link problems of daycare to other economic and social issues (e.g. "Should women's struggles be concentrated on economic issues?" "Should women organize separately from men?") to questions on a broader level, such as "Is patriarchy the main enemy for women?" "What would the politics of the unconscious be like?" Although Louise cannot find answers, there is hope in her having even begun to ask the questions.

The three sections that follow – 10 through 12 – return to the level of the first three, before Louise went out into the world; but now she is more confident and able to explore what is going on inside her. Louise finds connections with her childhood through participating in Anna's life; there is a calm afternoon at Louise's mother's house, where she and Maxine laugh at photographs of Louise as a child. This is followed by a scene in Chris's editing room where the distance Louise has come is clear in her firm stance toward her husband. The women's discourse is here nicely contrasted with that of Chris: while Chris wants to deal in very practical terms, either setting up the film he is going to show or discussing the selling of the house, Louise and Maxine spend their time looking at a Camel cigarette cover, noting how the image is not reversed in the mirror because of the cellophane, and appreciating the lumpy, baggy shape of the camel set against the endlessness of the desert. The women are allowing other parts of themselves to function while Chris is locked into tasks and material matters.

Chris shows Louise and Maxine a film of Mary Kelly (the British feminist artist) reading from some diaries. The Lacanian analysis of her separation from her child is perhaps rather artificially introduced, but it provides an occasion for recalling Louise's earlier problems and giving her intellectual understanding of what went on as part of the growth that the film is charting. Louise learns that with language a Third Term intervenes between the mother–child dyad:

> This intervention situates the imaginary "Third Term" of the primordial triangle (that is the child as phallus) and the paternal "image" of the mirror phase within the dominance of the symbolic structure through the Word of the father. That is, the mother's words referring to the authority of the "father" to which the real father may or may not conform.

The clinical language here breaks the rhythm of the inner language that Louise, and the women generally, have used in opposition to the "male" language dominant in the culture. But it is immediately balanced by Louise reading Maxine's dream in the next sequence, which takes place in Maxine's unusual room, full of primitive objects.

The dream is quite compelling and filled with obvious sexual and Oedipal connotations, but it is unclear just what Mulvey and Wollen intend with it. Most likely, the dream represents yet one more form of language, one more mode of reaching into the unconscious to discourses unmediated by official male culture. The dream is an important way for women to reach back into mythology, to the realm inhabited by the sphinx that pre-dated Oedipus and male culture.

The last section of Louise's story emphasizes the themes in the dream scene, since now we see Louise and Anna walking through the British Museum, looking at the mummified bodies with their enigmatic scripts. The intertitle voice now seems to be Anna's, not Chris's, and the voice off, the sphinx, reflects Anna's thoughts, not those of Louise. Anna's inner speech is significant in that she begins by trying to solve the dilemma of women in patriarchy through reason and logic, through the theories of male writers like Bachofen and Freud, but "she found her mind wandering, mislaying the thread of logical reconstruction and returning to images from her own childhood." By the end of her speech, Anna has finally managed to hear the voice of the sphinx – to reach, that is, a part of herself known but somehow up to then inaccessible – and this resolves her complex problem about the words "capital," "delay," "body." She has attained a level of freedom symbolized by some acrobats she recalled drawing.

The last three sections of the film parallel those from the start. In place of the montage of sphinx monuments, there is now a beautiful series of women acrobats in various colors suggesting freedom, versatility, energy, life. The juxtaposition of the opening sphinx montage and these women acrobats is perhaps intended to suggest the release of energy in women once they connect with the world of the sphinx. Section 6 of the film parallels Laura's opening speech, only now we see her playing back what she said at the beginning, listening reflectively to parts of it. For us, the section works to remind us of some of the main themes that Louise's story has demonstrated. Included also is a small part of Maxine's dream, to remind us of the importance of the dream as access to the unconscious. The film ends with a close-up of a mercury puzzle in which the mercury pieces have to find their way through a labyrinth to the center; a fitting image for the dilemmas that face women in patriarchy as we struggle to interpret the patterns we are given, find our way among them, and reach some safe center from which we may take our bearings.

While the first three sections of the film presented the dilemmas that face women in patriarchy, the last three suggest that Anna, benefiting from her mother's growth, may find a way to break out of the old forms; or at least to decipher them, to read them for what they are. The film is about ways of thinking, about languages, and about finding new words for new ideas. It asks the question: How can women think in a patriarchal culture that is not theirs?

In *Riddles*, Mulvey and Wollen have in fact begun to answer one of Louise's questions and to show us what a "politics of the unconscious" might look like. It is not surprising that people approaching the film from the vantage point of traditional left theory of the media either did not like it, or did not understand it. Historically, this position has reflected an external, rational way of looking at people and society, with a view of the mind as a *tabula rasa*, lacking its own internal energies and dynamics. Everything is presented as a one-way process without a recognition of the complex, dialectical relationship between media productions and the people who watch them.

The negative reactions to *Riddles* validate Mulvey and Wollen's theories that avant-garde cinema frustrates the deep-seated need for ego-ideals that Hollywood films manipulate and satisfy. People get bored with the film, not so much because of its slow pace or formal devices (the same people are entertained by Buñuel or Godard films), but because Louise is not set up as an object of our gaze. The 360° pan prevents Louise from being focused on in the way that women – or significantly sexual parts of women – are in Hollywood films. While Buñuel and Godard were rebelling against a familiar bourgeois culture by parodying it, Mulvey and Wollen attempt to present a new, rarely heard discourse that is difficult to appreciate because it is unfamiliar.

Some people may complain that the attention to beauty in the film reflects a concern with form for its own sake. It is true that Mulvey and Wollen have carefully chosen and arranged for their shapes and colors the objects that the camera pans on its journey. The scene in the supermarket is beautifully filmed, as is that toward the end in the British Museum. But the formal beauty has a function quite other than that in the Hollywood film, where it depends largely on the very fetishizing of the female form that Mulvey and Wollen have taken pains to avoid. Here it is always linked to Louise's state of mind. In the early scenes, where Louise is happy with her child, the objects reflect her sense of peace, warmth, and security. The scenes when Louise first goes to work lack this kind of beauty because she is troubled, confused, uncertain. And the beauty in later scenes reflects Louise's new peace with herself, and her happiness in being with Maxine.

The more specific political objections to the film take three main forms: first, some people object because the film does not show Louise winning any of the battles about daycare and because it offers no solutions to her political dilemma as a single, working mother; second, people object to the use of the black actress for the role of Maxine, suggesting that this is confusing since her dilemma specifically as a *black* woman is not confronted; and finally, the film's inaccessibility to a general audience is criticized.

The first two criticisms are problematic in applying social-realist standards to what is a film on a very different level. To begin with, this is not a political film in the sense of suggesting ways of winning daycare or of how to deal with unions, or of explaining how capitalism exploits women workers. Not located on the level of social reality *per se*, the film positions itself rather in Louise's unconscious, in the language and thought that are limited by the male culture in which she lives.

The second criticism has more validity but for a different reason. The figure of Maxine is indeed troubling because the treatment of the image, in a film that is, after all, about representation, either ignores our cultural, mythic associations with the black image or, worse still, fails to provide a *critique* of the associations that the image inevitably evokes. In terms of the erotic female bonding between the two women, Mulvey/Wollen replace the sexual difference that characterizes heterosexual relationships with a visual difference. But why is this necessary? That it is a racial difference simply compounds the problems. The association of Maxine's blackness with primitivism and mythology may indeed underscore the themes introduced by the sphinx legend, but it is problematic to use such links uncritically.

The final objection which condemns the film's inaccessibility reflects the genuine problem that I discussed in chapter 10. It is hard to see, by virtue of Mulvey and Wollen's theoretical position itself, how non-traditional film can change consciousness. How are people to get into these films, given their "alien" (although *in fact* more "real") discourse? Because of the complex theoretical underpinnings of a film like *Riddles*, it only reaches, and can be fully appreciated by, students and intellectuals.

Yet *Riddles* is important, first because of the implicit critique of capitalism and of old ideology, particularly in relation to the mother; and second because of the attempt to find theoretical links between Marxist economics, with its model of dialectical progress toward revolution, and new notions of patriarchal structures, including psychoanalytic concepts of repression and displacement as these function in relation to women. But the problem is how to create a counter-cinema that is accessible to a general audience while not being propagandistic and rhetorical (as are many new left and feminist films) in ways that simply duplicate how bourgeois ideology is communicated. I am not as convinced as the British group that forms so unequivocally carry ideology, and believe that a way out of the dilemma may be to use forms familiar to people in new ways that challenge old concepts, while still permitting people to understand what is going on.[7]

Michelle Citron's *Daughter-Rite*, in fact, sets itself this very challenge, to provide a film that is at once theoretical and uses the necessary avant-garde techniques but that, at the same time, arises out of people's concrete experiences and speaks to them in a familiar way.

The process that Citron used in making her film is by now quite well known: she had always had her eye on some home-movie footage but had not been sure of how to use it. Once she had the idea of the daughter theme, she saw a use for the movies, but she also began doing extensive interviews with women about their mother–daughter inter-relationships. A script was written in collaboration with her actresses, who improvised in addition, so that the narrative became the expression of women's voices combined.

Citron decided to construct the film out of two different tracks. There is first a track containing the home-movie footage, slowed down, often repeated, and accompanied by a voice-over narration consisting of excerpts from a diary belonging to a person designated within the film text as the "author" of the film. Also in this narration some dreams are recounted. Second, intercut with the slowed home-movie footage, there is a track consisting of two actresses supposedly being interviewed by the filmmaker, cinema-vérité style. In the fiction, they are sisters, evidently returning temporarily to their mother's house while she is away (in hospital?) and sharing memories of growing up.

Now, both Citron and her critics[8] have discussed these two tracks mainly in terms of the formal intervention involved: that is, the home-movie footage is seen as "deconstructing" a familiar "realist" film mode, bearing the weight of realist assumptions about "capturing" lived experience on film; it is also seen as demonstrating male domination in filmmaking practice in that the mother and daughters are constant "objects" of the father's camera, performing for his (voyeuristic) camera eye; they look out to the camera, aware of its presence and of the need to present the "ideal family look" for that camera. The slow-motion device, together with the film loops that repeatedly show certain gestures and actions, further deconstruct the very ideal family that the group is supposedly reconstructing for the film record. The images reveal, first, the way the little girls are socialized into the patriarchal idea of "the feminine"; and second, the brittleness of the flashy smiles that are constantly demanded (occasionally the camera captures a terribly strained, or downright miserable,

Plate 20 Citron constructs the film out of two tracks. Here the slowed-down home-movie footage deconstructs the familiar "realist" mode, commenting on the limitations of realism as a cinematic form. Further, Citron highlights male domination in filmmaking practice in that the mother and daughters are always objects for the father's camera, performing for *his* eye. Here, they walk up and down in their summer outfits.

expression that would pass by unnoticed in the normal speed of the film).

This track, then, functions in a non-realist manner, commenting *on* the limitations of realism as a cinematic mode, i.e. revealing that realism indeed is an artificial construction of what is desirable in dominant ideology. The voice-over narration further deconstructs realism in having nothing particularly to do with the images we see, other than as a general counterpoint to the ideal family representation (the voice, that is, describes all kinds of problems within the family relationships that are represented as functioning smoothly and harmoniously in the home movies).

Meanwhile, on first viewing, the cinema-vérité-style track gives us the illusion (since we do not yet know that it is fictional) of a familiar, realist form, common to independent women's films and totally accessible. We can enjoy these scenes (which are often filmed for humor), yet, at the end of the film, when we realize the enactment, we reflect on the vérité style, apprehending its construction also. We understand that our vérité movies have all along been painfully close to "home movies" in assuming (as I showed in chapter 10) that we could capture the truth of our oppression unproblematically on film. The

Plate 21　The second, cinema-vérité-style track gives us the illusion of a familiar realist form common to independent women's films. When we realize the scenes were enacted, we reflect on the construction of *all* images. Here the "sisters" reminisce about their experiences with their mother.

deliberately overdramatic narration and enacted vérité conversations further draw attention to, and critique, a dominant, realist women's film form, melodrama, that is epitomized in the television soap opera.

While Citron's cinematic strategies do indeed raise these formal issues, they are not inserted *only* to make formal points: each set of strategies is geared also to distinguishing the two distinct levels of discourse that I mentioned in talking about feminists' difficulties in approaching the topic of mothering, namely the psychoanalytic discourse and the social-personal-political discourse. The voice-over narration embodies the level of the unconscious on which the diarist–daughter(s) struggle(s) to separate from the mother and discover her/their identity(ies); the enacted vérité sections represent the conscious level of discourse where the daughters' anger is directed at the mother's collusion in perpetuating a patriarchal domination that ensures the negative, repressive feminine socialization. This level offers an implicit critique of the nuclear family.

Now, the film is clearly constructed for the female spectator, but it seems to me that she can be positioned in one of two ways: either the spectator positions herself as *daughter*, identifying with the various daughter voices on the two filmic tracks and possibly spurred to reflect on her own daughter–mother interactions; or the spectator perceives the interweaving of the tracks, with their distinct levels of discourse, as an invitation to meditate on what the voices and images reveal: here, the spectator is encouraged to become a "spectator–therapist," analyzing the narrations and conversations as they expose the very blocks that have prevented feminists from studying the mother's construction in patriarchy, her particular form of silence, absence, and marginality. In fact, the spectator in this position is made increasingly aware (as the film continues) of the mother's *absence* and *silence*: not allowed to speak for herself, the mother is heard only through the daughter voices, seen only through the father's camera eye ("I"), to which she constantly turns for affirmation that she is fulfilling her prescribed role as socializer of the patriarchal feminine. The spectator then is made to *experience* the repression of the mother that patriarchal culture insists on: she sees how patriarchy has gotten the daughter's collusion in this repression through the very mechanisms of the Oedipal process that the daughters are struggling to overcome.

For my purpose here, the position of spectator–therapist will provide the most appropriate critical stance. In the first diarist–daughter track, with the voice-over narration accompanied by the slow-motion home movies, we hear the daughter's unconscious anger at the mother. (We should, I think, assume that this is not the continuous narration of one daughter, but a series of moments or modes that represent different phases and types of the daughter–mother relationship. That the spectator may unconsciously strive not only to link the various diarist narrations, but also to link the narration moments to the vérité conversations, reflects a fascinating phenomenon – that of the spectator's urge to create coherent narratives even when the evidence, in this case the varying names, suggests that there is no coherence. I am not sure that Citron had taken this tendency into account, as perhaps she had also not realized the violation that spectators feel when they learn that the supposed vérité sections were indeed enactments.) That the level of the unconscious is involved is signaled by the slow, monotone voice of the narration. The voice has a disconnected, disembodied effect, emerging as it does from nowhere, and not directly linked to the images we see. Who is speaking? And to whom? Where is she located? We do not know, and gradually we realize that the voice of the unconscious is at work.

One set of themes and attitudes to the mother that emerges from the diarist narration is that of anger and impatience at the mother for nearly everything she does, or does not, do. The daughter is irritated with her mother's decision to move to Hawaii, impatient when her mother is scared, and accuses her mother of dishonesty. But indications of the underlying anxiety that the mother's departure has evoked, and that the daughter cannot face, slip out in certain comments, such as where the diarist says that the mother's going away signals the end of childhood, even the end of "mother" (i.e. mother as to be depended upon). So, it seems that this set of themes reveals the daughter's problem in separating from the mother; she simultaneously needs her, yet must reject her if she (the daughter) is to gain her own identity. And the form that this rejection most naturally takes is that of disparagement of the mother.

But this disparagement is made uncomfortable for the speaker because of her fears of being *like* the mother: in one sequence, the voice tells of the fear that, like her mother, she will make the wrong decisions and notes that deep down she is as weak and vulnerable as her mother; in another episode, the voice expresses her fears of getting fat and depressed like her mother, of hating her life but not daring to change it; later on again, we hear: "I hate my weaknesses that are those of my mother; but in hating her, I hate myself."

Citron's film thus begins to articulate the dilemma for daughters growing up in patriarchy, positioned as they are to depend on and identify with the mother who, meanwhile, is positioned so as to necessitate engendering her daughter's hatred through the very requirement of separation, individuation, and socialization in an oppressive feminine. Daughters who reject the ideology of this socialization have a particularly difficult time, as these voices in the film show, because they have inevitably modeled themselves on their mothers, only later to realize that this is not how they want to be, or how they want to live.

Occasionally, a different note enters into the narration: that of feeling sympathy for the mother. This note is heard once early on, is eclipsed, and then emerges more forcefully towards the end of the film. The early example shows the daughter's sympathy for the mother's loneliness in her new home, although this is still accompanied by impatience because the mother will not admit her plight (yet the daughter lies in dread of the mother's articulating it because of the demands that would ensue). Later on, a poignant empathy is aroused as the mother sits and talks on the daughter's couch: "I am filled with sadness and love for this woman," the voice says. A little later on, a similar poignancy emerges when the mother gives the daughter some silk pajamas that she has kept since her honeymoon, but which she has long outgrown. The daughter feels the pathos of the mother's situation, but again fears that she too will get fat and be unable to wear the clothes of her young adulthood.

The three dreams that are narrated on this track of the film epitomize the range of attitudes to the mother, and go further in raising the sibling rivalry which is evident in the vérité conversations between two "sisters." The first dream reflects the empathy for the mother that is the least frequent stance, for reasons noted above, while the second two show, first, a mother and a grandmother in collusion to kill the speaker and, second, the speaker and her mother colluding to murder an already sick and dying sister. All three dreams reveal the centrality of the mother for daughters and the pain of sibling rivalry around the mother figure.

The themes that the diarist-daughter(s) articulate(s) are counterpointed, as it were, by the home-movie images that accompany the narrations. Most of these show the little girls with their mother in a variety of situations that demonstrate, first, the mother's constant surveillance of the children; second, her efforts to make them into properly feminine products; and finally, the supposedly happy, ideal nuclear family, which is, of course, completed by the father off frame but in the observer position within the home-movie text, a position that duplicates his "real life" one as off frame to the close mother–daughter inter-relationships – the father does not engage the children's intense emotions.

We see the girls, in slow motion, running in an egg-and-spoon race – a sport suitable for girls; or parading back and forth, back and forth, on the suburban pavement, clearly showing off their new outfits; or busily pushing flower-laden carriages, all dressed up in curls and frills, participating in a local festival; or opening presents at a birthday party and clearly being told to be "grateful" and "happy;" or washing dishes at a young age, being socialized into their domestic role; or having the hair that has become unruly tied firmly back into its barrette to yield a neat, tidy look. These movies, awesomely silent in slow motion, seem to function on their own, without effort, slowly unfolding – uncanny because of their jerky, broken-down movements which expose the shallowness of the attempt to present a perfectly happy, harmonious image, such as that society demands of the nuclear family. They function like the superego to the id that is escaping through the voice-over narrations.

The sibling rivalry, for instance, is completely hidden in the home movies (we see rather the little girls kissing and helping each other), but it becomes clear in the vérité conversations, where, however, it is an underlying tension rather than an explicit antagonism. It emerges in the sisters' discussion about lending money to their mother and also, in a muted fashion, in the salad-making scene. The five vérité conversations, set up as spontaneous "live" interviews and discussions, reflect the discourse of consciousness-raising and political activism. Two main themes run throughout these discussions and monologues. There is first that of the mother's unwelcome invasion of the daughters' privacy (the discussion about the birth of one sister's baby; the talk about the mother opening mail and ransacking drawers and interfering in friendships). The mother is blamed for not accepting her children's separate existences, and for being concerned at how they turned out. Here, her preference for one daughter over the other is seen as a result of the favored daughter being more obedient and tractable; she was thus not so carefully scrutinized and invaded. The second theme is that of the mother's failure to protect her daughters from the abuses that patriarchal fathers can enact on the vulnerable children. This is most evident in the monologue about the daughter's rape by a stepfather – a rape that the mother did not want to hear or do anything about.

Often the discussions are more conscious dramatizations of issues that the diarist narrator raises: perhaps most shocking of all is the way the daughters in the last vérité sequence actually become what they had accused their mother of being – a snooper, a person who did not know boundaries, who invaded privacy. As they pick up one object after another, they cannot contain their surprise that their mother was into this or that; we in turn cannot help but feel that all the fears mentioned by the diarist have materialized in these daughters – they have indeed taken on one of their mother's negative characteristics and, without realizing it, reveal their socialization into adults like the mother.

Citron's film thus reveals from two different standpoints the need for accepting, confronting, and then working through the daughter's anger at the mother: there is, first, the need from the daughter's own position; and second, there is the need arising from the mother's position, i.e. to enable us to *see* the mother.

Although Citron's film does not explicitly articulate the reasons for anger at the mother, it provides the material from which we can draw some conclusions. These have to do with the way both mothers and daughters are positioned in patriarchy; and with the way the father, outside of and observing the intense relating, is idealized. The diarist narrator's ambivalent feelings about her mother in the film arise from her rejection of her socialization and her blaming the mother for it.

The daughter cannot thus speak from the mother's position; in the film, relegated to silence, absence, and marginality, by the daughters as well as by patriarchy, the mother suffers a double negation mandated by patriarchal structures. Her very role as the sole actively parenting figure (her function then being the one setting controls) has inevitably stimulated the child's love–hate feelings. Meanwhile, her role demands that she have no voice, that she be at the service of the nuclear family, abnegating herself. Thus, paradoxically, while literally present and fulfilling enormous demands physically and emotionally, the mother is psychologically *repressed*; qua herself, she is absent to the family and society. The father on the other hand represents the dominant Law and is thus psychoanalytically present, while literally absent. He is subject, in control, and given the voice, in contrast to the silence forced on the mother.

It is this silence that feminists must now seek to redress; Citron's film prepares us for undertaking the task since it forces us to see what *we* have done to the mother, as well as what *patriarchy* has done to her. Some negative responses to the film by feminists only underscore the difficulty we have in seeing how the mother has been positioned in culture. It is unfair to complain about the negative view of the mother in the film when this is a view we have all shared at one time or another, but have preferred to deny or avoid dealing with. And I do not think that the film *itself* takes the position of the critical daughters, just because they are the narrators and speakers: as I tried to show, the position of the mother emerges through her very repression in the discourse of the film, so that by the end the spectator is inevitably on her side. Citron's honesty in exposing our complicity in patriarchal patterns is important in enabling us to move beyond a socialization we could do little about while it was happening to us. We can now look toward explorations of the way the mother has been constructed, and to attempts to give her the voice she has so long been denied.[9]

13 | The woman director in the Third World: Sara Gomez's *One Way or Another* (1974)

For obvious reasons, this book has focused on female representation within capitalist cultures. But as I began to think about the future for the independent feminist film and about the influence on independent filmmaking of contexts for production, exhibition, and distribution of movies in America, it seemed important to look, however briefly and inadequately, at what women directors are able to do in the non-capitalist sphere.[1]

The situation of filmmakers in postrevolutionary Cuba differs from that of directors in America in two important ways, the first, institutional, and the second, ideological. As in most socialist nations, the Cuban film industry is a state institution as is also the film school that prepares future directors for their careers. Whatever the limitations and problems may be in such a situation (and this is not the place to deal with them),[2] Cuban filmmakers are able to experiment with film form and to deal with controversial and serious subjects without having to be concerned about commercial success.[3] On this level, somewhat paradoxically, Cuba's official, state-funded cinema has much in common with the American independent cinema, which, while lacking any official sanction, and obtaining little state funding, shares many of the same aims as the Cuban cinema for a film form that challenges people's beliefs and aims to bring about change.[4]

Second, on the level of ideology, Cuban filmmakers find themselves in a very different situation from their American counterparts. In terms of sex relations, no one is pretending that socialism magically produced female liberation (which was nevertheless idealistically anticipated); the difference lies rather in the attitude of the culture generally toward the patriarchal stances and behavior that remain in the postrevolutionary era. While the women's movement in America has achieved a surprising amount, capitalist commercial structures (movies, television, advertising, journalism, radio, music), while paying lip service to some aspects of female liberation (as we saw for instance in the analysis of *Looking for Mr Goodbar*), still essentially propagate male domination and exploit the female body for their own ends. By contrast, the official stance in Cuba is for total equality between men and women and against exploitation of the female form.

It is this stance that makes the difference, rather than men's actual behavior in the social formation. Indeed, one could argue that Latin American men generally are still embedded in a machismo ideology the proportions of which always went beyond those in North America, while their American analogues have begun to move out of chauvinist positions. It is this fact that makes the critique of machismo in Gomez's film all the more significant. It is a critique begun right after the revolution (for example in Humberto Solas's well-known *Lucia* (1969)) and that is continuing (as for example in Pastor Vegas's recent *Portrait of Teresa* (1979)); the time between these two films in itself exposes the resistance to change in this area, the difficulties of bringing about such change, and the government's determination nevertheless to keep insisting on its importance.

On one level, Gomez's film, *One Way or Another*, is addressed precisely to the complexity of change in the interpersonal, sexual sphere, placed as this is in the context of the (relatively) straightforward process of change in the economic and physical reality. As Julia LeSage notes, the film "examines Cuban revolutionary process from the vantage point of the neighborhood and the domestic sphere."[5] The two levels of change are signaled by using the documentary form to represent external change and the narrative form to represent problems of internal change. The intercutting of the two forms gives the film its power, for the juxtaposition provides a commentary on the capabilities of each cinematic form, as well as on the change that is involved.

The film opens with a sequence showing a worker being investigated in an increasingly heated atmosphere for his absence from work. While the first man, Humberto, is challenged by another, Mario, there is suddenly a cut to shots of buildings being torn down, with music now on the sound track. The camera then cuts to shots of slums contrasted immediately with shots of new buildings. A woman's voice on the track now informs us that the film is about both real people and fictitious ones, and we then have a title telling us that the people we are watching are "real." The narration continues, giving us facts about the new neighborhoods that have been created, but also showing that all the slums have not yet gone. The old capitalist system of poor, marginal people continues beneath the new one, while education is being pushed as the principal tool for bringing about transformation. While the revolution has put the old order aside, we are told that "the culture that lives in the depth of the subconscious can put up strong resistance to social change." It is the marginal sectors resistant to cultural change that the film will study.

These two sections function as the prologue to the film establishing, first, the crucial narrative climax to the fictional part of the film, and second, the

Plate 22 Early on in the film, there are enacted narrative sections. Here Yolanda and Mario share their past experiences with one another. Their narration is intercut with documentary sections relevant to what they are describing and setting their personal experiences in social and historical contexts. The camera focuses on the characters' emotions, while the park setting suggests romance.

documentary level with which the fiction will be intertwined. The narrative portion will be a retelling of the events that lead up to the climax we have just witnessed and an analysis of a developing love affair between Mario, born in a Havana slum, and his middle-class girlfriend, Yolanda. Yolanda has been sent to work as a primary-school teacher in the residential district of Miraflores, constructed by the revolution for the slum inhabitants, and it is here that she has met Mario. Meanwhile, the documentary level will underscore the narrative events, sometimes providing historical background, sometimes simply providing a kind of "evidence" to support narrative dilemmas. Throughout, the emphasis is on sex relations as foreground, but as LeSage has noted,[6] the social and political context for these relations, and the stresses involved, are always emphasized.

For example, after Mario describes his inability to attend school, and his subsequent life on the streets, there is a documentary analysis of life in Cuba under colonialism, when the violence and male chauvinism spawned by colonialism fitted into the existing primitive culture, with its grotesque rituals, representing a social relating based on marginality rather than on integration. It is suggested that Mario's behavior is a result of this colonial heritage.

Yolanda's story differs significantly, largely because she is a woman and because marriage was staked out for her. The marriage broke up when she wouldn't leave school to follow her husband in the army. The situation of women is further documented by a sequence with the mother of one of Yolanda's pupils (we presume this is documentary, but it is unclear) who, left with five children and no male support, simply cannot manage and ends up beating the one child whom she relies on.

Male machismo is stressed in the interactions among men when no women are around: Mario's friend (whom we recognize as the man "on trial" at the start of the film) talks about the woman he is going away with in derogatory, sexual terms, while on a double date, Mario's friend degrades and then ignores the woman he is with because she is not sexy in the right way.

A documentary section illustrates the ambiguity about the position for girls even after the revolution: Yolanda is seen pitying the plight of her female students, who have no future but a miserable marriage, while other teachers talk of the new possibilities for girls in careers like agriculture.

The climax in the Yolanda/Mario relationship happens when Yolanda keeps Mario waiting because of a meeting with teachers. When he yells: "Nobody makes me wait an hour," Yolanda decides to end the relationship. Although he is dejected, Mario perks up when he meets his friend Guillermo and, ignoring Yolanda (she is positioned at the very left of the frame, barely visible, squeezed out, iconographically, as well as psychologically, by the male bonding), he launches into a long discussion.

Again, a documentary section tells us who Guillermo is – a failed boxer turned singer who, through his travels, has acquired some wisdom. At one point he tells Mario that most people are afraid to leave what they know. "It takes courage to cut loose," he says. This is immediately followed by a documentary section showing buildings being torn down and giving us statistics about the families who had lived in the slums.

In a touching fictional scene, Yolanda shows Mario how different he is with his buddies, when he adopts a swaggering, bombastic manner. Mario appears to be taking her criticism in, but he cannot change all at once. In the following scene, which is Humberto's trial for being away from work, Mario is finally brought to tell the truth, namely that, far from visiting a sick mother, Humberto was shacked up with a woman. Afterwards, Mario is disgusted with himself for "acting like a woman" and for "betraying the male loyalty codes." But his friend argues that these codes are now out of date – that building a new society is what they should be doing, not making others do one's work while one slacks off. The men are seen eagerly debating the rights and wrongs of the case, while, on the other side of a wire fence, we see Yolanda walking by. Mario turns, and watches her, but it is not clear whether they will stay together, whether or not Mario can change so as to keep her. It is an appropriately ambiguous ending, leaving the male spectator without any firm resolution which might enable him simply to put the film out of his mind.

But more than the ending is involved in the overall impact of the film, which concerns the interesting use of both documentary and fiction. Indeed, the film raises many of the issues about the relative merits of documentary realism and of narrative fiction in the cinema that were discussed in chapter 10. The problem of personal and social change in a socialist society is extended to a reflection on the most effective cinematic strategies for facilitating acceptance of change in *both* levels. For if men resisted change in sexual relations, obviously, the ruling classes in Cuba resisted change in the economic/physical sphere.

On the level of cinematic strategy, the film seems to be asking two important and inter-related questions. First, how effective is the traditional, propagandist documentary, which works through voice-over narration, shocking footage, and juxtaposition of shots so as to make moral points persuading the spectator to the film's point of view? And second, how effective is the narrative fiction form for bringing about personal change, or for exposing complex issues about sex relations? These are questions that emerge simply through the juxtaposition of what are essentially two separate films, strategically, although they are connected thematically through the concept of change and through the way in which the documentary shots (for example, those of buildings being torn down) come to function as a metaphor for the "tearing down" of the equally horrendous "remains" of the patriarchal constructions of both sexes.

The juxtaposition of the two cinematic strategies forces the spectator to become aware of his/her need for narrative. For, as one watches, one becomes impatient with the documentary sections; one always wants to get back to the story. The disruption caused by the jarring cuts to the documentary film makes us realize a certain seductive power even of a narrative as "realistic" and unsensational as is this one. This question of the power of the narrative film preoccupies Cuban filmmakers and critics because of the continued public interest in the classical Hollywood cinema. According to Enrique Colina, 50 per cent of the films shown in Cuba every year are "capitalist" entertainment films,[7] playing to packed audiences. What is it about the kind of imaginary world that dominant cinema projects that so attracts people worldwide? What basic need is being tapped? One of these needs is, obviously, for the sheer pleasure that the narrative process itself affords, which I discussed in chapter 10. But the question that then emerges (and it is one, as we've seen, that American independent filmmakers are currently facing), has to do with the possibility of narrative not only to entertain but to "teach" in a way that challenges rather than simply confirms (as do Hollywood films) existing ideology.

In other words, do we have to believe, with Plato, that all poetry is corrupting, because able to deal only with things at such a far remove, and must be banned? Or was Sidney (writing in Elizabethan England) correct in seeing poetry as the best moral teacher because able to "sweeten" its lessons through the pleasure it afforded at the same time?

It seems to me that Sara Gomez is attempting in *One Way or Another* to follow

Philip Sidney and to give us our moral lesson in a pleasing way. But she is further exposing the very mechanisms through which we find the message "pleasurable," so that we are being taught at the same time about the cinematic apparatus itself. The jumps away from the narrative are jarring because they force us out of the realm of the imaginary and into the symbolic sphere. We must listen to arguments, statistics, politics; we must think about people in abstract, global terms as against the easy, pleasurable identification with a man or a woman like ourselves. The shift in modes makes us aware of our "addiction" to narrative; it makes us think about that addiction, and about our resistance to the more difficult, cognitive mode.

At the same time, the juxtaposition of styles makes us aware also of the highly "constructed" representations in the *documentary* form. Each cinematic form, that is, makes us aware of the construction of the *other*. While we are in one form, we do not particularly notice that it is "constructed," simply because of the persuasive power of the cinematic apparatus itself. But the change from one form to the other reveals the fact that all is being made for us, it is not simply and naturally "there."

It is at this point that the documentary footage may begin to assume its metaphorical dimension and to emphasize the film's basic theme, which is that our ways of behaving sexually are so deeply embedded that it takes enormous power, energy, and commitment (analogous to what is needed to tear down buildings and to create enough new, clean, orderly houses and parks for everyone) to alter our relations with the other sex. In other words, were this just a narrative film about Yolanda and Mario, we may leave the theatre having been entertained and having had some pleasure, but not changed *internally*. A male spectator would have identified with Mario's struggle while the narrative went on, and have had to recognize some parts of himself that usually go unnoticed, but with the film's end (even though it actually has no closure) he would leave the cinema forgetting the relationship between what he had seen and his daily behavior. It is possible, however, that with the documentary analogy to a more readily perceptible kind of change, the need for inner change has been more firmly anchored in the spectator's mind.

14 | The future of the independent feminist film: strategies of production, exhibition, and distribution in the USA

We have seen that the Cuban filmmaker faces a number of complicated dilemmas about the most effective cinematic strategies for bringing about needed social and psychological change, but s/he has a relatively easy situation in terms of production, exhibition, and distribution of works when compared to the American independent director. While Cuban audiences still enjoy commercial Hollywood films, they evidently have a sophisticated critical awareness about them, and they are able to appreciate the documentary and experimental films that Cuban directors have been exhibiting.[1] The Cuban filmmaker benefits (again relatively) from political goals generally agreed upon by both the government and the people. Although evidently a number of Cubans have not yet accepted the revolution psychologically or politically, the dominant cultural stance is that the revolution was a good thing and that Cubans should continually work to implement its ideals, no matter what the odds against it may be.[2]

The American independent filmmaker who is seeking to bring about change finds him/herself in quite another situation. With the experience of ten years or so behind us, feminist directors now need to pay attention specifically to issues of production, exhibition, and distribution which may be affecting film practice in ways we are not aware of. The problem is that the debate that I traced in chapter 10 has taken place mainly on an abstract, theoretical level, divorced from the concrete situation of production, exhibition, and reception. We have been so concerned with figuring out the "correct" theoretical position, the "correct" strategies *theoretically*, that we forgot to pay attention, first, to the way subjects "receive" (read) films; and second, to the contexts of production and reception, particularly as these affect what films can be made and *how* films are read.[3]

That criticism is finally turning to this area may be seen from some recent articles in *Screen* and elsewhere,[4] and from the publication of the book by

MacPherson and Willemen on British independence, which looks back at the 1930s in order to discover how production, exhibition, and distribution practices shaped, or influenced, certain documentary forms.[5] Although it is hard to grasp the implications of practices as one is living with them, MacPherson and Willemen's book shows the importance of attempting to understand the ways in which *apparently* independent practice is in fact formed by the social institutions in which it is inevitably embedded. Totally independent cinematic practice is a utopian myth.

Let me substantiate this last statement by looking briefly at some of the contradictions which have dominated alternate practices of all kinds during the very years when critics have been debating cinematic strategy.

(1) Filmmakers have had to rely for funding on the very system they oppose.
(2) In the case of anti-illusionist films, directors have been using cinematic strategies that are difficult for the majority of people, who are raised on narrative and commercial films.
(3) Having made the films, directors have not had any mechanism for the distribution and exhibition of their films on a large scale. (Showings have been by necessity limited to small art cinemas in a few large cities and to college campuses. It is important to note that the situation is rather different, and slightly better, in Europe.)
(4) The culminating contradiction is that filmmakers whose whole purpose was to change people's ways of seeing, believing, and behaving have only been able to reach an audience already committed to their values.

Thus, critics (increasingly, it is hoped, with independent filmmakers) need to discuss cinematic strategies not only in terms of the most correct theory, but also in relation to the contradictions outlined above. We have to re-examine together (as a unit, that is) our theory, our cinematic strategies, and the strategies of reception as they affect the way a film is "read." But even before doing this, we need to look carefully at the economic base for film production and at the possible influence that funding agencies have had on the very shape of alternate practice.

Much of the recent independent American filmmaking was made possible by the new government-funding agencies (nationally, the National Endowment for the Humanities and the National Endowment for the Arts; locally, various state agencies) and by the interest that private funding agencies began to show in film projects in the 1970s. But the question is: to what extent did funding sources condition the shape of the films produced? To what extent, that is, did funding agencies refuse projects that did not fit their ideologies or their notions of cinematic practice? And how far did filmmakers begin to gear their cinematic strategies to pleasing funding agencies, once they realized the kinds of film that did receive money?

A full study along these lines would reveal the degree to which the history of independent cinema, as we can now reconstruct it, is itself a construction of funding agencies. We would see how the history of independent cinema, as of commercial cinema, is governed by the economic relations in which the practices are embedded. The study would no doubt reveal a host of projects reflecting various kinds of innovation that did not get funded and that therefore never materialized. Other films may be discovered that were indeed made through independent means but which never got seen for the same reasons that they were not funded in the first place. For at least in America the films that were officially funded were also the ones that were shown in film festivals, that won awards, and that reached the attention of librarians who would then buy the films, providing them with a college or community audience. (A cross-cultural study would be very useful in illuminating particular American political and cultural constraints by contrast with the different European situations. The differences in alternate cinematic practice between Europe and America would in part be explained by the different cultural discourses and operations.)

If a study such as the one outlined would tell us a lot about how "history" gets made, it would also reveal the way in which alternate practice is never independent of the society in which it is embedded. Alternate cinema, that is, cannot stand outside of the dominant discourses that construct it through its very position in opposition to mainstream cinema. We can begin to see that alternate practices are to an extent bound by the very signifying practices they aim to subvert. Perhaps it is necessary for feminist film practices to move through a series of stages analogous to those that, according to Franz Fanon, primitive cultures have to move through in relation to colonialism: we may currently be at the stage where the only strategies available to us are those conditioned by being in opposition to dominant ones. We need to think about how to move beyond merely reversing what is established to creating truly alternative films, but this involves the basic problems of how to move beyond discourses that are dominant. As I mentioned earlier, it may well be that we can only free ourselves by moving *through* dominant discourse.

Once we understand the situation we are in, it is possible to phrase, and then choose among, a number of alternatives in relation, first, to producing films and, second, to the exhibition and reception of independent films. In terms of the first, filmmakers will have to choose between (a) continuing to make the films they want to, experimenting with theory and the cinematic apparatus, but raising their own money and reaching only a small, already committed audience; (b) obtaining government or private corporation funding and paying a certain cost in compromising on form and content – although there is often more latitude than might be expected and there *are* some non-Establishment backers interested in unconventional texts; and (c) moving into dominant cinema practice and waging the struggle there; in this case, there are real dangers of co-optation or of a far higher degree of compromise on ideology and form than in the other options (viz. Claudia Weill, Lina Wertmuller, Gillian Armstrong).

All three alternatives are challenging for the filmmakers in requiring close attention to the structuring by dominant discourses: people will have to examine ways to work with available discourses without being overwhelmed by them. It is through precisely this kind of tension, this sort of enlightened struggle, that a dent in dominant discourse can be made, which can begin to alter the modes through which we apprehend reality.

The second issue, about strategies for reception and exhibition, is necessarily linked to questions about the cinematic strategies we use. Those of us who teach, for example, are well aware of the difficulties that the avant-garde theory films pose for an average student audience. A great deal of work is demanded of the spectator, and it is work of a very special kind. A high level of sophistication, both about cinema and about certain philosophical and other matters, is needed in order to grasp what is going on in many of the films. For people brought up on Hollywood, totally new film-viewing habits are required, especially in relation to pleasure.

This pleasure is, as we know, linked to a particular kind of narrative structure that binds the spectator to the screen, mainly through the family romance and recognition/identification mechanisms, and that keeps us fixed in the established positions in patriarchal culture. Many of the new films quite deliberately (as we saw in chapter 1) deny people the pleasure they are used to. We need now to think whether it would be possible to use a narrative form that is pleasurable and that does not produce the retrogressive effects of the commercial cinema, or whether we can educate people to like the pleasure of learning (i.e. a cognitive process) as against the pleasure of recognition/identification (i.e. an emotional process).[6]

In order to answer these questions adequately, we need to know more about how change takes place: does it happen through consciousness (including the unconscious), through example (imitation of models), or through working on people's emotions? We also need to know more about how people "read" films, in the concrete as against theoretically. Helpful here, for instance, would be information about where both realist and theory films have been shown and with what results. In which contexts did the theory films seem to work? How were the realist films "read" in different contexts?[7] Films receive quite different responses in, for example, a New York Film Festival showing, a classroom, and a Labor Hall. What precisely are these differences? How can we account for them?[8]

In terms of strategies for reception of independent films, we need to think about new viewing contexts which would produce better results, particularly with the theory films. Many directors of theory films have been experimenting with viewings prepared for by notes explaining something about the film's aims and intellectual context and followed by discussion with the director in the viewing hall.[9] Another idea is to make films for specifically targeted audiences so that the filmmakers and spectators share a common framework of concerns and the audience can thus immediately relate to the film's intervention in a specific area.[10] This would be useful for both theory and realist films; for perhaps the most functional use of realism is around specific political actions at a specific historical moment (e.g. a strike, abortion, childcare), when immediate and accessible information is needed to develop support and to clarify strategies.

The larger problem of exhibiting independent films would remain even were we able to improve the situation of reaching the small, specialized audiences we already have, or to find ways to create more such audiences. We will never have in America the kind of access to mass audiences that ideally we would desire. As I noted, the situation is slightly better in Europe, where television has become a viable outlet for radical films of all kinds (especially in Germany and Britain[11]). And some of the independent films get theatrical release in a manner that is rare here.[12] Obviously, the way dominant discourses function varies from culture to culture, and a look at these variations might tell us a lot about America and about what strategies might work to achieve greater access to large audiences without severely compromising what we want to say and how we want to say it.

It is essential for both feminist films theorists and feminist filmmakers to focus on these central questions if we are to move beyond the impasse that I think we have reached after ten years of intensive, varied, and exciting work. We must begin to create institutions in which feminist theorists and filmmakers can work together for the benefit of both groups. As I've shown, at least in Britain an apparently beneficial collaboration between filmmakers and theorists has resulted in a group of interesting and innovative films. Such a collaboration is just beginning over here (for example, Michelle Citron's *Daughter-Rite*, analyzed in chapter 12, which shows the influence of the new theories on her filmmaking practice in her attempt to bridge the gap between the early realist vérité films and the new anti-illusionist ones). Such collaboration will produce interesting work in the near future if we can work together in developing new strategies for production, exhibition, and reception. It is also necessary, however, to develop theories about how to break through dominant discourses in patriarchy. I will deal briefly with this issue in the following, and concluding, chapter.

15 | Conclusion: Motherhood and patriarchal discourse

In this second half of the book, we have looked at the various ways in which women directors in Europe, America, and the Third World have responded to the Hollywood appropriation of the female image and begun to explore the possibilities for giving women the voice and status as subject. The constant underlying issue in the new films by women has been that of knowing what the feminine might be outside of patriarchal constructs. Is it enough simply to "give women the voice," if women can only speak from a position already defined by patriarchy? If male discourse is monolithic and all-controlling, how can women ever insert another "reality" into it? From what place would women come to know any other "reality?"

We have looked at the different theoretical positions taken by new women directors in relation to these questions; some women believe that by simply speaking our experiences and showing our everyday images we can bring about change; others think that all we can do is to demonstrate our oppressive placing in art and in culture, and to raise questions about the repression of the feminine outside of patriarchal images.

Here I want briefly to develop a position that lies somewhere in between these two extremes and that was raised in the discussion of the films about mothering in chapter 12. Using different theoretical approaches, various writers (including Dorothy Dinnerstein, Adrienne Rich, Julia Kristeva, Laura Mulvey, and Nancy Chodorow) have suggested that we go back to the basic mother–child relationship to discover why the feminine has been repressed, why patriarchy seeks to control women. In some ways, the boy child can never recover from the fact of having been mothered and totally dependent on a figure who is, first, castrated, and second, possesses a genital organ (the vagina) that seems sinister to him. In addition, the boy child is threatened by knowing that his small genital organ could never satisfy the mother. Women theorists have argued that in various ways some or all of these factors have contributed to the patriarchal need to position women so that the threat they offer is mitigated.

But the girl child's experience with mothering is quite different, as I noted in chapter 12. The fact that the differences have not been dealt with adequately in psychoanalytic theory is part of the perpetuation of the repression of the feminine, as is also the fact that psychoanalysis has omitted looking at the mother from her position. Seeking to correct the eliding of different gender experiences in being mothered, Nancy Chodorow has perhaps most clearly demonstrated that the girl's relationship with her mother remains forever unresolved, incomplete. In heterosexuality, she is forced to turn away from her primary love object, and is destined never to return to it, while the boy, through marrying someone like his mother, can regain his original plenitude in another form. The girl must transfer her need for love to her father, whom, as Chodorow shows, never completely satisfies it.[1]

Laura Mulvey and Peter Wollen sought to correct the repression of the mother in patriarchal culture by confronting it directly in their *Riddles of the Sphinx*, as we saw in chapter 12. The film argued that women "live in a society ruled by the father, in which the place of the mother is repressed. Motherhood, and how to live it or not to live it, lies at the root of the dilemma."[2] In an interview, Mulvey noted the influence of psychoanalysis on her conception of the mother–child exchange ("the identification between the two, and the implications that has for narcissism and recognition of the self in the 'other' "), but she went on to say that this is an area rarely read from the mother's point of view.[3]

Meanwhile, the directors of *Sigmund Freud's Dora*, as we saw in chapter 11, foreground the way psychoanalysis omits the mother. The daughter's comments (in the letters read by the mother at the end) stress that Freud dismisses Dora's mother in his case history instead of talking about her as "the site of the intersection of many representations" (of which the historical mother is just one). The omission was not merely an oversight, but, given Freud's system, a necessity.[4]

But both Laura Mulvey and Julia Kristeva have shown, in different ways, that this omission of the mother provides some hope since it shows that patriarchal culture is not monolithic, not cleanly sealed. There are gaps through which women can begin to ask questions and introduce change. Motherhood becomes one place from which to begin to reformulate our position as women just because patriarchy has not dealt with it theoretically or in the social realm (i.e. by providing free childcare, free abortions, maternal leave, after-school child programs, etc.). Motherhood has been repressed on all levels except that of hypostatization, romanticization, and idealization.[5] Yet women have been struggling with lives as mothers – silently, quietly, often in agony, often in bliss, but always on the periphery of a society that tries to make us all (men and women) forget our mothers.

But what impresses me is that Motherhood, and the fact that we are all mothered, will not be repressed; or, if the attempt is made, there will be effects signaling "the return of the repressed." The entire construction of woman in patriarchy as a "lack" could be viewed as emerging from the need to repress mothering and the painful memory traces it has left in the man. The phallus as signified can only be set in motion given the Other with a lack, and this has resulted in the male focus on castration. But is it possible that this focus was designed to mask the even greater threat that mothering poses? The notion of woman as castrated that hides the fear of the mother has led me to focus, first, on the repression of mothering in one of the Hollywood films (*Blonde Venus*), and in the second half of the book, on recent women's films that raise the whole issue of how the mother is constructed in patriarchy. Here I want briefly to lay out the reasons why a focus on Motherhood is important if women are to move forward.

Using some traditional Freudian concepts, both Dorothy Dinnerstein and Adrienne Rich have extended Karen Horney's analysis of the dread of woman generally to a dread of the mother specifically. Rich, for instance, notes that "the ancient, continuing envy, awe and dread of the male for the female capacity to create life has repeatedly taken the form of hatred for every other female aspect of creativity." Rich notes how fear of the mother gets displaced to a kind of revenge for evoking fear.[6] Dinnerstein meanwhile develops ideas from Melanie Klein and Simone de Beauvoir to show first the deep ambivalence that surrounds the figure of the mother, split as she is into the "good" object and the "bad" object;[7] and second, that the mother is disparaged by association with non-human, natural, and supernatural forces.[8] We can conclude that the intense feelings aroused by early experience with the female parent cause patriarchy to repress the mother and to emphasize rather woman's lack.

If we look from the position of women, however, need this lack have the dire implications that patriarchy insists on? The focus on woman as (simply) sex object or (more complexly) as fetishized (narcissistic male desire), which we have been tracing through Hollywood films, may be part of the apparatus that represses mothering. The insistence on rigidly defined sex roles, and the dominance–submission, voyeurism–fetishism mechanisms, may be constructed to this end.

In foregrounding the issue of mothering in this way, one is not necessarily falling into the trap of essentialism. First, I am not denying that Motherhood has been constructed in patriarchy by its very place as repressed; nor, second, am I saying that women are inherently mothers; nor, third, that the only ideal relationship that can express female specificity is mothering. I am saying, rather, that Motherhood is one of the areas that has been left vague, allowing us to reformulate the position as given, rather than discovering a specificity outside the system we are in. It is a place to start rethinking sex difference, not an end.

Let me review briefly some of the main ways in which Motherhood can be regarded within psychoanalysis. First, and most conservatively, Motherhood has been analyzed as an essentially narcissistic relationship, and as involved with the problem of castration. In this way, it parallels male fetishism; just as men fetishize women in order to reduce their threat (finding themselves in the Other), so women "fetishize" the child, looking in the child for the phallus to "make up" for castration. In her re-reading of the classic Freudian position, Kristeva calls this the "paternal symbolic" axis of mothering:

> The discourse of analysis proves that the desire for motherhood is without fail a desire to bear a child of the father (a child of her own father) who, as a result, is often assimilated to the baby itself and thus returned to its place as *devalorized man*, summoned only to accomplish his function, which is to originate and justify reproductive desire.[9]

Second, Motherhood can be seen as narcissistic, not in the sense of finding the phallus in the child, but of finding *oneself* in the child (this parallels male fetishizing of women in another way); women here do not relate to the child as Other, but as an extension of their own egos. Third, and most radically (but this is also the position that can lead to essentialism), one could argue that since the Law represses mothering, a gap is left through which it may be possible to subvert patriarchy.

This latter position reflects Kristeva's second possibility for Motherhood, namely what she calls "the non-symbolic, non-paternal causality," reflecting a "pre-linguistic, unrepresentable memory" that is unable to be verbalized, an "excursion to the limits of primal repression."[10] Kristeva interestingly goes on to speak of mothering as the only way for "reunion of a woman-mother with the body of *her* mother." For Kristeva, the mother's body is that toward which all women aspire, just because it lacks a penis; here women actualize "the homosexual facet of motherhood" where woman is "closer to her instinctual memory, more open to her own psychosis, and consequently, more negatory of the social, symbolic bond."[11] In Motherhood, then, a woman becomes her mother, in total identification. Kristeva here finds a position that compensates for what heterosexuality cannot do, i.e. offer (as it does for men) a refusion with the mother.

There are unfortunately two problems with these last (and most hopeful) positions: the first is the danger of essentialism, while the second is the problem of how to *express* Motherhood in a symbolic world that represses it. As Laura Mulvey puts it, women are faced with an impossible dilemma: to remain in illusory unity with the child in the realm of the imaginary (to hold onto this realm), or to enter the symbolic where mothering cannot be "spoken," cannot "represent a position of power."[12] For Kristeva, it seems, since the homosexual facet of mothering is "a whirl of words, a complete absence of meaning and seeing, feeling, displacement, rhythm, sound and fantasied clinging to the maternal body as a screen against the plunge,"[13] the only resistance is silence.

But isn't this one of those places where a rigid adherence to the theoretical formulations about essentialism and about the split between the imaginary and the symbolic betrays the limitations of theoretical formulations? In a recent essay, Mary Ann Doane demonstrates the need (in feminist film practice and theory) to move beyond the impasse caused by the opposition between essentialism and anti-essentialism. The goal of essentialist feminist film practice, Doane notes, is "the production of images which provide a pure reflection of the real woman, thus returning the real female body to the woman as her rightful property."[14] This position assumes that the body is "accessible to a transparent cinematic discourse," as if signification could be outside of the psychic. In pointing out the error of the position, anti-essentialists show how it "retains patriarchy's strongest rationalization of itself," assuming an inevitable alliance between "feminine essence" and "the natural, the given, or precisely what is outside the range of political action, and thus not amenable to change."[15]

Yet the danger of this anti-essentialist position, in turn, is the absolute exclusion of the female body, "the refusal of any attempt to figure or represent that body." Both positions then, Doane argues, deny "the necessity of posing a complex relation between the body and the psychic" and reveal the need for "a syntax which constitutes the female body as a term."[16] Recent theoretical writings about Motherhood (especially those from France) and some feminist avant-garde films have begun to develop such a new syntax[17]; while, as we have seen, some American scholars (like Nancy Chodorow and Dorothy Dinnerstein), using more traditional Freudian concepts, have begun to "speak" a discourse about mothering, as it were, "through" patriarchal discourse (i.e. they remain within psychoanalysis while offering new insights about the position of the mother, and about the girl's Oedipal cycle[18]).

From a sociological perspective, we are, in addition, living in a period when mothers increasingly reside alone with their children, offering the possibility for new psychic patterns to emerge; fathers are increasingly becoming involved with child-rearing, and also living alone with their children. Freud's own kind of science (which involved studying the people brought up in strict Victorian, bourgeois households) applied rigorously to people today results in very different conclusions. Single mothers are forced to make themselves subject in relation to their children; they are forced to invent new symbolic roles, which combine positions previously assigned to fathers with traditional female ones. The child cannot position the mother as object to the Law of the Father, since in single-parent households, *her* desire sets things in motion.

A methodology is often not *per se* either revolutionary or reactionary, but open to appropriation for a variety of usages. At this point, feminists may have to use psychoanalysis, but in a manner opposite to the traditional one. Other kinds of psychic processes obviously can exist and may stand as models for when we have worked our way through the morass that confronts us as people having grown up in western capitalist culture. Julia Kristeva, for example, suggests that desire functions in a very different manner in China, and urges us to explore Chinese culture, from a very careful psychoanalytic point of view, to see what is possible. She says that she did not get the impression "that reproductive and symbolic representations were determined by what we, in the West, call the 'phallic principle.'" Although Kristeva later on warns about the danger of equating the problems of the Chinese with our own, she nevertheless sees their situation as a starting point for a critique of "a metaphysical tradition and a mode of production which have functioned in this part of the world because of the complicity of our language and our dead silence."[19]

Many of the mechanisms we have found in Hollywood films which echo deeply embedded myths in western capitalist culture are thus not inviolable, eternal, unchanging, or inherently necessary. They reflect rather the unconscious of patriarchy, including a fear of the pre-Oedipal plenitude with the mother. The domination of women by the male gaze is part of patriarchal strategy to contain the threat that the mother embodies, and to control the positive and negative impulses that memory traces of being mothered have left in the male unconscious. Women, in turn, have learned to associate their sexuality with domination by the male gaze, a position involving a degree of masochism in finding their objectification erotic. We have participated in, and perpetuated, our domination by following the pleasure principle, which leaves us no options given our positioning.

Everything, thus, revolves around the issue of pleasure, and it is here that patriarchal repression has been most negative. For patriarchal structures have been designed to make us forget the mutual, pleasurable bonding that we all, male and female, enjoyed with our mothers. Some recent experimental (as against psychoanalytic) studies have shown that the gaze is first set in motion in the mother–child relationship.[20] But this is a *mutual* gazing, rather than the subject–object kind that reduces one of the parties to the place of submission. Patriarchy has worked hard to prevent the eruption of a (mythically) feared return of the matriarchy which might take place were the close mother–child bonding to return to dominance, or allowed to stand in place of the Law of the Father.

What I have been trying to show here is that while female sexuality has, perhaps inevitably, become enmeshed in the symbolic, this is not totally true for Motherhood. Female sexuality has been taken over by the male gaze, and, in addition, the domination–submission modes may be an inherent component of eroticism for both sexes in western capitalist culture. Because of patriarchy's intricate involvement in heterosexuality, its discourse has been able to control female sexuality, including lesbian relations.[21] But while Motherhood has of course been annexed by the symbolic, Kristeva and others have shown that some part remains unviolated, unable to be penetrated by patriarchy. This is because, unlike in the realm of sexuality, some part of Motherhood lies outside of patriarchal concerns, networks, economy. It is this part that eludes control. The extremity of patriarchal domination of female sexuality may be a reaction to helplessness in the face of the threat that Motherhood represents.

This is by no means to argue that return to a matriarchy would be either possible or desirable. What rather has to happen is that we move beyond long-held cultural and linguistic patterns of oppositions: male/female (as these terms currently signify); dominant/submissive; active/passive; nature/civilization; order/chaos; matriarchal/patriarchal. If rigidly defined sex differences have been constructed around fear of the Other, we need to think about ways of transcending a polarity that has only brought us all pain.[22]

Notes

Introduction

1 See the discussion of Foucault's *Archeology of Knowledge* in Frank Lentricchia (1980) *After the New Criticism*, Chicago, The University of Chicago Press, and London, The Athlone Press (hardback) and Methuen (paperback), pp. 190–5.

2 Throughout this book I am using the word "essentialism" as it has been used by feminists and others, i.e. as a theory that posits an *essence* that is uniquely feminine, somehow exists outside of dominant culture, and is largely biological.

3 For a short, clear discussion of this evolution, see Christine Gledhill (1978) "Recent developments in feminist film criticism," *Quarterly Review of Film Studies*, Vol. 3, No. 4, pp. 469–73.

4 E. Ann Kaplan (1980) "Integrating Marxist and psychoanalytical approaches in feminist film criticism," *Millenium Film Journal*, No. 6, pp. 8–17.

5 British feminist film critics (Claire Johnston and Pam Cook especially) first articulated this notion, but it has been presented most thoroughly perhaps in Judith Mayne (1981) "The woman at the keyhole: women's cinema and feminist criticism," *New German Critique*, No. 23, pp. 27–43.

6 Molly Haskell (1973) *From Reverence to Rape: the Treatment of Women in the Movies*, New York, Holt, Rinehart & Winston.

7 Jacqueline Rose (1978) "'Dora' – fragment of an analysis," *m/f*, No. 2, pp. 5–21.

8 Julia Kristeva (1980) "Motherhood according to Bellini," trans. Thomas Gora, Alice Jardine, and Leon S. Roudiez, in Leon S. Roudiez (ed.) *Desire in Language: A Semiotic Approach to Literature and Art*, New York, Columbia University Press, p. 238.

9 ibid., p. 239.

10 Haskell, *From Reverence to Rape*.

11 *Camera Obscura* editors (1976) "Yvonne Rainer: interview," *Camera Obscura*, No. 1, pp. 5–96.

1 Is the gaze male?

1 See Kate Millett (1970) *Sexual Politics*, New York, Doubleday; Thomas B. Hess and Linda Nochlin (eds) (1972) *Woman as Sex Object: Studies in Erotic Art, 1730–1970*, New York, Newsweek; Molly Haskell (1973) *From Reverence to Rape: The Treatment of Women in the Movies*, New York, Holt, Rinehart & Winston; *Screen Education*,

throughout the 1970s. See Lucy Arbuthnot (1982) "Main trends in feminist criticism: film, literature, art history – the decade of the '70's," unpublished dissertation, New York University, for a summary of early developments across the arts.

2 This argument is inserted by a figure, Talking Lips, at the start of the film *Sigmund Freud's Dora* (Anthony McCall, Andrew Tyndall, Claire Pajaczkowska, Jane Weinstock). "Psychoanalysis," the figure says, "may be seen as a discourse shot through with bourgeois ideology, functioning almost as an ideological state apparatus," with its focus on the individual, "outside of real history and real struggle." This is not necessarily the position that the film itself takes up. For analysis, see chapter 10.

3 Peter Brooks (1976) *The Melodramatic Imagination*, New Haven and London, Yale University Press, p. 17.

4 ibid., p. 15.

5 ibid., p. 201.

6 Laura Mulvey (1976–7) "Notes on Sirk and melodrama," *Movie*, Nos 25–6, p. 54.

7 Freud's work is, of course, central to any discussion of sadism and masochism, especially his "Beyond the pleasure principle," *Standard Edition*, Vol. 17, pp. 3–44, "A child is being beaten," *Standard Edition*, Vol. 17, pp. 175–204, and "The economic problem in masochism," *Standard Edition*, Vol. 19, pp. 157 ff. Since I wrote this, the issues have been taken up in Kaja Silverman (1981) "Masochism and subjectivity," *Framework*, No. 12, pp. 2–9, and (in terms of case histories) in Joel Kovel (1981) *The Age of Desire: Reflections of a Radical Psychoanalyst*, New York, Pantheon.

8 Nancy Friday (1974) *My Secret Garden: Women's Sexual Fantasies*, New York, Pocket Books, pp. 100–9.

9 ibid., pp. 80–90. There is obviously a problem with assuming that to be in the dominant position is to be in the "male" position; when critics talk in this way, it seems to me that they are using the term metaphorically (i.e. in this culture, the dominant position has been associated with the male gender). Clearly, in any new construction of society, gender connotations would be fundamentally changed to avoid any such identifications.

10 Unpublished transcript of a discussion, organized by Julia LeSage, at the Conference on Feminist Film Criticism, Northwestern University, Nov. 1980. See also, for discussion of dominance–submission patterns, Pat Califa (1981) "Feminism and sadomasochism," *Heresies*, Vol. 3, No. 4, pp. 30–4, and Robert Stoller (1975) *Perversions: The Erotic Form of Hatred*, New York, Pantheon.

11 Since I wrote this, the whole issue of sadomasochism has exploded in feminist circles; Pat Califa's article (1979) "Unraveling the sexual fringe: a secret side of lesbian sexuality," *The Advocate*, 27 Dec., pp. 19–23, had inserted a position that was highly controversial, and increasing tension over women's sexual choices finally culminated in the heated debate about the Barnard Women Scholars Conference on Sexuality in April 1982. The resulting booklet, *Diary of a Conference on Sexuality*, New York, Faculty Press, 1982, describes the debates about sexuality that took place among the co-ordinators, and in the process many crucial issues are raised.

12 Nancy Friday (1980) *Men in Love*, New York, Dell Publishing.

13 Claude Lévi-Strauss (1969) *The Elementary Structures of Kinship*, London, Eyre & Spottiswoode.

14 Kaja Silverman's article ("Masochism and subjectivity") is important in underscoring some of Freud's observations about masochism and sadism. She stresses that both male and female subjects are attracted to passivity and masochism, to

negativity and loss. It is this lure toward what has been defined as the "feminine" position that male subjects must resist and repress, since to recognize it would be to admit insufficiency, castration.

15 See Mary Ann Doane, "The woman's film: possession and address," paper delivered at the Conference on Cinema History, Asilomar, Monterey, May 1981, pp. 3–8, forthcoming in P. Mellencamp, L. Williams, and M. A. Doane (eds) *Re-Visions: Feminist Essays in Film Analysis*, Los Angeles, American Film Institute.

16 ibid., p. 17.

17 Laura Mulvey (1975) "Visual pleasure and narrative cinema," *Screen*, Vol. 16, No. 3, pp. 12–13.

18 ibid., pp. 6–18.

19 Karen Horney (1932) "The dread of woman," reprinted in Harold Kelman (ed.) (1967) *Feminine Psychology*, New York, Norton, p. 134.

20 ibid., p. 136.

21 For a useful discussion of fetishism, see Otto Fenichel (1945) *The Psychoanalytic Theory of Neurosis*, New York, Norton, pp. 341–5.

22 Mulvey, "Visual pleasure," p. 14.

23 ibid.

24 Claire Johnston (1973) "Woman's cinema as counter-cinema," in Claire Johnston (ed.) *Notes on Women's Cinema*, London, Society for Education in Film and Television, p. 26.

25 For a full discussion of this, see chapter 9.

26 This has been evident in feminist film sessions at conferences, but was particularly clear at the Lolita Rodgers Memorial Conference on Feminist Film Criticism, held at Northwestern University, Nov. 1980. For a report of some differences, see Barbara Klinger (1981) "Conference report," *Camera Obscura*, No. 7, pp. 137–43.

27 In "Women and film: a discussion of feminist aesthetics," *New German Critique*, No. 13 (1978), p. 93.

28 ibid., p. 87.

29 Judith Mayne (1981) "The woman at the keyhole: women's cinema and feminist criticism," *New German Critique*, No. 23, pp. 27–43.

30 Lucy Arbuthnot and Gail Seneca, "Pre-text and text in *Gentlemen Prefer Blondes*," paper delivered at the Conference on Feminist Film Criticism, Northwestern University, Nov. 1980, and published in *Film Reader*, No. 5 (1982), p. 14.

31 See Maureen Turim (1979) "Gentlemen consume blondes," *Wide Angle*, Vol. 1, No. 1, pp. 52–9. Carol Rowe also (if somewhat mockingly) shows Monroe's phallicism in her film *Grand Delusion* (1977).

32 Julia Kristeva (1980) "Woman can never be defined," trans. of "La Femme, ce n'est jamais ça" by Marilyn A. August, in Isabelle de Courtivron and Elaine Marks (eds) *New French Feminisms*, Amherst, Mass., University of Massachusetts Press, pp. 137–8.

33 Judith Barry and Sandy Flitterman (1980) "Textual strategies: the politics of art-making," *Screen*, Vol. 21, No. 2, p. 37.

34 ibid.

35 Mulvey, "Visual pleasure," pp. 7–8, 18. It is true that "Women whose image has continually been stolen and used for this end (i.e., satisfaction, pleasure, etc.) cannot view the decline of the traditional film form with anything much more than sentimental regret," but the question remains as to what the pleasure in cinema will be replaced *with*.

36 See, for example, the essays in *Edinburgh Magazine*, No. 1 (1976), especially those by Rosalind Coward, "Lacan and signification: an introduction," pp. 6–20; Christian

Metz, "History/discourse: notes on two voyeurisms," pp. 21–5; Stephen Heath, "Screen images, film memory," pp. 33–42; Claire Johnston, "Towards a feminist film practice: some theses," pp. 50–9. Cf. also issue of *Screen* devoted to "Psychoanalysis and cinema," Vol. 16, No. 2 (1975), in which articles of particular interest are Christian Metz, "The imaginary signifier," pp. 14–76, and Stephen Heath, "Film and system: terms of analysis, Part II," pp. 91–113.

37 See Jane Clarke, Sue Clayton, Joanna Clelland, Rosie Elliott, and Mandy Merck (1979) "Women and representation: a discussion with Laura Mulvey," *Wedge* (London), No. 2, p. 49.

2 Patriarchy and the male gaze in Cukor's "Camille" (1936)

1 Stephen S. Stanton (ed.) (1957) "Introduction" to *Camille and Other Plays*, New York, Hill & Wang, p. xxx.

2 Famous stage actresses who have played Marguerite Gautier include Sarah Bernhardt, Eleanora Duse, Lillian Gish, Ethel Barrymore, and Eva LeGallienne; at least five film versions predate Cukor's 1936 version (which marked the 84th anniversary of the play's original stage production in 1852), including the 1917 version with Theda Bara, the 1921 version starring Nazimova and Valentino, and the 1927 version with Norma Talmadge. In 1980 Mauro Bolognini produced an Italian version.

3 I.e. *Gaslight* and *Born Yesterday*. For discussion of Cukor as a woman's director, see Gary Carey (1971) *Cukor and Co: The Films of George Cukor and His Collaborators*, New York, Museum of Modern Art.

4 Posters for the film are available in the Lincoln Center Library, New York, as are also the reviews written at the time of the film's appearance.

5 Stanton (ed.) *Camille and Other Plays*, p. xxx.

6 ibid., pp. xxxi–xxxii.

7 ibid., p. xxxi.

8 H. S. Schwarz is quoted ibid., p. xxx.

9 ibid., p. xxxi.

10 For an important analysis of the evolution of the melodramatic form and its essential characteristics, see Peter Brooks (1976) *The Melodramatic Imagination*, New Haven and London, Yale University Press, especially chapters 1 to 4; for more specifically film-related studies of melodrama, see Griselda Pollock (ed.) (1977) "Dossier on melodrama," *Screen*, Vol. 18, No. 2, pp. 105–19, and Laura Mulvey (1976) "Notes on Sirk and melodrama," *Movie*, No. 25, pp. 53–6.

11 See Sandra M. Gilbert (1978) "Patriarchal poetry and women readers: reflections on Milton's bogey," in *PMLA*, Vol. 93, No. 3, pp. 368–82.

12 Stanton (ed.) *Camille and Other Plays*, p. xxxi.

13 Jacqueline Rose (1978) "'Dora' – fragment of an analysis," *m/f*, No. 2, p. 18.

14 This phenomenon is discussed in Joel Kovel (1981) *The Age of Desire: Reflections of a Radical Psychoanalyst*, New York, Pantheon. See, for example, his chapter "Desire and the transhistorical," where he says:

> The point is that political economy is constituted so as to be indifferent to desire. That is just what makes it so galling. The very heartlessness of the economic system is historically decisive precisely because our history is made by passionate creatures whose yearning is thwarted by the impersonal world wrought by the class antagonism of capital. . . . In late capitalism, desire festers . . . desire becomes the location of the concrete and the irrational. It is hell to the heaven of political economy. (op. cit., pp. 84–5)

15 This is evident, for example, in the second generation of British Romantic poets, especially Keats and Shelley, who yearned to transcend the material realm and find peace in illusory unity with the loved one.
16 Sigmund Freud (1955) "Mourning and melancholia," *Standard Edition*, Vol. 14, London, The Hogarth Press, p. 237 ff.
17 ibid., p. 241.
18 "J'ai eu tout à l'heure un moment de colère contre la mort; je m'en repens; elle est nécessaire, et je l'aime, puisqu'elle t'a attendu pour me frapper. Si ma mort n'eût été certaine, ton pere ne t'eût pas écrit de revenir." Elliott M. Grant (ed.) (1934) *Chief French Plays of the Nineteenth Century*, New York, Harper & Row, p. 477.

3 Fetishism and the repression of Motherhood in Von Sternberg's "Blonde Venus" (1932)

1 See Gary Carey (1971) *Cukor and Co: The Films of George Cukor and His Collaborators*, New York, Museum of Modern Art.
2 A good analysis of the function soap operas serve may be found in Tania Modleski (1983) "The rhythms of day-time soap operas," in E. Ann Kaplan (ed.) *Re-Garding Television: A Critical Anthology*, Los Angeles, American Film Institute.
3 Claire Johnston (1973) "Women's cinema as counter-cinema," in Claire Johnston (ed.) *Notes on Women's Cinema*, London, Society for Education in Film and Television, p. 26.
4 Laura Mulvey (1975) "Visual pleasure and narrative cinema," *Screen*, Vol. 16, No. 3, p. 14.
5 This statement by Von Sternberg is quoted by Richard Dyer (1979) *Stars*, London, British Film Institute, p. 179. A similar sense of Dietrich as his "creation" appears in Von Sternberg (1965) *Fun in a Chinese Laundry*, New York, Macmillan, where Sternberg says:

> I then put her into the crucible of my conception, blended her image to correspond with mine, and, pouring lights on her until the alchemy was complete, proceeded with the test. She came to life and responded to my instructions with an ease that I had never encountered. (p. 237)

Earlier in the book, Von Sternberg reveals his underlying assumptions about women that account for his unabashed way of taking control of Dietrich:

> It is the nature of woman to be passive, receptive, dependent on male aggression and capable of enduring pain. In other words, she is not normally outraged by being manipulated. On the contrary, she usually enjoys it. (p. 120)

6 See Charles Silver (1974) *Marlene Dietrich*, New York, Pyramid, pp. 39–45, and John Baxter (1971) *The Cinema of Joseph Von Sternberg*, London, Zwemmer, pp. 102, 108.
7 Julia Kristeva (1980) "Motherhood according to Bellini," trans. Thomas Gora, Alice Jardine, and Leon S. Roudiez, in Leon S. Roudiez (ed.) *Desire in Language: A Semiotic Approach to Literature and Art*, New York, Columbia University Press, p. 238.
8 ibid., p. 239.
9 Baxter, *The Cinema of Joseph Von Sternberg*, pp. 103, 106–7.
10 Bill Nichols (1981) *Ideology and the Image*, Bloomington, Ind., Indiana University Press, pp. 113–19.
11 See Baxter, *The Cinema of Joseph Von Sternberg*.
12 Nichols, *Ideology and the Image*, pp. 119–22.
13 See comments by panelists in "Women in film: a discussion of feminist aesthetics," *New German Critique*, No. 13 (1978), pp. 93–7.

4 The struggle for control over the female discourse and female sexuality in Welles's "Lady from Shanghai" (1946)

1 Sylvia Harvey (1978) "Woman's place: the absent family in film noir," in E. Ann Kaplan (ed) *Women in Film Noir*, London, British Film Institute, p. 22.
2 ibid., p. 25.
3 ibid.
4 Christine Gledhill (1980) "Klute I: a contemporary film noir and feminist criticism," in Kaplan, *Women in Film Noir*, p. 19.
5 ibid., p. 19.
6 ibid., p. 16.
7 Laura Mulvey (1975) "Visual pleasure and narrative cinema," *Screen*, Vol. 16, No. 3, p. 10.
8 ibid.
9 ibid.
10 For issues to do with cinematic identification and primary and secondary process, see Christian Metz "The imaginary signifier," *Screen*, Vol. 16, No. 2, pp. 46–59 especially.
11 Longtemps, le spectateur ne se doute pas de la hideuse réalité cachée sous la divine apparence de Rita. Blonde, superbe, sculpturale, elle continue à incarner un idéal fondé avant tout sur la fascination physique qu'elle exerce. Sa beauté la met au-dessus de tout soupçon. Elle est Rosalinde. Elle est l'innocence et la pureté. Souveraine d'un univers ignoré (et qui restera à cause des coupures. On sait seulement que le Chinois lui obéissent avec dévotion), une Déesse, assurément, habitant pour quelque temps un corps terrestre et qui semble pourtant inaccessible. (Jean-Claude Allais (1961) "Orson Welles", *Premier Plan*, March, p. 32).
12 Karen Horney (1932) "The dread of woman," reprinted in Harold Kelman (ed.) (1967) *Feminine Psychology*, New York, Norton, p. 134.
13 Mulvey, "Visual pleasure," p. 12.
14 See Serge Daney (1966) "Welles au pouvoir," in *Cahiers du Cinéma*, No. 181, pp. 27–8; also Maurice Bessy (1963) *Orson Welles*, Paris, Editions Seghers, p. 62.

5 Forms of phallic domination in the contemporary Hollywood film: Brooks's "Looking for Mr Goodbar" (1977)

1 The construction of woman as spectacle, internalized, leads women to offer their bodies in professions like modeling and advertising, and film acting, and to be generally susceptible to demands to be made "spectacle." For a detailed study of women's socialization into being object of the gaze and illustration of how this is played out in the history of painting and in advertising, see John Berger (1977) *Ways of Seeing*, New York, Penguin.
2 In Lazarus and Wunderlish's *Rape Culture* (1975), there is an interview with a young rapist who outlines his fantasy that he will force himself on a woman, obtaining satisfaction from asserting his control in this way, but that she will turn out to want him and will make him feel sexually desirable. This interview, together with others in the film, exposes the fact that an insufficient sense of manliness can only be assuaged through dominating women sexually or through being wanted by a woman.
3 It is interesting to speculate about the underlying reasons for these new images of avenging women, which evidently appeal to the male audience. Perhaps the images play to a male fantasy of suffering at the hands of a castrating woman –

being punished for their hostility to women in a kind of reversion to the Oedipal fantasies about the Mother.

4 Cf. Charlotte Brunsdon (1982) "A subject for the seventies," in *Screen*, Vol. 23, Nos 3–4, pp. 22–3.

5 ibid., p. 20.

6 The prohibition against mothers being sexual is a traditional one, exemplified, for instance, in Curtiz's *Mildred Pierce* (1945). More recent films like *An Unmarried Woman* (1978) begin to allow mothers to also have sexual needs, but in that case the daughter was grown up and herself already dating. In the case of a film like *Shoot the Moon* (1982), the mother, now of small children, is allowed a full-blown sexuality, but it is significant that at the end all she has built up is totally destroyed by a jealous ex-husband.

7 At one point, Tony shows his distaste for the fact that Teresa, a promiscuous bar-hopper, should actually be a teacher of small children. His comment reveals his underlying scorn for her, although he is, of course, perfectly willing to use her. In other words, men like Tony, despite their own promiscuity and bar-hopping, still retain the old virgin–whore dichotomy and basically *respect* only virgins.

8 In Judith Rossner's novel (1975), from which the film was made, this psycho-analytic discourse is foregrounded. We learn in much more detail, and from Teresa's own point of view, the facts about her family situation, and her Oedipal crisis. The interior monologue of the written text makes this possible in a way not equalled by the fantasies and flashbacks that dot the film in an effort to bring in some of the material we are told by Terry in the book.

9 For more discussion of the problems James presents as a character, see Robin Wood (1980–1) "The incoherent text: narrative in the 70s," *Movie* (UK), Nos 27–8, pp. 33–6.

10 Karen Horney (1932) "The dread of woman," reprinted in Harold Kelman (ed.) (1967) *Feminine Psychology*, New York, Norton.

6 The avant-gardes in Europe and the USA

1 Peter Wollen (1976) "The two avant-gardes," *Edinburgh Magazine*, Summer, p. 77.

2 Peter Wollen (1981) "The avant gardes: Europe and America," *Framework*, Spring, p. 10.

3 ibid., p. 10.

4 ibid., p. 9.

5 See Peter Gidal "Theory and definition of structural materialist film," pp. 1–21, and his "Deke Dusinberre," pp. 109–13, in Peter Gidal (ed.) (1976) *Structural Film Anthology*, London, British Film Institute.

6 Wollen, "The avant gardes: Europe and America," p. 10.

7 See Wollen's discussion in "The two avant-gardes," pp. 81–2.

8 Dulac evidently did identify with feminism, according to Wendy Dozoretz (1982) "Germaine Dulac: filmmaker, polemicist, theoretician," unpublished dissertation, New York University, but there was as yet no full-fledged movement in France and no specific attention to feminism in relation to representation. Deren was exposed to very little feminist thinking of any kind, given the war and its aftermath, and thus developed little conscious feminism. However, her own career, and the focus in her films on women's psyches, bodies, placings, show her sensitivity to what we now define as feminist issues.

9 See the discussion of influences on Dulac in Dozoretz, "Germaine Dulac."

10 Both women wrote and lectured extensively about cinema as an art form. See the

many essays by Dulac in film journals in the 1920s (e.g. *Cinémagazine, Le Rouge et le noir,* and *Les Cahiers du mois*); a long essay by her, "Le Cinéma d'avant-garde," was published in H. Fescourt (ed.) (1932) *Le Cinéma des origines à nos jours,* Paris, Editions des Cygne, pp. 341–53. See M. Deren (1946) "Cinema as an art form," *New Directions,* No. 9, reprinted in Charles T. Samuels (1970) *A Casebook on Film,* New York, Van Nostrand Reinhold, pp. 47–55; and "A letter to James Card" (1965), reprinted in Gerry Peary and Karyn Kay (eds) (1977) *Women in the Cinema: A Critical Anthology,* New York, Dutton, pp. 224–30; in addition to many short articles, Deren wrote a long essay on film form, "An anagram of ideas on art, form and film," reprinted in George Amberg (ed.) (1972) *The Art of Cinema: Selected Essays,* New York, Arno Press.

11 Jacqueline Zita (1981) "Films of Barbara Hammer: counter-currencies of a lesbian iconography," *Jump Cut,* Nos 24–5, p. 27.

12 So far as I know, no one has satisfactorily explained male interest in images of women making love to one another. Perhaps it has to do with the male fantasy of being made love to by two women (i.e. the man can put himself into the representation of the women lovers). Male lovers in pornography are amazingly virile and superhuman in their performance: images of women alone may therefore evoke far less competitiveness in the male spectator. But this is a complex issue which requires a lot more work.

7 Silence as female resistance in Marguerite Duras's "Nathalie Granger" (1972)

1 Marguerite Duras wrote her first novel, *Les Impudents,* in 1943, and had written eleven novels by 1966, when she made her first film, *La Musica.* Several of her novels have been made into films, and a few works exist in drama form as well. For a complete bibliography/filmography, see Elisabeth Lyon (1980) "Marguerite Duras: Bibliography/Filmography," *Camera Obscura,* No. 6, pp. 50–4.

2 Duras, in an interview with Jacques Rivette and Jean Narboni (1969) *Cahiers du Cinéma,* No. 217, pp. 45–57, trans. Helen Lane Cumberford (1970) *Destroy, She Said,* New York, Grove Press.

3 ibid., p. 115.

4 ibid., p. 117.

5 ibid., p. 120.

6 ibid., p. 121.

7 ibid., pp. 119–20.

8 ibid., p. 127.

9 See Introduction II: "Histories of France and of feminism in France," in Courtivron and Marks (eds) (1980) *New French Feminisms,* Amherst, Mass., University of Massachusetts Press, pp. 24–5. The main events were the fusion of smaller women's groups, bringing about consciousness of a movement; the placing of a wreath dedicated to the "Unknown Wife of the Soldier" on the Tomb of the Unknown Soldier by Wittig, Rochefort, and others; the founding of "Feministes révolution-naires," who aimed at destroying patriarchal order and carried out several disruptive actions and demonstrations; and in 1972, the founding of a group to study women's culture and to liberate "smothered creation."

10 Xavière Gauthier, "Is there such a thing as women's writing?", trans. Marilyn A. August, in Courtivron and Marks (eds) *New French Feminisms,* pp. 162–3.

11 Claudine Herrmann, "Women in space and time," trans. Marilyn R. Schuster, ibid., p. 169.

12 Julia Kristeva, "Oscillation between 'power' and 'denial'," trans. Marilyn A. August, ibid., p. 166.

13 ibid., p. 167.
14 As the editors note, "in French *nom* (name) and *non* (no) are homophonic words. Lacanian psychoanalysis has used this resemblance to underline the role of the father in the child's coming to language and the child's separation from the desired mother. In the Lacanian paradigm, this coming to language marks the passage into the symbolic world governed by the laws of language." Gauthier, "Is there such a thing as women's writing?", p. 163.
15 Gauthier, ibid., p. 163.
16 Duras, in an interview with Susan Husserl-Kapit in *Signs* (1975); reprinted in Courtivron and Marks, *New French Feminisms*, p. 174.
17 ibid., p. 175.
18 ibid.
19 Duras, in an interview in Suzanne Horer and Jeanne Soquet (eds) (1973) *La Création étouffée*, reprinted as "Smothered creativity," in Courtivron and Marks (eds) *New French Feminisms*, p. 111–13.
20 Kristeva, "Oscillation between 'power' and 'denial' ".
21 Duras (1973) *Nathalie Granger*, Paris, Gallimard, p. 33.
22 Suter and Flitterman (1979) "Textual riddles: woman as enigma or site of social meanings? An interview with Laura Mulvey," *Discourse*, No. 1, p. 111.
23 Sigmund Freud, *Civilization and Its Discontents*, trans. James Strachey, New York, Norton (1961), pp. 37, 47.
24 Duras (1973) *Nathalie Granger*, p. 31.
25 Mulvey, "Women and representation," p. 51.
26 Duras, *Nathalie Granger*, p. 78.

8 Female politics in the symbolic realm: Von Trotta's "Marianne and Juliane" ("The German Sisters") (1981)

1 Vincent Canby (1982) *New York Times*, 7 March.
2 See Charlotte Delorme (1982) "Zum Film *Die bleierne Zeit* von Margarethe von Trotta," *Frauen und Film*, No. 31, p. 52, who argues that, in addition to the clichés, the film follows reactionary family psychologists and simplifies issues.

9 The American experimental woman's film: Yvonne Rainer's "Lives of Performers" and "Film about a Woman Who . . ." (1972–4)

1 For background to Rainer's work, see Annette Michaelson (1974) "Yvonne Rainer, Part one: the dancer and the dance," *Artforum* (Jan.); "Yvonne Rainer, Part two: lives of performers," *Artforum* (Feb.).
2 *Camera Obscura* editors (1976) "Yvonne Rainer: interview," *Camera Obscura*, No. 1, pp. 76–96; also Rainer's comments to me in a personal conversation.
3 Interview with Lucy Lippard (1975) in *Feminist Art Journal*, Vol. 4, No. 2.
4 ibid., p. 6.
5 *Camera Obscura* editors (1976) "Yvonne Rainer: an introduction," *Camera Obscura*, No. 1, p. 59.
6 See chapter 10 for more discussion of the issues arising out of realism.
7 "Yvonne Rainer: an Introduction," p. 59.
8 ibid.
9 ibid., pp. 81–5.
10 ibid., p. 65.
11 ibid., p. 80.
12 See chapter 10 for a fuller discussion of these issues.

13 The issue of spectator response is hampered by inadequate research into ways in which audiences in fact "receive" specific films.
14 "Yvonne Rainer: an introduction," p. 61.
15 Cindy Nemser (1975), editorial, *Feminist Art Journal*, Vol. 4, No. 2, p. 4.
16 ibid., p. 4.
17 "Yvonne Rainer: interview," pp. 80–1.
18 Fredric Jameson (1981) *The Political Unconscious*, Ithaca, N.Y., Cornell University Press, p. 180.
19 ibid., p. 183.
20 ibid., p. 175.
21 The script of *Lives of Performers* is printed in Yvonne Rainer (1974) *Work 1961–73*, New York, New York University Press. This quotation, used in the script, is taken from Vladimir Nizhny (1969) *Lessons with Eisenstein*, New York, Hill & Wang.
22 Ruby Rich (1980) *Yvonne Rainer*, Minneapolis, The Walker Art Center, p. 7.
23 ibid., pp. 7–8.
24 "Yvonne Rainer: interview," p. 81.
25 ibid.
26 See Rich, *Yvonne Rainer*, p. 8.
27 "Yvonne Rainer: interview," p. 95.
28 There simply was not room in the book to do in-depth analyses of both the early films and *Journeys from Berlin* (1980). While it is true that *Journeys* deals with issues central to the book, it is a much less accessible film than the ones dealt with here. Readers should look at Ruby Rich's discussion of *Journeys* in *Yvonne Rainer*; Noel Carroll (1980–1) "Interview with a woman who . . .," *Millenium Film Journal*, Nos 7–9, pp. 37–68; and Jan Dawson's extended review of *Journeys* in *Sight and Sound*, Vol. 49, No. 3, pp. 196–7.

10 The realist debate in the feminist film: a historical overview of theories and strategies in realism and the avant-garde theory film (1971–81)

1 I am thinking here particularly of filmmakers like Barbara Loden, Elaine May, and Claudia Weill.
2 Eileen McGarry (1975) "Documentary realism and women's cinema," in *Women and Film*, Vol. 2, No. 7, p. 50.
3 ibid.
4 ibid., p. 51.
5 See E. Ann Kaplan (1976) "Aspects of British feminist film theory: a critical evaluation of texts by Claire Johnston and Pam Cook," *Jump Cut*, Nos 12–13, pp. 52–5, and Julia LeSage (1978) "The political aesthetics of the feminist documentary film," *Quarterly Review of Film Studies*, Vol. 3, No. 4, pp. 507–23.
6 See LeSage, "The political aesthetics of the feminist documentary film."
7 Jacques Derrida (1976) *Of Grammatology*, trans. Gayatri Spivak, Baltimore and London, Johns Hopkins Press, quoted in Terence Hawkes (1977) *Structuralism and Semiology*, London, Methuen, p. 146.
8 ibid., p. 145.
9 ibid., p. 143.
10 Siegfried Kracauer (1960) *Theory of Film: The Redemption of Physical Reality*, Oxford, Oxford University Press; and André Bazin (1967) *What is Cinema?*, Vol. 1, trans. Hugh Gray, Berkeley, Calif., University of California Press.
11 Claire Johnston (1973) "Women's cinema as counter-cinema," in Claire Johnston

(ed.) *Notes on Women's Cinema*, London, Society for Education in Film and Television, p. 28.

12 Noel King (1981) "Recent 'political' documentary – notes on *Union Maids* and *Harlan County, U.S.A.*," *Screen*, Vol. 22, No. 2, p. 9.

13 Cf. Steve Neale (1973) "Propaganda," *Screen*, Vol. 18, No. 3, p. 25.

14 King, "Recent 'political' documentary," p. 12.

15 ibid., p. 5.

16 ibid., p. 17.

17 ibid., p. 18.

18 M. H. Abrams (1953) *The Mirror and the Lamp: Romantic Theory and the Critical Tradition*, London, Oxford University Press, p. 267. Chapter 10 as a whole explores the issues of "truth to nature."

19 ibid., chapters 5, 6, on the development of the Romantic theory of poetry.

20 Terry Eagleton (1978) "Aesthetics and politics," *New Left Review*, No. 107, p. 22.

21 What I have in mind here is the danger of a theory that ignores the need for emotional identification with people suffering oppression. We may be able to explain the situation of a strike, for example, in terms of dominant versus minority discourses; the dominant discourse in the factory is that of the owners who construct the position of the workers to suit their (the bosses) own interests. One of the few reactions to domination available to the oppressed group is that of striking, although it is clear that this position is very much a defensive one, constructed by the dominant discourse and causing the workers themselves a lot of hardship. The workers are, thus, on a basic material level, in need of support (food, clothing), and on the psychological level, in need of emotional support. The level of abstraction on which the theory functions often makes it seem as if these other levels are unimportant or not worth mentioning. That Metz is one of the few critics who retains constant awareness of the level of the social formation is evident not only in his discussion of realism in *Film Language: A Semiotics of the Cinema* (trans. Michael Taylor, New York, Oxford University Press (1974)), but also in an interview in *Discourse* (paradoxically his statements here prompted Noel King's article referred to in note 12 above), where he supports the "naively" realist documentary, like *Harlan County, U.S.A.* Asked if he thinks a documentary of a strike could be misleading "insofar as it assumes that knowledge is unproblematic, and on the surface," Metz replies: "If the film has a very precise, political and immediate aim; if the filmmakers shoot a film in order to support a given strike . . . what could I say? Of course, it's O.K." Talking specifically about *Harlan County*, Metz continues:

> It is the kind of film that has nothing really new on the level of primary/secondary identification, but it's a very good film. . . . It is unfair, in a sense, to call a film into question on terms which are not within the filmmaker's purpose. She intended to . . . support the strike and she did it. It's a marvelous film and I support it. ("The cinematic apparatus as social institution: an interview with Christian Metz," *Discourse*, No. 1 (1979), p. 30)

22 See Dana Polan (1982) "Discourses of rationality and the rationality of discourse in avant-garde political film culture," paper presented at the Ohio University Film Conference, April 1982.

23 Metz, *Film Language*, p. 4.

24 ibid., p. 5.

25 ibid., p. 22.

26 ibid., pp. 21–2.

27 McGarry, "Documentary realism and women's cinema."

28 Michael Ryan (1981) "Militant documentary: Mai '68 par lui," *Ciné-Tracts*, Nos 7–8.
29 Many women, of course, continued to make realist films, especially in America. Two recent and interesting examples are Connie Field's *Rosie the Riveter* and Pat Ferrero's *Quilts in Women's Lives*.
30 Sylvia Harvey (1981) "An introduction to *Song of the Shirt*," *Undercut*, No. 1, p. 46.
31 ibid.
32 ibid., p. 47.
33 For a full discussion of realist theories of knowledge and society, together with a critique of Althusserian theories, see Terry Lovell (1980) *Pictures of Reality: Aesthetics, Politics and Pleasure*, London, British Film Institute.
34 Christine Gledhill (1978) "Recent developments in feminist film criticism," *Quarterly Review of Film Studies*, Vol. 3, No. 4, pp. 469–73.

11 The avant-garde theory film: three case studies from Britain and the USA: "Sigmund Freud's Dora" (1979), "Thriller" (1979), Mulvey/Wollen's "Amy!" (1980)

1 I am here referring to films like Godard's *Letter to Jane*, works by Chantal Ackerman, *The Amazing Equal Pay Show* (made by the London Women's Film Group, later called the London Women Filmmakers' Cooperative), *Rapunzel* (made by another British women's film group), and Mulvey and Wollen's first film, *Penthesilea*, as well as the second two works, considered here and in chapter 12.
2 *Argument* (90 mins, McCall/Tyndall, 1978), provided the basis for *Sigmund Freud's Dora* in that *Dora* was an attempt to deal with issues *Argument* avoided. Cf. essays by Claire Pajaczkowska (who worked as production assistant on *Argument*) and Jane Weinstock in the booklet *Argument*, published with the film. See also Anthony McCall and Andrew Tyndall (1978) "Sixteen working statements," *Millenium Film Journal*, Vol. 1, No. 2, pp. 29–37. My unpublished interviews with McCall and Tyndall are also relevant here.
3 Laura Mulvey (1975) "Visual pleasure and narrative cinema," *Screen*, Vol. 16, No. 3, pp. 6–18.
4 See Jacqueline Rose (1978) "'Dora' – fragment of an analysis," *m/f*, No. 2, pp. 5–21. Rose argues that the intimacy of Dora and Frau K. functions "as the 'secret' of the case . . . which thus cuts straight across from the 'manifest' behavior of the participants to the 'latent' aetiology of the symptoms (Freud's theory of hysteria)." She shows how keen Freud is to hang onto a notion of heterosexual desire.
5 Freud did not publish *Dora* until 1905 because he was unsatisfied with the case history. When he did so, he left the text unchanged but added many footnotes commenting on the analysis. He realized that the analysis suffered from his lack of understanding of transference at the time, together with his lack of a theory of homosexuality.
6 The information about the filmmakers' views is taken from two separate, unpublished, interviews that I did with them. I have at various points in the chapter developed certain statements along my own lines. Tyndall is however responsible for the notion of the three parts of the text.
7 Jacqueline Rose, "'Dora.'"
8 The different views of the mother in the film emerged from the two sets of interviews with the filmmakers. Both male directors saw the mother as tragic and placed much meaning on her affect; Pajaczkowska was interested in the symbolic meanings of the mother, while Weinstock was concerned with the tension between real and symbolic mothers. All mentioned the varied audience responses to the mother.

9 Dora herself mentions this possibility in the fifth letter. For the full script of the film, see *Framework*, Nos 15–17 (1981) pp. 75–81, introduced by Claire Pajaczkowska.

10 This came up in the unpublished interviews, as did the comments on history referred to below.

11 See George Marek (1951) *Puccini: A Biography*, New York, Simon & Schuster, pp. 247–60.

12 See Giuseppe Adami (ed.) (1931) *Letters of Giacomo Puccini*, trans. and ed. for the English edn by Eva Makin, Philadelphia and London, Lippincott, pp. 96–7.

13 Briefly, the plot of the opera is as follows: A young seamstress, Mimi, suffering from consumption, meets and falls in love with Rodolfo, a painter, living in the room beneath her attic. Passionately happy, Mimi and Rodolfo celebrate their love with the artist's friends, who include the lively prostitute, Musetta, whom the men joke about. Realizing that Rodolfo is unable to endure Mimi's illness, and that he is unreasonably jealous, Mimi leaves Rodolfo and goes to live with a rich man. Since she can barely endure the separation, Mimi's health declines; finding her near death, Musetta brings Mimi to Rodolfo's room where she and her lover are briefly reconciled. The opera ends with the artists mourning Mimi's death. (For a useful, translated edition of *La Bohème*, complete with supporting materials, see Ellen H. Beiler's version (1982), New York, Dover.)

14 Jane Weinstock (1981) "She who laughs first, laughs last," *Camera Obscura*, No. 11, pp. 73–9.

15 For a psychoanalytic reading of *Thriller*, see Joan Kopjec (1981) "*Thriller*: an intrigue of identification," *Ciné-Tracts*, No. 11, pp. 33–8.

16 See Ruby Rich's review of *Thriller* in *The Chicago Reader* (March 1980), pp. 14, 16.

17 See their much quoted articles: Mulvey, "Visual pleasure," and Claire Johnston (1973) "Woman's cinema as counter-cinema," in Claire Johnston (ed.) *Notes on Women's Cinema*, London, Society for Education in Film and Television.

18 Christine Gledhill (1978) "Recent developments in feminist film criticism," *Quarterly Review of Film Studies*, Vol. 3, No. 4, p. 484.

19 Peter Wollen, lecture given at the Collective for Living Cinema, New York, April 1981. Wollen has also written (1981) about the films that he and Laura Mulvey made in "The field of language in film," *October*, No. 17, pp. 53–60.

20 "Interview about *Penthesilea*" (with Laura Mulvey and Peter Wollen) *Screen*, Vol. 15, No. 3 (1974), p. 129.

21 ibid.

22 "Women and representation: a discussion with Laura Mulvey," *Wedge* (London), No. 2 (1979), p. 47.

23 Script of *Amy!* in *Framework*, No. 14 (1981), p. 38.

24 Gerald Peary and Karyn Kay, "Interview with Dorothy Arzner," reprinted in Peary and Kay (eds) (1977) *Women in the Cinema: A Critical Anthology*, New York, Dutton, p. 164.

25 In his lecture at the Collective for Living Cinema and in "The field of language in film."

26 Script of *Amy!*, p. 38.

27 Mulvey and Wollen evidently joined the Haverfield Flying Club in order to obtain authentic photographs of the type of plane used by Amy Johnston.

28 Peter Wollen's voice-over in the script of *Amy!*, p. 39.

29 ibid.

30 ibid., p. 40.

31 ibid.

32 ibid., p. 41.

12 Mothers and daughters in two recent women's films: Mulvey/Wollen's "Riddles of the Sphinx" (1976) and Michelle Citron's "Daughter-Rite" (1978)

1 Dorothy Dinnerstein (1977) *The Mermaid and the Minotaur*, New York, Harper, pp. 97–111. Cf. Adrienne Rich (1976) *Of Woman Born*, New York, Norton.

2 See Nancy Chodorow (1978) *The Reproduction of Mothering: Psychoanalysis and the Sociology of Gender*, Berkeley, Calif., University of California Press, especially ch. 5.

3 A recent book exploring the anger of daughters at inadequate protection by their mothers is Lucy Gilbert and Paula Webster (1982) *Bound by Love: The Sweet Trap of Daughterhood*, Boston, Beacon Press, especially chapters 2 and 3.

4 Laura Mulvey (1975) "Visual pleasure and narrative cinema," *Screen*, Vol. 16, No. 3, p. 18.

5 Much of the following discussion is taken from my article "Avant-garde feminist cinema," *Quarterly Review of Film Studies* (Spring 1979), pp. 136–41.

6 This and other quotations are taken from the script of *Riddles of the Sphinx*, printed in *Screen*, Vol. 18, No. 2 (1977), pp. 61–78.

7 See E. Ann Kaplan (1976) "Aspects of British feminist film theory," *Jump Cut*, Nos 12–13, pp. 52–5; also Christine Gledhill (1977) "Whose choice? – Teaching films about abortion," *Screen Education*, No. 24, p. 44. Gledhill does not believe "that all that remains open to the radical filmmaker is opposition, counter-cinema, negation," or that "ideology can only be exposed through the *experience* of contradiction, the subject disoriented, language ruptured."

8 See Jane Feuer (1980) "Daughter-Rite: living with our pain and love," *Jump Cut*, No. 23, pp. 12–13; and Linda Williams and B. Ruby Rich (1981) "The right of re-vision: Michelle Citron's *Daughter-Rite*," *Film Quarterly*, Vol. 35, No. 1, pp. 17–21.

9 Citron herself went on to make a realist documentary giving her own mother a voice, to remedy the mother's repression here.

13 The woman director in the Third World: Sara Gomez's "One Way or Another" (1974)

1 It is, however, significant that Sara Gomez is the only female director to have made a feature film in Cuba. Clearly, the biases and the problems with the old sexual ideology that Gomez deals with in her film partly account for this lack of female directors. Tragically, Gomez died shortly after editing the film. Julia LeSage points out that "her associates Tomas Guitierrez Alea and Rigoberto Lopez supervised the sound-mix and post production stages of preparing *One Way or Another* for theatrical release." See Julia LeSage (1979) "*One Way or Another*: dialectical, revolutionary, feminist" *Jump Cut*, No. 20, p. 23.

2 See "Artistic freedom, political tasks," a discussion between Michael Scrivener, Chuck Kleinhans, John Hess, and Julia LeSage, *Jump Cut*, No. 21 (1979), pp. 28–9. *Jump Cut* is one of the few film journals to pay substantial attention to Cuban cinema. The three special sections on Cuban cinema (*Jump Cut*, Nos 19, 20, 22) contain invaluable overviews of the development of Cuban cinema, reviews of specific films (sometimes translated from Cuban film journals), interviews with Cuban filmmakers (also often translated from Cuban film magazines), and bibliographies of articles in English.

3 Humberto Solas (1978) makes this clear in his interview with Julianne Burton in *Jump Cut*, No. 19, pp. 27–33; note also Carlos Galiano's comment, in his review of Gomez's film, that "*One Way or Another* has contributed to one of the Cuban film industry's fundamental purposes, that is, to approach our present problems from a

critical standpoint" (ibid., p. 33).

4 The degree to which this is the aim in Cuba is clear from the discussion between Jorge Silva and Enrique Colina in *Jump Cut*, No. 22 (1980), pp. 32–3. Colina says:

> We feel that our work in film has what we might call a meta-goal: To enable people to take a more critical, more reflective and analytic attitude. We strive to encourage people to take on the kind of serious intellectual effort which is the precondition of that state of readiness which any transformation of reality requires. . . . We also try to increase people's understanding of everything having to do with the distribution network, the commercialization of film as merchandise, and the political and ideological – as well as artistic – implications which this market imposes upon the film product.

5 Julia LeSage, "*One Way or Another,*" pp. 20–3. Aside from Galiano's short review, LeSage's article is the only other full-length treatment of Gomez's film that I know.

6 LeSage (ibid.) says:

> Every moment and aspect of the characters' lives is seen in terms of the complex social relations that form and condition them. In turn, each aspect of the characters' lives and each interaction between characters influences both their own future and that of others.

7 Silva and Colina, discussion in *Jump Cut*, p. 32. Colina notes that this proportion is better than before the revolution (when 70 per cent of the films were from the United States). The concern with how Hollywood narrative actually works is clear in Colina's discussion of the American thriller, *Bullit*; he says:

> Let's try to define the particular expressive devices which prevent us from making a moral judgement about the hero when we see the film and instead lead us to identify with him in a positive way. . . . We might also refer to literary antecedents in our attempt to explain why this particular kind of hero is presented as entertainment in a capitalist society.

Colina concludes that "Our goal is to develop analytical tools in the reader or spectator which will permit them to defend themselves against cultural penetration."

14 The future of the independent feminist film: strategies of production, exhibition, and distribution in the USA

1 See the interviews with Humberto Solas in *Jump Cut*, No. 19 (1978), pp. 27–33; and with Enrique Colina in *Jump Cut*, No. 22 (1980), pp. 32–3.

2 Cf. Julia LeSage (1979) "*One Way or Another*: dialectical, revolutionary, feminist," *Jump Cut*, No. 20, p. 20.

3 Julia LeSage began to think about problems of production, exhibition, and distribution in a 1974 article, "Feminist film criticism: theory and practice," *Women and Film*, Vol. 1, Nos 5–6, pp. 12–19; and in general the journal *Jump Cut* focused more than others on matters of the social and political context for feminist films. Julia LeSage's article is reprinted in slightly revised version in Patricia Erens (ed.) (1979) *Sexual Stratagems: The World of Women in Film*, New York, Horizon Press, pp. 156–67.

4 See, for example, Marc Karlin et al. (1980–1) "Problems of independent cinema," *Screen*, Vol. 21, No. 4, pp. 19–43; John Hill, "Ideology, economy and British cinema," in Michèle Barrett et al. (eds) (1979) *Ideology and Cultural Production*,

London, Croom Helm; Anthony McCall and Andrew Tyndall (1978) "Sixteen working statements," *Millenium Film Journal*, Vol. 1, No. 2, pp. 29–37; Steve Neale (1980) "Oppositional exhibition: notes and problems," *Screen*, Vol. 21, No. 3, pp. 45–56; Michael O'Pray (1980) "Authorship and independent film exhibition," *Screen*, Vol. 21, No. 2, pp. 73–8; Susan Clayton and Jonathan Curling (1981) "Feminist history and *The Song of the Shirt*," *Camera Obscura*, No. 7, pp. 111–27; Susan Clayton and Jonathan Curling (1979) "On authorship," *Screen*, Vol. 20, No. 1, pp. 35–61; John Caughie (1980–1) "*Because I Am King* and independent cinema," *Screen*, Vol. 21, No. 4, pp. 9–18; Steve Neale (1981) "Art cinema as institution," *Screen*, Vol. 22, No. 1, pp. 11–41.

5 Don MacPherson (ed.) (1980) *Traditions of Independence: British Cinema in the Thirties* (with Paul Willemen), London, British Film Institute, especially, Claire Johnston, "'Independence' and the thirties – ideologies in history: an introduction," pp. 9–23, and Annette Kuhn, "British documentary in the 1930s and 'independence' – recontextualizing a film movement," pp. 24–35.

6 Christian Metz (1979) discusses these very issues in some detail in "The cinematic apparatus as social institution: an interview with Christian Metz," *Discourse*, No. 1, pp. 20–8.

7 See McCall and Tyndall, "Sixteen working statements," where they argue that realist films often have no lasting impact on audiences.

8 Pat Ferrero's *Quilts* (1980), for instance, evoked laughter when shown to the 1980 New York Film Festival audience (it is a significant criticism of this kind of vérité-realism that its cinematic strategies didn't protect its subjects from such a response), while in a women's studies classroom the film is a moving and illuminating experience.

9 Peter Wollen and Laura Mulvey have made a practice of being present at film viewings, as have Sally Potter, Susan Clayton, Jonathan Curling, and Michelle Citron, among others. It would be interesting to compile evidence from such filmmakers about their experiences with audiences.

10 See McCall and Tyndall, "Sixteen working statements."

11 In Britain, the fourth television channel has just opened, providing an outlet for independent filmmakers. It will be interesting to see what the results are and what the filmmakers' experience is in working for Channel 4.

12 For instance, Sally Potter's film was shown commercially; in America, an independent film occasionally gets released, as did, for example, Kopple's *Harlan County, U.S.A.*, but it is then always in the realist mode.

15 Conclusion: Motherhood and patriarchal discourse

1 Nancy Chodorow (1978) "Psychodynamics of the family," in Nancy Chodorow (ed.) *The Reproduction of Mothering*, Berkeley, Calif., University of California Press, pp. 191–209.

2 "*Riddles of the Sphinx*: a film by Laura Mulvey and Peter Wollen; script," *Screen*, Vol. 18, No. 2 (1977), p. 62.

3 Sandy Flitterman and Jacquelyn Suter (1979) "Textual riddles: woman as enigma or site of social meanings? An interview with Laura Mulvey," *Discourse*, Vol. 1, No. 1, p. 107.

4 Claire Pajaczkowska (ed.) (1981) "Introduction to script for *Sigmund Freud's Dora*, *Framework*, Nos 15–17, pp. 75–81.

5 Flitterman and Suter, "Textual riddles," pp. 109–20.

6 Adrienne Rich (1976) *Of Woman Born*, New York, Norton, pp. 40, 44.

7 Dorothy Dinnerstein (1977) *The Mermaid and the Minotaur*, New York, Harper, pp. 95, 97–8, 105–6.

8 ibid., pp. 116–19.

9 Julia Kristeva (1980) "Motherhood according to Bellini," trans. Thomas Gora, Alice Jardine, and Leon S. Roudiez, in Leon S. Roudiez (ed.) *Desire in Language: A Semiotic Approach to Literature and Art*, New York, Columbia University Press, p. 238.

10 ibid., p. 239.

11 ibid., p. 239.

12 "Women and representation: a discussion with Laura Mulvey," *Wedge* (London), No. 2 (1979), p. 49.

13 Kristeva, "Motherhood according to Bellini," pp. 239–40.

14 Mary Ann Doane, "Woman's stake in representation: filming the female body," *October*, No. 17 (1981), p. 33.

15 ibid., p. 26.

16 ibid.

17 For representative examples of French theory about mothering, see Isabelle de Courtivron and Elaine Marks (eds) (1980) *New French Feminisms*, Amherst, Mass., University of Massachusetts Press, and films by Laura Mulvey and Peter Wollen (*Riddles of the Sphinx*), Michelle Citron (*Daughter-Rite*), Marjorie Keller (*Misconception*), and Helke Sanders (*All Round Redupers*).

18 Nancy Chodorow, "Psychodynamics of the family."

19 Julia Kristeva, "Chinese women against the tide," trans. of "Les Chinoises à 'contre-courant'" by Elaine Marks, in Courtivron and Marks, *New French Feminisms*, p. 240. (Unfortunately some recent work by Marilyn Young suggests that all may not be so well in China after all.)

20 Eleanor Maccoby and John Martin (1983) "Parent–child interaction," in E. M. Hetherington (ed.) *Handbook of Child Psychology*, New York, Wiley. One has obviously to be careful here about introducing discourses that work on an entirely different level than the theoretical, psychoanalytic discourse that I have mainly been considering. It may be, however, that confronting the psychoanalytic discourse with more empirically based kinds of discourse could lead to an opening up of the theory, to suggestions for a way out of the theoretical impasse in which psychoanalytic frameworks place women. But that is another book.

21 By this I mean that since heterosexuality is made the "norm," lesbian relations often have no choice but to be set up as antithetic to the "norm" (and thus to an extent have their shape controlled by the norm), or to *mimic* the "normal" heterosexual coupling.

22 Cf. an important article by Jessica Benjamin (1980) "The bonds of love: rational violence and erotic domination," *Feminist Studies*, Vol. 6, No. 1, pp. 144–73.

Filmographies and synopses

Hollywood films

CAMILLE (1936)

Credits

Producers:	Irving Thalberg, Bernard Hyman
Director:	George Cukor
Screenplay:	Zoë Atkins, Frances Marion, James Hilton, from Alexander Dumas's *La Dame aux camélias*
Photography:	William Daniels, Karl Freund
Art direction:	Cedric Gibbons
Editor:	Margaret Booth
Music:	Herbert Stothart
Dances:	Val Raset
Cast:	Greta Garbo (Marguerite Gautier); Robert Taylor (Armand Duval); Lionel Barrymore (Monsieur Duval); Elizabeth Allan (Nichette); Jessie Ralph (Nanine); Henry Daniell (Baron de Varville); Lenore Ulric (Olympe); Laura Hope Crews (Prudence); Rex O'Malley (Gaston); Russell Hardle (Gustave); E. E. Clive (Saint Gaudens); Douglas Walton (Henri); Marion Ballou (Corinne); Joan Brodel (Marie Jeanette); June Wilkins (Louise); Fritz Leiber, Jr (Valentin); Elsie Esmonds (Mme. Duval); Edwin Maxwell (Doctor); Eily Malyon (Thérèse); Mariska Aldrich (Friend of Marguerite); John Bryan (DeMusset); Rex Evans (Companion); Eugene King (Gypsy Leader); Adrienne Matzenauer (Singer); Georgia Caine (Streetwalker); Mabel Colcord (Madame Barjon); Chappel Dossett (Priest); Elspeth Dudgeon (Attendant); Effie Ellsler (Grandma Duval); Sibyl Harris (Georges Sand); Maude Hume (Aunt Henriette); Olaf Hytten (Croupier); Gwendolyn Kogan (Governess); Ferdinand Munier (Priest); Barry Norton (Emile); John Picorri (Orchestra Leader); Guy Bates (Auctioneer); Zeffie Tilbury (Old Duchess)
Filmed at:	Metro-Goldwyn-Mayer Studios
Completed:	December 1936
Released:	January 1937
Running time:	108 minutes

Synopsis

Set in Paris of the 1840s, *Camille* traces the story of a woman, Marguerite Gautier, who lives by winning rich lovers. Already sick (with tuberculosis) as the film opens, she persists in her gay life, going to the theatre nightly, buying extravagant gowns from her friend, Prudence, and always wearing expensive white camellias in her hair.

Mistaking Armand Duval (the son of a middle-class lawyer) for the rich Baron de Varville, Marguerite falls in love for the first time; but she rejects Armand for his rich rival. Some time passes; we learn that Marguerite has been ill, and that the Baron is leaving on a trip. Marguerite goes to an auction where she meets Armand and learns that he visited her every day when she was ill. She invites him to a party at her house that night.

The party is a raucous affair, Marguerite's friends being loud and vulgar. Alienated, Armand follows Marguerite into her room when a coughing fit seizes her. They declare their love for one another, and Marguerite gives Armand key so that he can return later. In the meantime, however, the Baron returns, having changed his plans, and Armand is unable to get in. The Baron suspects Marguerite of treachery, while she believes that her one chance of happiness has slipped by.

Armand visits his family and asks his father for money to go abroad. When Marguerite receives a letter telling her of Armand's plans, she visits him and their passion resurges. Marguerite promises to go to the country with Armand, but she first has to disentangle herself from the Baron and settle her financial affairs, which she does by taking money from the Baron.

An idyllic period in the country follows: Armand and Marguerite are blissfully happy with one another and with the simple joys of country life which replace the city extravagances. Marguerite and Armand learn, however, that the castle on the hill belongs to the Baron de Varville.

One day when Armand is in Paris, sorting out his affairs so that he and Marguerite can have money to live on, Monsieur Duval visits Marguerite and persuades her to give up Armand for Armand's own sake; he points out that Armand could never live the life he should with a woman who would be excluded from his circles. Heartbroken, Marguerite pretends that she no longer loves Armand and goes back to the Baron. Distraught in turn, Armand rejects Marguerite and goes abroad.

Time passes; at a club one night, Armand and Marguerite meet. Still hurt, Armand scorns Marguerite but his passion has not abated. Winning a great deal of money from the Baron, Armand begs Marguerite to leave with him. Shaken badly, Marguerite clings to her promise, and Armand throws his money at Marguerite. The Baron and Armand challenge each other to a duel in which the Baron is wounded, requiring Armand's flight from France.

Abandoned now also by the Baron, Marguerite sickens. Close to death, and bereft of all money and possessions, Marguerite waits only for Armand's return. He comes to town, finally relents and visits Marguerite, just in time. The lovers are blissfully united for a brief moment before Marguerite dies, forgiven.

BLONDE VENUS (1932)

Credits

Director:	Joseph Von Sternberg
Screenplay:	Jules Furthman, S. K. Lauren; based on an original story by Joseph Von Sternberg
Photography:	Bert Glennon
Art direction:	Wiard B. Ihnen
Songs:	"Hot Voodoo" and "You little so and so" by Ralph Rainger,

	lyrics by Sam Coslow; "I could be annoyed" by Dick Whiting and Leo Robin (lyrics)
Music:	Oskar Potoker
Cast:	Marlene Dietrich (Helen Faraday); Herbert Marshall (Edward Faraday); Cary Grant (Nick Townsend); Dickie Moore (Johnny); Gene Morgan (Ben Smith); Rita La Roy ("Taxi Belle" Hooper); Robert Emmett O'Connor (Dan O'Connor); Sidney Toler (Detective Wilson); Cecil Cunningham (Night-Club Owner); Hattie McDaniel, Mildred Washington (Black Maids); Francis Sayles (Charlie Blaine); Morgan Wallace (Dr Pierce); Evelyn Preer (Iola); Robert Grave (La Farge); Lloyd Whitlock Baltimore (Manager); Emile Chautard (Chautard); James Kilgannon (Janitor); Sterling Holloway (Joe); Charles Morton (Bob); Ferdinand Schumann-Heink (Henry); Jerry Tucker (Otto); Harold Berquist (Big Fellow); Dewey Robinson (Greek Restaurant-Owner); Clifford Dempsey (Night Court Judge); Bessie Lyle (Grace); Gertrude Short (Receptionist); Brad Kline (New Orleans Policeman)
Filmed at:	Paramount Studios
Completed:	1932
Released:	1932
Running time:	80 minutes

Synopsis

Edward Faraday, touring in Germany, meets Helen, an actress, as she swims in a lake with friends. Falling in love immediately, Faraday engineers a meeting and marries Helen. Time passes; we cut to the New York apartment where Helen is bathing their son, Johnny. We soon learn that the family is in trouble since Edward has contracted a serious disease through his scientific research. As his formula is not quite complete, the family has little money, so Helen decides to get a job as a singer in order to pay for Edward's trip to Germany where there is a doctor who might be able to cure him.

At the agency, Helen immediately attracts the attention of the manager, Ben Smith, who finds her a job in a club frequented by the politician Nick Townsend. Fascinated by Helen's performance, Nick pursues her and invites her to meet him after the show. Helen returns home very late with a check to cover the cost of her husband's journey.

During Edward's absence, Nick and Helen fall in love. Nick sees that Helen leaves her job, and takes care of her and Johnny at his luxurious house.

Returning home cured, unexpectedly early, Edward finds the apartment empty and unlived in. He is unable to find out exactly where Helen is, but one day he surprises her at the apartment when she returns to pick up mail. She tells him about the affair, but declares her readiness to return to him. He rejects her scornfully, but demands to have Johnny back. Helen agrees to bring him, but has in fact already decided to run away.

The next section of the film traces Helen and Johnny on their wanderings, hotly pursued by detectives whom Edward has hired to capture them. Forced further and further south, Helen has to abandon singing because it is too public, and resorts finally to prostitution. She takes good care of Johnny, teaching him to read and write, and to remember his father.

Finally, exhausted by the long pursuit, Helen gives herself up to the detective who had not even recognized her, and Edward comes to collect Johnny and to give Helen back the money she earned for his medical expenses. Helen throws the money away in a shelter for homeless women, determined to make her own way up.

A quick montage sequence shows us Helen's meteoric rise to fame. We find her in Paris's most fashionable club, in a dazzling-white male outfit. Nick Townsend is there, and again comes to her dressing-room after the show. Beautiful, but cold as ice, Helen pretends to be happy and carefree; but Nick mentions her son, and, suggesting that Helen still cares for him, offers her a ticket on the boat he is going home on the following day.

Helen and Nick arrive in New York, and go to the Faraday apartment. Edward finally agrees to let Helen see Johnny, but, sullen and angry, refuses Nick's proffer of money. Johnny is delighted to see his mother, and Helen quickly sets about preparing him for bed. Seeing her thus involved, Nick quietly leaves. Johnny insists on the old nightly ritual – the story of how his parents met – and Edward softens. He and Helen are reconciled.

LADY FROM SHANGHAI (1946)

Credits

Producer:	Harry Cohn
Associate producers:	Richard Wilson, William Castle
Director:	Orson Welles
Assistant director:	Sam Nelson
Screenplay:	Orson Welles; freely adapted from the novel, *If I Die Before I Wake*, by Sherwood King
Photography:	Charles Lawton, Jr
Camera:	Irving Klein
Editor:	Viola Lawrence
Art direction:	Stephen Goosson, Sturges Carne
Set decoration:	Wilbur Menefee, Herman Schoenbrun
Special effects:	Lawrence Butler
Music:	Heinz Roemheld
Musical director:	M. W. Stoloff
Orchestrations:	Herschel Burke Gilbert
Song:	"Please don't kiss me" by Allan Roberts, Doris Fisher
Costumes:	Jean Louis
Sound:	Lodge Cunningham
Cast:	Orson Welles (Michael O'Hara); Rita Hayworth (Elsa Bannister); Everett Sloane (Arthur Bannister); Glenn Anders (George Grisby); Ted de Corsia (Sidney Broom); Gus Schilling (Goldie); Louis Merrill (Jake); Erskine Sanford (Judge); Carl Frank (District Attorney Galloway); Evelyn Ellis (Bessie); Wong Show Chong (Li); Harry Shannon (Horse-cab Driver); Sam Nelson (Captain); Richard Wilson (District Attorney's Assistant); players of the Mandarin Theatre of San Francisco
Filmed at:	Columbia Studios, Hollywood, and on location in Mexico and San Francisco
Completed:	1946
Released:	Great Britain, March 1948; USA, May 1948
Running time:	86 mins
Distributed by:	Columbia

Synopsis

Wandering in Central Park, New York, one summer night, Michael O'Hara, an unemployed, Irish, would-be novelist, happens upon Elsa Bannister, beautiful young wife of Arthur Bannister, the ageing, crippled, but famous criminal-defense lawyer. In flashback, voice-over narration, O'Hara tells us that he was immediately fascinated by her seductive beauty, and he leaps to her aid when her horse and carriage are held up by some petty thieves. He takes her to her garage, where Elsa wants to hire him to work on the boat that she and her husband are taking to San Francisco. Afraid of his attraction to her, and sensing some danger, O'Hara declines.

At the employment agency, Arthur Bannister seeks O'Hara; the men get drunk together, and O'Hara feels obliged to deposit Bannister safely on his boat. There, Elsa and her crew persuade him and his friend to take the job after all.

The boat sets out; one day, when Bannister is ashore and Elsa swimming nearby, George Grisby comes aboard and taunts O'Hara about Elsa's interest in him, to Michael's disgust. Elsa returns to the boat and seduces Michael, who first slaps her and then responds to her embrace. We learn that Grisby has seen the whole event from his boat, and he goes off laughing hysterically.

During the voyage, Michael tells Bannister that he plans to leave the crew at San Francisco; Bannister mocks him, while Elsa sings a song so haunting that all the men are enthralled. At an elaborate picnic shortly afterwards, Elsa finds time to tell Michael that Bannister suspects her of infidelity and has Broom, a detective disguised as the cook, watching her every move. Later on, Grisby and Bannister get drunk and send for O'Hara; disgusted by them, O'Hara lets them know how he scorns them. Elsa watches the scene intently, and hears Bannister mention some hold he has over her. Later that night, Michael and Elsa manage to get together, and Michael begs her to go away with him. She points out that he has no money and that she is used to an extravagant lifestyle.

Shortly afterwards, Grisby makes O'Hara a proposal; O'Hara will pretend to kill Grisby, for a large sum of money. Grisby plans to retire to a remote island with the insurance money he would receive. He assures O'Hara that he cannot be convicted since Grisby's body will never be found. O'Hara agrees to the deal.

They arrive in San Francisco. Elsa agrees to meet O'Hara secretly at a museum. There, O'Hara tells her about the Grisby deal, and that now he will have enough money to take her away. But the plan to fake Grisby's death backfires when Broom discovers the plot and, before dying from a gunshot wound fired by Grisby, warns O'Hara that he is about to be framed. He says that Grisby, with Elsa's help, is going to kill Bannister for his money and let O'Hara take the fall. When O'Hara arrives at Bannister's office to warn Bannister that Grisby may be going to kill him, he finds that Grisby is already dead there, and that the murder is pinned on him.

Bannister defends O'Hara, but really intends to see him convicted. At the trial, Elsa indicates that O'Hara should feign a suicide in order to escape. This he manages, but by this time he has faced the fact that Elsa must be behind the whole plot. Elsa sees O'Hara run into the Chinese quarter, where she has friends. She alerts these men, who capture O'Hara and take him to a closed fairground. O'Hara awakens in the Hall of Mirrors, and Elsa arrives with a gun, planning to kill him. Bannister interrupts them, however, telling Elsa that he has left a note to the District Attorney explaining that she killed Grisby because he lost his head and killed Broom, thus jeopardizing her plans. Husband and wife shoot at each other amongst the flying shards of glass, and their images reflect many times in the shattering mirrors. Bannister dies first, while Elsa struggles up, wounded, and out of the broken glass. O'Hara confronts her with her evil deeds, and with his knowledge that she was behind everything. He leaves her dying, determined to get over her, even if it takes him the rest of his life.

Like *The Big Sleep*, this is a film that never quite clears up its complicated plot, and questions are inevitably left unanswered.

LOOKING FOR MR GOODBAR (1977)

Credits

Producer:	Freddie Fields
Director:	Richard Brooks
Screenplay:	Richard Brooks; adapted from the novel by Judith Rossner
Photography:	William A. Fraker
Art direction:	Edward Carfagno
Editor:	George Grenville
Music:	Artie Kane
Costumes:	Jodie Lynn Tillen
Assistant director:	David Silver
Cast:	Diane Keaton (Teresa Dunn); Tuesday Weld (Katherine Dunn); William Atherton (James Morrissey); Richard Kiley (Mr Dunn); Richard Gere (Tony Lopanto); Alan Feinstein (Prof. Engle); Tom Berenger (Gary Cooper White); Priscilla Pointer (Mrs Dunn); Laurie Pranger (Brigid Dunn); Joel Fabiani (Barney); Julius Harris (Black Cat); Richard Bright (George); LeVar Burton (Capt. Jackson); Marilyn Coleman (Mrs Jackson); Elizabeth Cheshire (Little Teresa)
Filmed at:	Paramount Studios and on location
Completed:	1977
Released:	October 1977
Running time:	135 minutes

Synopsis

As the film opens, Teresa (Terry) Dunn is daydreaming about seducing her married college English teacher, and shortly afterwards manages to get a job as his assistant. Working in his apartment one day, she gets him to make love to her, rather hastily, and from then on is completely infatuated with him.

Back at home, Terry's lovely younger sister, Kathy, an air stewardess, has returned for a brief visit. She tells Terry that she is pregnant, does not know who the father is, and that she is on her way to Puerto Rico for an abortion. Weeping, Terry recalls how jealous of Kathy she used to be as a child, since their father so favored Kathy.

Flashbacks during this first part of the film explain Terry's difficult childhood. Diagnosed too late as having scoliosis, Terry spent months on her back in a plaster cast, after a difficult operation that has left a long scar down her back. Unable to deal adequately with the situation, Terry's parents isolated her so that she grew up feeling that she did not belong and that she could never compensate for the death of a much loved son. Terry's other sister, Brigid, has won the family's goodwill by marrying locally and producing babies.

Terry continues to meet her professor, Martin Engle, whenever she can, rushing out whenever he 'phones but being unable to call him because of his wife. He finally tires of her, and takes the opportunity of the summer break to end their relationship.

Meanwhile, Terry's sister, Kathy, has moved into New York City, with her new husband, Brooks, and she invites Terry to a party. There for the first time, Terry is introduced to marijuana, pornography movies, and an orgy. Arriving home the following morning, and unable to explain where she has been, she is thrown out of the house by her irate father. Kathy finds her an apartment in her building.

Terry gets a job as a teacher in a school for deaf and dumb children. Her patience is rewarded by the children's love and dedication. She is able particularly to help a young black girl, Amy.

At night, Terry haunts the singles bars, looking for men. One night, she meets an exciting, but wild man, Tony, who dazzles her with his neon knife and who thrills her physically. From then on, he drops in and out of her life as he pleases.

Taking Amy home one day, Terry meets the family's social worker, James, and begs him to get a proper hearing-aid for Amy. She and James become friends, and she invites him to her parents' home for dinner. Her father takes to Jim right away, and seems set on Terry marrying him. Terry is not sure that she is attracted to Jim, or that he is the man she loves, particularly since Jim has trouble making proper love to her.

One day, Tony arrives suddenly and tells her he has no place to stay; Terry refuses to let him be in her apartment, and he flies into a rage, and leaves, cursing. His pranks get more and more violent, and Terry plans to end the relationship with him. Jim begs her to marry him, but she refuses, still unsure about him.

Kathy meanwhile has divorced Brooks and married her psychology professor, turning over a new leaf. Terry plans to do the same thing as the new year starts. She throws her drugs away, and cleans and brightens her apartment. Jim phones and asks her to spend New Year's Eve with him, but she declines, as she does also the offer to go out with Kathy and her husband. She decides to spend one last night cruising the singles bars and then start out on a new footing.

At her usual bar, Terry meets an insecure young man, George, whom we have previously seen having a quarrel with his drunken male lover. Terry likes the look of George, and invites him up to her apartment. There, George has difficulty making love to her, and begins to talk about his time in jail, where he feared being called effeminate. Finally, he and Terry lie down, and George falls asleep. Terry wakes him up, and tells him he must leave. He becomes enraged, and, suddenly potent, begins to make love to her violently, simultaneously stabbing her when she begins to scream hysterically. The film ends with the two silhouetted figures, struggling bizarrely in Terry's flickering light.

The independent feminist film

NATHALIE GRANGER (1972)

Credits

Director:	Marguerite Duras
Screenplay:	Marguerite Duras
Director of photography:	Ghislain Cloquet
First cameraman:	Bruno Nuytten
Second cameraman:	Jean-Michel Carré
First assistant director:	Benoît Jacquot
Second assistant director:	Remy Duchemin
Editor:	Nicole Lubchansky
Assistant editor:	Michèle Muller
Sound:	Paul Laîné
Sound assistants:	Michel Vionnet, Michèle Muller
Continuity:	Geneviève Dufour
Production photography:	Jean Mascolo
Technical crew:	Daniel Arlet
Sound mix:	Paul Bertault
Cast:	Lucia Bose (Isabelle Granger); Jeanne Moreau (L'Amie); Luce Garcia Ville (Director of the School); Gérard Depardieu (Salesman); Dionys Mascolo (Father); Valérie Mascolo (Nathalie Granger); Nathalie

	Bourgeois (Laurence Granger)
Filmed:	On location, in a village in Yvelines, France, starting 2 April 1972
Completed:	16 April 1972
Released:	1972
Note:	In the text of the film, Duras appends a note about the house where the filming took place. Built in 1750, it is situated about 14 kilometers from Versailles, and now belongs to Duras. Among many interesting details, Duras notes that it was occupied by Germans in 1940.
Distributed by:	The French Consulate, 934 Fifth Avenue, New York, N.Y. 10021

Synopsis

As the film opens, Isabelle Granger, her husband, her friend, and her two children, Nathalie and Laurence, are finishing lunch. The parents talk about whether or not they will send Nathalie away to another school since she has been acting violently in the present one.

Soon, husband and children leave, and silence settles on the house. Silently, the two women clear the table and wash the dishes. We hear a voice on the radio talking about the rape and murder of two young girls in a nearby forest, and about the search for the killers. The silence of the afternoon is periodically punctuated by updates on the progress and capture of the suspects.

Isabelle 'phones the music teacher to discuss whether or not Nathalie will continue with the lessons that are apparently viewed as crucial to her psychological wellbeing; the teacher says that it is up to Nathalie. The friend goes outside and begins to collect wood in preparation for a bonfire. She then phones the Immigration Office about the Portuguese maid, Marie, who, not knowing the language, signed away her right to stay in France. She is told that nothing can be done.

After standing over the fire, the two women visit Nathalie's principal, and are told about her intractable behavior; the principal stresses how unusual such violence is in a little girl. These words haunt Isabelle once they are home again, and she 'phones the Datkin Boarding School to tell them to expect Nathalie.

As the afternoon wears on, Isabelle irons, prepares, and packs Nathalie's clothes, very upset about the turn of events. Her friend helps her.

A washing-machine salesman arrives, and tries to sell them a machine that, it turns out, they already have. He blurts out his sales talk, nervously, while the women sit quietly and watch him. He is trapped by his own language. Unsuccessful, he leaves, and through the windows, we see him try other doors and then drive off.

It is finally time to fetch the children from school. The friend brings them in, and makes them a snack. Nathalie plays in the garden with her pram and her cats, while Laurence and the friend get in a boat and clean up the pond. Isabelle watches.

The music teacher arrives, and Nathalie and the friend sit and watch Laurence have her lesson, while Isabelle walks around nervously outside, peeking in through the windows. Finally, Nathalie decides to take her lesson, to the relief of her mother and the friend.

This step is significant enough for Isabelle to 'phone the Datkin School to tell them that after all, Nathalie will not be coming. The two women then settle down for a nap, as do also the children in another room. Isabelle tears up the newspaper, mail, and Nathalie's exercise books.

The salesman comes in again; he sits down in the kitchen, with Isabelle, and tells her how he hates his work and wishes he could go back to being a laundry man. As he weeps, Isabelle goes out quietly into the garden. The salesman gets up, and wanders round the house as if in an alien, frightening realm. He leaves hurriedly, and from the silence of the now peaceful old house, we see him get into his car. In the garden, we see Isabelle's slight, dark frame moving amongst the trees.

MARIANNE AND JULIANE (DIE BLEIERNE ZEIT) (THE GERMAN SISTERS) (1981)

Credits

Producer:	Eberhard Junkersdorf
Production manager:	Gudrun Ruzickova
Assistant producer:	Gerrit Schwarz
Director:	Margarethe Von Trotta
Screenplay:	Margarethe Von Trotta
Assistant director:	Helenka Hummel
Photography:	Franz Rath
Camera assistant:	Werner Deml
Editor:	Dagmar Hirtz
Assistant editor:	Uwe Lauterkorn
Music:	Nicolas Economou
Sound:	Vladimir Vizner
Sound assistant:	Hieronymus Würden
Costumes:	Monika Hasse
Wardrobe:	Petra Kray
Make-up:	Rüdiger Knoll, Jutta Stroppe
Still photography:	Ralf Tooten
Lighting:	Rudolf Hartl, Uli Lotze, Wolf-Dieter Fallert
Continuity:	Margit Czenki
Props:	Robert Reitberger
Set decoration:	Georg von Kieseritzky
Cast:	Jutta Lampe (Juliane); Barbara Sukowa (Marianne); Rüdiger Vogler (Wolfgang); Verenice Rudolph (Sabine); Luc Bondy (Werner); Doris Schade (Mother); Franz Rudnick (Father); Ina Robinski (Juliane at 17 years); Julia Biedermann (Marianne at 16 years); Ingeborg Weber, Carola Hembus, Margit Czenki, Wulfhild Sydow, Anna Steinmann (Feminist Journal Editors); Samir Jawad (Jan at 4 years); Patrick Estrada-Pox (Jan at 10 years); Barbara Paepcke (Juliane at 6 years); Rebecca Paepcke (Marianne at 5 years); Karin Bremer (Officer); Hannelore Minkus (Teacher); Rolf Schult (Newspaper Editor); Anton Rattinger (Priest); Satan Deutscher (Marianne's friend); Michael Sellmann (Second Man with Marianne); Lydia Billiet (Nurse); Wilbert Steinmann (Lawyer); Felix Moeller (Rolf); Christoph Parge (Dieter); Dieter Baier (Cascadeur)
Filmed by:	Bioskop-Film München, and Sender Fries Berlin, starting 23 February 1981, and on location in West Berlin, Italy, and Tunisia
Completed:	September 1981
Released:	Festival premiere, 11 September 1981; cinema release, 25 September 1981
Running time:	109 minutes
Distributed by:	Filmverlag der Autoren, München, and New Yorker Films, New York

Synopsis

At the start of the film, Juliane's quiet research for the feminist journal she helps to edit is rudely interrupted by her brother-in-law, Werner, who has brought his son, Jan, to leave with Juliane. Resentful at being imposed upon because her sister, Marianne, has chosen to be a terrorist, Juliane agrees only to keep Jan for a day or two. Werner's suicide, however, puts her in a difficult position, and she reluctantly decides to place Jan in a foster home.

About this time, Marianne contacts Juliane and the different paths the sisters have taken becomes clear. Although Juliane shares Marianne's desire to correct the abuses of bourgeois capitalism, including the brutalization of the Third World, she cannot support her strategies. Marianne, for her part, scorns Juliane's liberal, reformist feminism. Flashbacks during this, and later, parts of the film reveal that in their childhood Marianne was the conformist, Juliane the rebel, and that nevertheless they had a strong, caring relationship. We also learn about the rigid conventional family that the sisters grew up in, dominated by an authoritarian father, who also ruled the obedient mother.

Time passes; Marianne and her friends descend rudely on Juliane and her middle-class, architect boyfriend, Wolfgang, in the early-morning hours.

Shortly afterwards, Marianne is captured and jailed. Juliane does all she can for her sister, who at first rebuffs her and then is grateful for the contact and for the little things Juliane is allowed to bring. A bond develops once more between them, although they still differ about politics and about their parents. Childhood memories haunt their meetings, and we learn a good deal about the Nazi and post-Nazi political climate whose legacy shaped the consciousness of the sisters and molded their political beliefs.

While Juliane is away with Wolfgang on a much-needed vacation, Marianne is discovered hanged in her cell. Convinced that it was murder, not suicide, Juliane goes all out to prove her case against the authorities. Her identification with Marianne develops into an obsession as she tries to recreate the precise conditions in which the alleged murder happened, and her sister's situation before and during her death. Becoming a fanatic in her research, Juliane forgets her work, her boyfriend, and her nephew, Jan. When she finally has the evidence she sought, Juliane finds that the outside world is not interested in what happened to a terrorist some years back.

Juliane suddenly gets an urgent call from Jan's foster parents, telling her that Jan was set on fire by boys who discovered that Marianne was his mother. Jan barely survives, but when he is ready to leave the hospital, Juliane decides to take him in.

The film ends with the two living together, bound by their relationship to Marianne and their desire to understand her and the past.

LIVES OF PERFORMERS (1972)

Credits

Director:	Yvonne Rainer
Screenplay:	Yvonne Rainer
Photography:	Babette Mangolte
Editors:	Yvonne Rainer, Babette Mangolte
Sound:	Gene De Fever, Gordon Mumma
Cast:	Yvonne Rainer, Valda Setterfield, Fernando Torm, James Barth, Epp Kotkas, John Erdman, Shirley Soffer, Sarah Soffer
Filmed in:	New York
Completed:	1972
Running time:	90 minutes
Distributed by:	Castelli-Sonnabend Tapes and Films Inc., 420 West Broadway, New York, N.Y. 10012

FILM ABOUT A WOMAN WHO . . . (1974)

Credits

Director: Yvonne Rainer
Screenplay: Yvonne Rainer
Photography: Babette Mangolte
Editors: Yvonne Rainer, Babette Mangolte
Sound: Deborah Freedman
Cast: Dempster Leach, Shirley Soffer, Sarah Soffer, John Erdman, Renfreu Neff, James Barth, Epp Kotkas
Filmed in: New York
Completed: 1974
Running time: 105 minutes
Distributed by: Castelli-Sonnabend Tapes and Films Inc., 420 West Broadway, New York, N.Y. 10012

SIGMUND FREUD'S DORA: A CASE OF MISTAKEN IDENTITY (1979)

Credits

Directors: Anthony McCall, Claire Pajaczkowska, Andrew Tyndall, Jane Weinstock
Screenplay: Same group, plus Ivan Ward
Camera: Babette Mangolte
Sound: Deedee Halleck
Cast: Joel Kovel (Sigmund Freud); Silvia Kolbowski (Dora); Anne Hegira (Dora's Mother); Suzanne Fletcher (Talking Lips)
Filmed in: New York City
Completed: 1979
Distributed by: McCall and Tyndall, 11 Jay Street, New York, N.Y. 10013

THRILLER (1979)

Credits

Director: ⎫
Camera: ⎪
Sound: ⎬   Sally Potter
Editing: ⎭
Cast: Colette Lafont, Rose English, Tony Gacon, Vincent Meehan
Filmed in: London
Completed: 1979
Released and distributed in USA by: Serious Business Company, 1145 Mandana Blvd, Oakland, Calif. 94610

DAUGHTER-RITE (1978)

Credits

Script: ⎫
Editor: ⎬   Michelle Citron
Director: ⎭
Sound assistants: Sharon Bement, Barbara Roos

Camera assistants:	Sharon Bement, Barbara Roos
Graphics:	Nancy Zucker
Closing quote:	Deena Metzger, "The book of hags," *Sinister Wisdom* (Fall 1976)
Cast:	Penelope Victor (Maggie); Anne Wilford (Stephanie); Jerri Hancock (Narrator)
Special thanks:	Irene Wilford, Emily McKenty, Jerri Hancock
Filmed in:	Chicago
Released:	1978
Distributed by:	Iris Films, Box 5353, Berkeley, Calif. 94705

RIDDLES OF THE SPHINX (1976)

Credits

Directors:	Laura Mulvey, Peter Wollen
Script:	Laura Mulvey, Peter Wollen
Cinematography:	Diane Tammes, assisted by Jane Jackson, Steve Shaw
Editing:	Carola Klein, Larry Sider
Sound:	Larry Sider
Music:	Mike Ratledge
Cast:	Dinah Stabb (Louise); Merdelle Jordine (Maxine); Rhiannon Tise (Anna); Clive Merrison (Chris); Marie Green (Acrobat); Paula Melbourne (Rope Act); Crissie Trigger (Juggler); Mary Maddox (Voice Off); Mary Kelly, Laura Mulvey
Produced by:	British Film Institute
Filmed:	On location in London, beginning August 1976
Completed:	October 1976
Distributed by:	The Museum of Modern Art, 11 West 53 Street, New York, N.Y. 10019

AMY! (1980)

Credits

Directors:	Laura Mulvey, Peter Wollen
Script:	Laura Mulvey, Peter Wollen
Camera:	Diane Tammes
Crew:	Jonathan Collinson, Anne Cottringer
2nd Camera:	Francine Winham
Sound:	Larry Sider
Editing:	Larry Sider
Design:	Michael Hurd
Cast:	Mary Maddox (Amy) (words from Amy Johnson's letters); Class Community Care Course, Paddington College; Yvonne Rainer (Voice of Bryher, Amelia Earhart, Lola Montez, 'S', and Gertrude Stein); Jonathan Eden (Headlines from *The Times*, May 1930); Laura Mulvey; Peter Wollen
Thanks:	Chris Berg, Ian Christie, Rosalind Delmar, Keith Griffiths, Ilona Halberstadt, John Howe, Tina Keane, Tamara Krikorian, Carol Laws, Patsy Nightingale, Geoffrey Nowell-Smith, Carl Teitelbaum, Chad Wollen, Evanston Percussion Unit, the De Havilland Moth Club

Special thanks: Feminist Improvising Group, Poly Styrene and X-Ray Spex, Jack Hylton and His Orchestra

Distributed by: The Museum of Modern Art, 11 West 53 Street, New York, N.Y. 10019

ONE WAY OR ANOTHER (DE CIERTA MANERA) (1974)

Credits

Director:	Sara Gomez Yara
Producer:	Camilo Vives
Script:	Sara Gomez Yara, Tomas Gonzalez Perez
Camera:	Luis Garcia
Music:	Sergio Vitier
Editing:	Ivan Arocha
Sound:	Germinal Fernandez
Cast:	Mario (Mario Balmaseda); Yolanda (Yolanda Cuellar); Humberto (Mario Limonta)
Additional work on the film:	Tomas Alea Gutierrez, Julio Garcia Espinosa
Distributed by:	Unifilm, Inc., 419 Park Avenue South, New York

Synopsis

At the start of the film, a worker, Humberto, is being tried by his mates for being absent from his job for dubious reasons. After much inner turmoil, his friend, Mario, reveals that, indeed, Humberto was away with a woman and not attending a sick mother.

The film flashes back to the events preceding the trial. We see Mario meeting Yolanda, a school teacher newly assigned to the area. As we follow their developing romance, Gomez intercuts documentary shots of the physical transformation of the neighborhood, from slums to neat high-rise apartments, under Castro's regime.

The story of Mario and Yolanda takes us back into their past lives; the difference in their struggles is explicitly related to gender, as part of an exploration that the film undertakes into sex roles in modern Cuba. The film shows how relatively easy it is to change things on the economic level; and how painfully slow change is on the psychological, personal level.

We return to Humberto's trial in the film's present; Mario feels guilty for having "betrayed" Humberto, but learns that such machismo codes no longer apply. Although he and Yolanda have broken up as a result of Mario's intractable machismo, the film's ending suggests that things may change.

Appendix for teachers

As I noted in the Preface, the idea for this book arose out of a series of courses on women in film that I have been teaching over the years. Since I found none of the available texts satisfactory, I had to rely on xeroxed articles left in the Rutgers Library Reserve room – a very inefficient and inadequate way of proceeding. I realized that if teacher and students had a book that not only placed issues clearly in their historical and theoretical context but that also provided in-depth readings of films, the discussion of any one film could start at a far higher and more coherent level. Obviously, not all teachers and students are going to agree with the readings I have given here; hopefully, however, the analyses will be provocative enough to stimulate a debate not only about the films themselves and what really goes-on in them, but also about the particular theoretical assumptions underlying each of the interpretations.

A class, that is, could be conceived as setting up a dialogue with the text, examining and testing its assumptions, and taking further the issues which may often have been only tentatively, and inadequately, explored. Sometimes a class may build on a reading; at other times, it may reject the reading and think through an alternative one, using different theoretical assumptions. The heavily psychoanalytic cast to the first half of the book could provide a testing-ground for the validity or not of the psychoanalytic approach to Hollywood films. Does the method illuminate films? Or does it mask other meanings that emerge when it is not applied?

Not all teachers will want to use the films that I have selected in an inevitably idiosyncratic manner. I will thus list here a few obvious "replacements" for each film, as well as mention films that I had no room to deal with in the book. Replacing at least some of the films could be useful in extending the students' repertoire: they will learn something about a film from reading about it, but will then be able to experience another film (from the same period and genre) in class. Teachers, meanwhile, can apply the approach given in the text to the new film to see if it works equally well on different material; or set up a different approach, thus extending students' awareness of possible theoretical methods, and of what each yields.

I usually begin the course with at least one silent film; for years I have been using Frank Powell's *A Fool There Was* (1914) because it lays out clearly the virgin–whore split. The virginal, but cheeky, blonde-haired sister and the saintly, long-suffering wife are set up against the dark, slinky, coal-eyed Theda Bara, originator of the Vamp à la Hollywood. The idyllic "Holy" family here is threatened by the Vamp, who becomes the serpent in the Garden of Eden. But almost any Griffiths work would lay out the basic positionings (e.g. *Broken Blossoms* (1919), *Way Down East* (1920), *Birth of a Nation* (1916), *Hearts of the World* (1918) although the better the director, the more complex matters become. Other possibilities, with slightly different emphases, would be: Von Stroheim's *Foolish Wives* (1921); a Lois Weber film (*Where Are My Children?* (1916) or *The Blot* (1921) would be interesting); or a Vidor film, like *The Crowd* (1928), where, however, there is a very sophisticated critique of Establishment culture along with the acceptance of certain sexual positionings.

In place of *Camille* I suggest: Von Sternberg's *Morocco* (1930), Fitzmaurice's *Mata Hari* (1932), Arzner's *Christopher Strong* (1932), Mervyn LeRoy's *Gold Diggers of 1933* (1933), or Cukor's *Sylvia Scarlett* (1935).

In place of *Blonde Venus*: John Stahl's *Imitation of Life* (1934), Arzner's *Craig's Wife* (1936), Vidor's *Stella Dallas* (1937), or, with slightly different emphasis, Cukor's *Dinner at Eight* (1933).

In place of *Lady from Shanghai*: *The Postman Always Rings Twice* (1946), *Out of the Past* (1947), *Double Indemnity* (1944), *Murder My Sweet* (1944), *Gilda* (1946), or, with slightly different emphasis, *Mildred Pierce* (1945), which would usefully pick up "mother" issues from the previous session.

If one were going to include a 1950s film, a Sirk or a Hitchcock would work well. For Sirk, I suggest, *Written on the Wind* (1957) or *All that Heaven Allows* (1956). Both films would enable instructors to develop issues around the melodrama, which would have been introduced with the first Hollywood film. Peter Brooks' work could now be complemented by that of Laura Mulvey and Mary Ann Doane since they deal with the 1950s in particular. For Hitchcock, *Rear Window* (1955) or, if available, *Vertigo* (1959) would be excellent for issues relevant to the course, but if one wanted to step over into the 1960s *The Birds* (1964) or *Marnie* (1966) would be useful, particularly since some work has been done on these films by Bill Nichols, and by Bellour and Flitterman.

Other 1950s films could be Mankiewicz's *All about Eve* (1950) or Joshua Logan's *Picnic* (1956).

In place of *Nathalie Granger*, one should, perhaps, first consider a later Duras film – *India Song* (1975), for example. But any Chantal Akerman film that is available would be excellent, especially *Jeanne Dielman* (1975). Other possibilities are an Agnes Varda film – *Cleo de 5 à 7* (1962) or *One Sings the Other Doesn't* (1979); or Nelly Kaplan's *A Very Curious Girl* (1971); although this last has not recently been available, it works well in a class because it is so provocative.

Von Trotta's earlier *The Second Awakening of Christa Klages* (1977) could replace her *Marianne and Juliane* (I would not recommend her second film *Sisters* (1979) because it is morbid). Other less well-known German women filmmakers would fit in well here, especially Helke Sander (her *All Round Reduced Personality/Redupers* is excellent); but a film by Ulrike Ottinger, such as *Ticket of No Return*, would also be good. Sometimes, I have paired the contemporary German film with Leontine Sagan's 1930 *Maedchen in Uniform*. This early film about female–female relationships in the pre-Nazi context establishes an interesting focus for the new films made in the post-Nazi era whose approach to female–female bonding, while different, nevertheless looks back in interesting ways to Sagan's work. Ruby Rich's excellent article on this film in *Jump Cut*, Nos 24–5 (March 1981), would be useful alongside the film.

It would be difficult to replace Yvonne Rainer, since her work is unique, especially in the American context. Her later *Journeys From Berlin* (1980) would be a better example of what she is now doing than the films I discuss. One could well add Jackie Raynal's *Deux Fois* (1970), a film that, along with work by Duras, Akerman, Godard, and Rainer, influenced the shape of the feminist avant-garde theory film. *Deux Fois* is particularly useful as a compendium of devices that deconstruct traditional Hollywood ones, as is clear from the essay on her film by the *Camera Obscura* editors (see Bibliography). If the film is used along with the essay, one would have a good introduction to the avant-garde theory films that follow later in the course.

I always begin the section on shorter independent women's films with Germaine Dulac's *The Smiling Madame Beudet* (1922) and Maya Deren's *Meshes of an Afternoon* and *At Land* (1943) to establish the historical context for recent films. While there is a lot of choice regarding contemporary European and American independent films, I suggest that teachers stick with the three groupings that I outline in chapter 6 (experimental film, realist documentary, and avant-garde theory film). One could obviously cover more or less of any grouping according to preference and desired emphasis. I often teach Connie Field's *Rosie the Riveter* (1980) for the realist documentary, or Wunderlish and Lazarus's *Rape Culture* (1975). *The Wilmar 8* (1979) or *With Babies and Banners* (1978) fit well here also, as do *Union Maids* or Kopple's *Harlan County, U.S.A.* Often I focus on mothering as a theme in this section of the course, and show films on it in various modes, including Marjorie Keller's *Misconception*, Choppra's *Joyce at 34*, Ashur's *Janie's Janie*, and Mulvey/Wollen's *Riddles*; Citron's *Daughter-Rite* is almost irreplaceable, given its particular daughter focus, and its unusual visual style. The avant-garde theory films *Thriller*, *Sigmund Freud's Dora*, and *Amy!* work very well as a unit, but one need not perhaps do all three. Curling/Clayton's *Song of a Shirt* is a very interesting and unique work, but students find it hard. I would recommend doing only one reel or so.

One would be hard put to replace the Gomez film with another by a woman director. There are so few in the Third World, and not all those are making films on women's topics. Films about women in the Third World (but by male directors) that could be used are Humberto Solas's *Lucia* (Cuba, 1969) or Pastor Vega's *Portrait of Teresa* (Cuba, 1979). Of the films by women available for distribution in the USA (most with Unifilm), one could use Anna Carolina's *Sea of Roses* (Brazil, 1978), Maria Del Rosario's *Branded for Life* (Brazil, 1975), Vera Figueiredo's *Feminine Plural* (Brazil, 1977), or Helena Sonbert-Ladd's documentaries – *The Double Day* (Brazil, 1975), or *Nicaragua from the Ashes* (Nicaragua, 1982).

Ultimately, teachers will gradually find their own ways of organizing a course on women in film. I hope simply that the material in this book has proved stimulating enough to spur efforts of varying kinds. We are only just beginning to mine the fascinating silent period for films relevant to female issues, and I can imagine that in future courses I will greatly expand this section.

Appended here is an outline of a course I recently taught at Rutgers University which will give teachers a more concrete idea of how films, lectures, and readings may be organized.

Course 1: Women in film

This course aims, first, to show the evolution of women's cinema from the 1920s to the present, and second, to analyze the differing theories about what a feminist cinema should look like. Since many of the theories take their shape from the critique of the commercial cinema, we will begin by looking at four representative examples of the Hollywood film, from the beginnings to the present, to see the various images of women and how the films construct a particular position for the male and female spectator. Third, we will examine the different theories that have been used to analyze both the independent and the commercial film – sociological, psychoanalytic, semiological – in order to evaluate their differences and assess their respective usefulness.

Required films will be shown in class *only*, so attendance is crucial.
Required texts: John Berger, *Ways of Seeing*
                Peter Filene, *Him/Her Self: Sex Roles in America*
                E. Ann Kaplan (ed.), *Women in Film Noir*
(These texts are listed in the syllabus by the author's name. Other required readings are xeroxes of published works and are on reserve at the Alexander Library; many are in the Bibliography, if fuller details are required.)

LIST OF REQUIRED FILMS AND READINGS

Part I: Women's absence, silence, or marginality in the classical Hollywood film
  9/9   **Introduction:** dominant images of women in mainstream culture – the virgin–whore split as a construction for the male spectator
        Films: *Killing Us Softly* (independent documentary) (USA, 1980)
        A Fool There Was (Hollywood, silent) (with Theda Bara) (USA, 1915)
        Reading: Berger, *Ways of Seeing*, chs 1, 2
  9/16 **Topic:** The relationship of social/political history to the female image
        (a) Basic cinematic terms (see Glossary Handout)
        (b) Woman as victim in history and in classical narrative
        Film: Cukor, *Camille* (Hollywood) (with Greta Garbo) (USA, 1936)
        Readings: Filene, *Him/Her Self*, ch. 1
        Kaplan, "Is the gaze male?" (xerox)
  9/23 **Topic:** The construction of mothering in the Hollywood film (1)   *Paper I*
        Film: Vidor, *Stella Dallas* (Hollywood) (with Barbara Stanwyck) (USA, 1937)
        Readings: Filene, *Him/Her Self*, ch. 2
        Berger, *Ways of Seeing*, chs 3, 4
  9/30 **Topic:** The construction of mothering in the Hollywood film (2)
        Film: Curtiz, *Mildred Pierce* (Hollywood) (with Joan Crawford) (USA, 1946), Part I
        Readings: Pam Cook, "Duplicity in *Mildred Pierce*," in Kaplan, *Women in Film Noir*, p. 68ff.
        Filene, *Him/Her Self*, ch. 3
  10/07 **Topic:** The struggle over the female discourse in film noir
        Film: *Mildred Pierce*, Part II
        Readings: Janey Place, "Women in film noir," in Kaplan, *Women in Film Noir*, pp. 53–62
        Berger, *Ways of Seeing* chs 5, 6
        Filene, *Him/Her Self*, ch. 4   *Mid-semester in-class writing*
  10/14 **Topic:** Transgressing the male discourse in the contemporary Hollywood film (punishing the independent woman)
        Film: Pakula, *Klute* (Hollywood) (with Jane Fonda) (USA, 1971)
        Readings: Gledhill, "*Klute* 2: feminism and *Klute*," in Kaplan, *Women in Film Noir*, pp. 112–28
        Berger, *Ways of Seeing*, chs 7, 8
        Mulvey, "Visual pleasure and narrative cinema" (xerox)

Part II: Discovering the female voice – experimental, avant-garde and foreign films by women
  10/21 **Topic:** Feminine discourse and cinematic innovation in Dulac and Deren's concept of counter-cinema

Films: Dulac, *The Smiling Madame Beudet* (France, 1922)
Deren, *Meshes in the Afternoon* (USA, 1943)
Readings: Deren, "A letter to James Card" (xerox)
Johnston, "Women's cinema as counter-cinema" (xerox)
Filene, *Him/Her Self*, ch. 5

10/28 **Topic:** The politics of female bonding in the German film (1)
Film: Leontine Sagan, *Maedchen in Uniform* (Germany, 1932)
Readings: Filene, *Him/Her Self*, ch. 6.
Horney, "The dread of woman" (xerox)
Mayne, "Women at the keyhole: women's cinema and feminist criticism" (xerox)

11/04 **Topic:** The politics of female bonding in the German film (2)
Film: Von Trotta, *The Second Awakening of Christa Klages* (Germany, 1977)
Readings: Filene, *Him/Her Self*, ch. 7
New German Critique, Nos 24–5 (1981–2), special issue on new German cinema (on reserve)

Part III: Realist documentary and avant-garde theory films by women
11/11 **Topic:** The construction of mothering in films by women (1)
Film: Citron, *Daughter-Rite* (USA, 1978)
Readings: LeSage, "Feminist criticism: theory and practice" (xerox)
Feuer, "*Daughter-Rite*: living with our pain and love"
Williams and Rich, "The right of re-vision: Michelle Citron's *Daughter-Rite*"
Paper II

11/18 **Topic:** The construction of mothering in films by women (2)
Films: Choppra, *Joyce at 34*;
Ashur, *Janie's Janie* (1971)
Keller, *Misconception* (1973–7)
Readings: McGarry, "Documentary realism and women's cinema" (xerox)

12/02 **Topic:** Strategies in the realist documentary film
Film: Field, *Rosie the Riveter* (USA, 1980)
Readings: Barry/Flitterman, "Textual strategies" (xerox)

12/09 **Topic:** Avant-garde and realist strategies for exposing patriarchal oppression
Films: Lazarus and Wunderlish, *Rape Culture*
Weinstock, et al., *Sigmund Freud's Dora*
Readings: Freud, "Dora: a case history" (recommended)
Pajaczkowska, *Dora*: script (xerox)

12/14 Investigating the heroine of classical narrative (and review)
Film: Potter, *Thriller* (UK, 1980)
Script of the film (xerox)

Final examination

Bibliography

Abrams, M. H. (1953) *The Mirror and the Lamp: Romantic Theory and the Critical Tradition*, London, Oxford University Press.

Adami, Giuseppe (1931) *Letters of Giacomo Puccini*, trans. and ed. for the English edn by Eva Makin, Philadelphia and London, Lippincott.

Allais, Jean-Claude (1961) "Orson Welles," *Premier Plan*, March, pp. 29–32.

Althusser, Louis (1969) *For Marx*, trans. Ben Brewster, New York, Vintage–Random House.

———— (1971) *Lenin and Philosophy and Other Essays*, trans. Ben Brewster, New York and London, Monthly Review Press.

Arbuthnot, Lucy (1982) "Main trends in feminist criticism: film, literature, art history – the decade of the '70s," Ph.D dissertation, New York University. (Includes a useful bibliography.)

———— and Seneca, Gail (1982) "Pre-text and text in *Gentlemen Prefer Blondes*," *Film Reader*, No. 5, pp. 13–23.

Barrett, Michèle, et al. (1979) "Representation and cultural production," in Michèle Barrett (ed.) *Ideology and Cultural Production*, London, Croom Helm.

Barry, Judith and Flitterman, Sandy (1980) "Textual strategies: the politics of art-making," *Screen*, Vol. 21, No. 2, pp. 35–48.

Barthes, Roland (1967) *Elements of Semiology*, London, Jonathan Cape.

———— (1971) "Rhetoric of the image," *Working Papers in Cultural Studies*, No. 1, pp. 37–52.

———— (1972) *Mythologies*, trans. Annette Lavers, London, Jonathan Cape.

———— (1974) *S/Z: An Essay*, trans. Richard Miller, New York, Hill & Wang.

———— (1975) *The Pleasure of the Text*, trans. Richard Miller, New York, Hill & Wang.

———— (1977) "Introduction to the structural analysis of narratives," in his *Image-Music-Text*, London, Fontana.

———— (1981) "Upon leaving the movie theater," in Theresa Hak Kyung Cha (ed.) *Apparatus*, New York, Tanam Press, pp. 1–4.

Baudry, Jean-Louis (1974–5) "Ideological effects of the basic cinematographic apparatus," trans. Alan Williams, *Film Quarterly*, Vol. 28, No. 2, pp. 39–47.

———— (1976) "The apparatus," trans. Bertrand August and Jean Andrews, *Camera Obscura*, No. 1, pp. 97–126.

Baxter, John (1971) *The Cinema of Josef Von Sternberg*, London, Zwemmer.

Baxter, Peter (1978) "On the naked thighs of Miss Dietrich," *Wide Angle*, Vol. 2, No. 2, pp. 19–25.

Benjamin, Jessica (1980) "The bonds of love: rational violence and erotic domination," *Feminist Studies*, Vol. 6, No. 1, pp. 144–73.

Berger, John (1977) *Ways of Seeing*, New York, Penguin.

Bergstrom, Janet (1977) "Jeanne Dielman, 23 Quai du Commerce, 1080 Bruxelles (Chantal Akerman)," *Camera Obscura*, No. 2, pp. 117–23.

—— (1979) "Enunciation and sexual difference (Part I)," *Camera Obscura*, Nos 3–4, pp. 33–70.

—— (1979) "Rereading the work of Claire Johnston," *Camera Obscura*, Nos 3–4, pp. 21–32.

Bessy, Maurice (1963) *Orson Welles*, Paris, Editions Seghers.

Bovenschen, Silvia (1977) "Is there a feminine aesthetic?" *New German Critique*, No. 10, pp. 111–37.

Brenner, Charles (1957) *An Elementary Textbook of Psychoanalysis*, New York, Anchor.

Brooks, Peter (1976) *The Melodramatic Imagination*, New Haven and London, Yale University Press.

Brunsdon, Charlotte (1982) "A subject for the seventies," *Screen*, Vol. 23, Nos 3–4, pp. 20–30.

Burton, Julianne (1981) "Seeing, being, being seen: *Portrait of Teresa*: or contradictions of sexual politics in contemporary Cuba," *Social Text*, No. 4, pp. 79–95.

Cahiers du Cinéma editors "John Ford's *Young Mr Lincoln*," reprinted in *Screen*, Vol. 13, No. 3 (1972), pp. 54–64.

Califa, Pat (1979) "Unraveling the sexual fringe: a secret side of lesbian sexuality," *The Advocate*, 27 Dec., pp. 19–23.

—— (1981) "Feminism and sadomasochism," *Heresies*, Vol. 3, No. 4, pp. 30–4.

Camera Obscura editors (1976) "An interrogation of the cinematic sign: woman as sexual signifier in Jackie Raynal's *Deux Fois*," *Camera Obscura*, No. 1, pp. 27–52.

—— (1976) "Yvonne Rainer: an introduction" and "Yvonne Rainer: interview," *Camera Obscura*, No. 1, pp. 5–96.

Carey, Gary (1971) *Cukor and Co: The Films of George Cukor and His Collaborators*, New York, Museum of Modern Art.

Carroll, Noel (1980–1) "Interview with a woman who . . ." (Yvonne Rainer), *Millenium Film Journal*, Nos 7–9, pp. 37–68.

—— (1983) "From real to reel: entangled in nonfiction film," *Philosophical Exchanges*, Fall.

Caws, Mary Ann (1981) *The Eye in the Text: Essays on Perception, Mannerist to Modern*, Princeton, N.J., Princeton University Press.

Chodorow, Nancy (1978) *The Reproduction of Mothering: Psychoanalysis and the Sociology of Gender*, Berkeley, Calif., University of California Press.

Cixous, Hélène (1976) "The laugh of the Medusa," *Signs*, Vol. 1, No. 4, pp. 875–93, reprinted in Isabelle de Courtivron and Elaine Marks (eds) (1980) *New French Feminisms*, Amherst, Mass., University of Massachusetts Press, pp. 245–64.

—— (1980) "Sorties," in Isabelle de Courtivron and Elaine Marks (eds) *New French Feminisms*, Amherst, Mass., University of Massachusetts Press, pp. 90–8.

Colina, Enrique and Silva, Jorge (1980) interview, in *Jump Cut*, No. 22, pp. 32–3.

Comolli, Jean and Narboni, Paul (1971) "Cinema/ideology/criticism," *Screen*, Vol. 12, No. 1, pp. 27–35.

Cook, Pam (1975) "Approaching the work of Dorothy Arzner," in Claire Johnston (ed.) *The Work of Dorothy Arzner: Towards a Feminist Cinema*, London, British Film Institute.

—— (1978) "Duplicity in *Mildred Pierce*," in E. Ann Kaplan (ed.) *Women in Film Noir*, London, British Film Institute.

—— and Johnston, Claire (1974) "The place of women in the cinema of Raoul Walsh," in Philip Hardy (ed.) *Raoul Walsh*, Edinburgh, Edinburgh Film Festival.

Courtivron, Isabelle de and Marks, Elaine (1980) *New French Feminisms*, Amherst, Mass., University of Massachusetts Press.

Coward, Rosalind (1976) "Lacan and signification: an introduction," *Edinburgh Magazine*, No. 1, pp. 6–20.

—— and John Ellis (1977) *Language and Materialism: Developments in Semiology and the Theory of the Subject*, London, Routledge & Kegan Paul. (Includes a bibliography.)

Cowie, Elizabeth (1977) "Women, representation and the image," *Screen Education*, No. 23, pp. 15–23.

Curling, Jonathan and Clayton, Susan (1981) "Feminist history and *The Song of the Shirt*," *Camera Obscura*, No. 7, pp. 111–28.

—— and McLean, Fran (1977) "The Independent Filmmakers' Association – Annual General Meeting and Conference," *Screen*, Vol. 18, No. 1, pp. 107–17.

Daney, Serge (1966) "Welles au pouvoir," *Cahiers du Cinéma*, No. 181, pp. 27–8.

Dawson, Jan (1980) Review of Yvonne Rainer's *Journeys from Berlin*, *Sight and Sound*, Vol. 49, No. 3, pp. 196–7.

de Courtivron, Isabelle, see Courtivron

de Lauretis, Teresa, see Lauretis

Delorme, Charlotte (1982) "Zum Film *Die bleierne Zeit* von Margarethe Von Trotta," *Frauen und Film*, No. 31, pp. 52–5.

Deren, Maya (1946) "Cinema as an art form," *New Directions*, No. 9, reprinted in Charles T. Samuels, *A Casebook on Film*, New York, Van Nostrand Reinhold, pp. 47–55.

—— "A letter to James Card," (1965) reprinted in Karyn Kay and Gerry Peary (eds) (1977) *Women in the Cinema: A Critical Anthology*, New York, Dutton.

—— "An Anagram of Ideas on Art, Form and Film," (1946) reprinted in George Amberg (ed.) (1972) *The Art of Cinema: Selected Essays*, New York, Arno Press.

—— (1980) "From the notebook of 1947," *October*, No. 14, pp. 21–46.

Derrida, Jacques (1976) *Of Grammatology*, trans. Gayatri Spivak, Baltimore and London, Johns Hopkins Press.

Diary of a Conference on Sexuality (1982) Barnard Women Scholars Conference, New York, Faculty Press.

Dinnerstein, Dorothy (1977) *The Mermaid and the Minotaur*, New York, Harper.

Doane, Mary Ann (1981) "Woman's stake in representation: filming the female body," *October*, No. 17, pp. 23–36.

—— (1982) "Film and the masquerade – theorizing the female spectator," *Screen*, Vol. 23, Nos 3–4, pp. 74–88.

—— "The woman's film: possession and address," paper delivered at the Conference on Cinema History, Asilomar Monterey, May 1981; forthcoming in P. Mellencamp, L. Williams, and M. A. Doane (eds) *Re-Visions: Feminist Essays in Film Analysis*, Los Angeles, American Film Institute.

Dozoretz, Wendy (1982) "Germaine Dulac: filmmaker, polemicist, theoretician," Ph.D dissertation, New York University.

Dulac, Germaine (1932) "Le Cinéma d'avant-garde," in H. Fescourt (ed.) *Le Cinéma des origines à nos jours*, Paris, Editions des Cygne.

—— Essays in *Le Rouge et le noir*, *Cinémagazine*, and *Les Cahiers du mois* during the 1930s.

Duras, Marguerite (1969) Interviewed by Jacques Rivette and Jean Narboni, *Cahiers du*

Cinéma, reprinted in *Destroy, She Said* (1970) trans. Helen Lane Cumberford, New York, Grove Press.

—— (1973) Interviewed in Suzanne Horer and Jeanne Soquet (eds) *La Création étouffée*, Paris, Horay, partly reprinted as "Smothered creativity," trans. Virginia Hules, in Isabelle de Courtivron and Elaine Marks (eds) (1980) *New French Feminisms*, Amherst, Mass., University of Massachusetts Press.

—— (1973) *Nathalie Granger*, Paris, Gallimard.

—— (1975) Interviewed by Susan Husserl-Kapit, *Signs*, reprinted in Isabelle de Courtivron and Elaine Marks (eds) (1980) *New French Feminisms*, Amherst, Mass., University of Massachusetts Press.

Dyer, Richard (1979) *Stars*, London, British Film Institute.

Eagleton, Terry (1978) "Aesthetics and politics," *New Left Review*, No. 107, pp. 21–34.

Eco, Umberto (1976) *A Theory of Semiotics*, Bloomington, Ind., Indiana University Press.

Ellis, John (1980) "On pornography," *Screen*, Vol. 21, No. 1, pp. 81–108.

Emmens, Carol (1975) "New Day Films: an alternative in distribution," *Women and Film*, No. 7, pp. 72–5.

Erens, Patricia (ed.) (1979) *Sexual Stratagems: The World of Women in Film*, New York, Horizon Press. (Includes a bibliography.)

Fenichel, Otto (1945) *The Psychoanalytic Theory of Neurosis*, New York, Norton.

Feuer, Jane (1980) "*Daughter-Rite*: living with our pain and love," *Jump Cut*, No. 23, pp. 12–13.

Fischer, Lucy and Landy, Marcia (1982) "The eyes of Laura Mars – a binocular critique," *Screen*, Vol. 23, Nos 3–4, pp. 4–19.

Flitterman, Sandy and Suter, Jacqueline (1979) "Textual riddles: woman as enigma or site of social meanings? An interview with Laura Mulvey," *Discourse*, Vol. 1, No. 1, pp. 86–127.

Foucault, Michel (1972) *The Archeology of Knowledge*, trans. Alan Sheridan, London, Tavistock; New York, Pantheon.

—— (1978) *The History of Sexuality*, Vol. 1: *An Introduction*, trans. Robert Hurley, New York, Pantheon (London, Allen Lane, 1979).

Freud, Sigmund "Dora: a case history," *Standard Edition*, Vol. 7, London, The Hogarth Press, 1953, pp. 3–112.

—— "Three essays on the theory of sexuality," *Standard Edition*, Vol. 7, London, The Hogarth Press, 1953, pp. 135–243 especially.

—— "A child is being beaten," *Standard Edition*, Vol. 17, London, The Hogarth Press, 1955, pp. 175–204.

—— "Mourning and melancholia," *Standard Edition*, Vol. 14, London, The Hogarth Press, 1957, p. 237ff.

—— *Civilization and Its Discontents*, *Standard Edition*, Vol. 21, London, The Hogarth Press, 1960, pp. 59–176.

—— "Fetishism," *Standard Edition*, Vol. 21, London, The Hogarth Press, 1961, pp. 152–9.

Friday, Nancy (1974) *My Secret Garden: Women's Sexual Fantasies*, New York, Pocket Books.

Galiano, Carlos (1979) Review of Sara Gomez's *One Way or Another*, *Jump Cut*, No. 20.

Gallop, Jane (1982) *The Daughter's Seduction*, Ithaca, N.Y., Cornell University Press.

Gauthier, Xavière (1980) "Is there such a thing as women's writing?", trans. Marilyn A. August, in Isabelle de Courtivron and Elaine Marks (eds) *New French Feminisms*, Amherst, Mass., University of Massachusetts Press, pp. 161–4.

"Gespräch zwischen Margarethe Von Trotta und Christel Buschmann" (1976) *Frauen und Film*, No. 8, pp. 29–33.

Gidal, Peter (ed.) (1976) *Structural Film Anthology*, London, British Film Institute. (See especially Gidal's own essay, "Theory and definition of structural-materialist film," pp. 1–21.)

Giddis, Diane (1973) "The divided woman; Bree Daniels in *Klute*," *Women and Film*, Vol. 1, Nos 3–4, pp. 57–61, reprinted in Bill Nichols (ed.) (1976) *Movies and Methods*, Berkeley, Calif., University of California Press.

Gilbert, Lucy and Webster, Paula (1982) *Bound by Love: The Sweet Trap of Daughterhood*, Boston, Beacon Press.

Gilbert, Sandra M. (1978) "Patriarchal poetry and women readers: reflections on Milton's bogey," *PMLA* (Publications of the Modern Language Association of America), Vol. 93, No. 3, pp. 368–82.

—— and Gubar, Susan (1979) *The Madwoman in the Attic*, New Haven, Conn. and London, Yale University Press.

Gledhill, Christine (1977) "Whose choice? – teaching films about abortion," *Screen Education*, No. 24, pp. 35–46.

—— (1978) "Recent developments in feminist film criticism," *Quarterly Review of Film Studies*, Vol. 3, No. 4, pp. 458–93.

Godard, Jean-Luc and Gorin, Jean-Pierre (1973) "Excerpts from the transcript of Godard–Gorin's *Letter to Jane*," *Women and Film*, Vol. 1, Nos 3–4, pp. 45–52.

Grant, Elliott M. (ed.) (1934) *Chief French Plays of the Nineteenth Century*, New York, Harper & Row.

Halberstadt, Ira (1976) "Independent distribution: New Day Films," *Filmmakers' Newsletter*, Vol. 10, No. 1, pp. 18–22.

Harvey, Sylvia (1978) *May '68 and Film Culture*, London, British Film Institute.

—— (1978) "Woman's place: the absent family in film noir," in E. Ann Kaplan (ed.) *Women in Film Noir*, London, British Film Institute.

—— (1981) "An introduction to *Song of the Shirt*," *Undercut*, No. 1.

Haskell, Molly (1973) *From Reverence to Rape: The Treatment of Women in the Movies*, New York, Holt, Rinehart & Winston.

Hawkes, Terence (1977) *Structuralism and Semiology*, London, Methuen.

Heath, Stephen (1975) "Film and system: terms of analysis, Part I," *Screen*, Vol. 16, No. 1, pp. 7–17.

—— (1975) "Film and system: terms of analysis, Part II," *Screen*, Vol. 16, No. 2, pp. 91–113.

—— (1976) "On screen, in frame: film and ideology," *Quarterly Review of Film Studies*. Vol. 1, No. 3, pp. 251–65.

—— (1976) "Screen images, film memory," *Edinburgh Magazine*, No. 1, pp. 33–42.

—— (1978) "Difference," *Screen*, Vol. 19, No. 3, pp. 51–112.

—— (1981) *Questions of Cinema*, Bloomington, Ind., Indiana University Press. ("On screen, in frame" is reprinted here, along with others not mentioned above.)

Herrmann, Claudine (1980) "The virile system," in Isabelle de Courtivron and Elaine Marks (eds) *New French Feminisms*, Amherst, Mass., University of Massachusetts Press, pp. 87–9.

—— (1980) "Woman in space and time," trans. Marilyn R. Schuster, in Isabelle de Courtivron and Elaine Marks (eds) *New French Feminisms*, Amherst, Mass., University of Massachusetts Press, pp. 168–73.

Horney, Karen (1932) "The dread of woman," in Harold Kelman (ed.) (1967) *Feminine Psychology*, New York, Norton.

—— (1933) "The denial of the vagina," in Harold Kelman (ed.) (1967) *Feminine Psychology*, New York, Norton.

—— (1933) "Maternal conflicts," in Harold Kelman (ed.) (1967) *Feminine Psychology*, New York, Norton.

Irigaray, Luce (1977) "Woman's exile," *Ideology and Consciousness*, No. 1, pp. 62–76.
—— (1980) "Ce sex qui n'en est pas un," reprinted as "This sex which is not one," trans. Claudia Reeder, in Isabelle de Courtivron and Elaine Marks (eds) *New French Feminisms*, Amherst, Mass., University of Massachusetts Press, pp. 99–110.
Jameson, Fredric (1981) *The Political Unconscious*, Ithaca, N.Y., Cornell University Press.
Johnston, Claire (1973) "Women's cinema as counter-cinema," in Claire Johnston (ed.) *Notes on Women's Cinema*, London, Society for Education in Film and Television.
—— (1975) "Dorothy Arzner: critical strategies," in *The Work of Dorothy Arzner: Towards a Feminist Cinema*, London, British Film Institute.
—— (1975) "Femininity and the masquerade: *Anne of the Indies*," in Claire Johnston and Paul Willemen (eds) *Jacques Tourneur*, Edinburgh, Edinburgh Film Festival, pp. 36–44.
—— (1975) "Feminist politics and film history," *Screen*, Vol. 16, No. 3, pp. 115–24.
—— (1976) "Towards a feminist film practice: some theses," *Edinburgh Magazine*, No. 1, pp. 50–9.
—— (1980) "'Independence' and the thirties: ideologies in history: an introduction," in Don MacPherson (ed.) *Traditions of Independence: British Cinema in the Thirties* (with Paul Willemen), London, British Film Institute, pp. 9–23.
—— (1980) "The subject of feminist film theory/practice," *Screen*, Vol. 21, No. 2, pp. 27–34.
Jump Cut, special issues on "The Cuban cinema," Nos 20 (May 1979) and 22 (May 1980); on "Lesbians and film," Nos 24–5 (March 1981); and on "Film and feminism in Germany today," No. 27 (July 1982).
Kaplan, E. Ann (1975) "Women's Happytime Commune: new departures in women's films," *Jump Cut*, No. 9, pp. 9–11.
—— (1976) "Aspects of British feminist film theory: a critical evaluation of texts by Claire Johnston and Pam Cook," *Jump Cut*, Nos 12–13, pp. 52–5.
—— (1977) "*Harlan County, U.S.A.*: the problem of the documentary," *Jump Cut*, No. 15, pp. 11–12, expanded and revised in Tom Waugh (ed.) (forthcoming 1983) *History and Theory of the Radical Documentary*, Metuchen, N.J., Scarecrow Press.
—— (1977) "Interview with British ciné-feminists," in Karyn Kay and Gerald Peary (eds) *Women and the Cinema: A Critical Anthology*, New York, Dutton.
—— (1978) "Lina Wertmuller's sexual politics," *Marxist Perspectives*, Vol. 1, No. 2, pp. 94–104.
—— (ed.) (1978) *Women in Film Noir*, London, British Film Institute.
—— (1980) "Integrating Marxist and psychoanalytical approaches in feminist film criticism," *Millenium Film Journal*, No. 6, pp. 8–17.
—— (1980) "Patterns of violence to women in Fritz Lang's *While the City Sleeps*," *Wide Angle*, Vol. 3, No. 3, pp. 55–60.
—— (1983) "Fritz Lang and German expressionism: a reading of *Dr Mabuse, der Spieler*," in Stephen Bronner and Doublas Kellner (eds) *Passion and Rebellion: the Expressionist heritage*, New York, Bergin Press.
—— (1982) "Movies and the women's movement: sexuality in recent European and American films," *Socialist Review*, No. 66, pp. 79–90.
—— (ed.) (1983) *Re-Garding Television: A Critical Anthology*, Los Angeles, American Film Institute. (Contains essays on soap operas relevant to issues of women in melodrama.)
—— "Cinematic form and ideology in Fritz Lang's *Scarlet Street* and Jean Renoir's *La Chienne*," *Wide Angle*, forthcoming.
—— "Feminism, mothering and the Hollywood film: the mother as spectator in Vidor's *Stella Dallas*," *Heresies*, forthcoming.
—— and Ellis, Kate (1981) "Feminism in Bronte's *Jane Eyre* and its film versions," in

M. Klein and G. Parker (eds) *The English Novel and the Movies*, New York, Ungar, pp. 83–94.

—— and Halley, Jeff (1980) "One plus one: ideology and deconstruction in Godard's *Ici et Ailleurs* and *Comment Ca Va*," *Millenium Film Journal*, No. 6, pp. 98–102.

Kay, Karyn and Peary, Gerald (eds) (1977) *Women and the Cinema: A Critical Anthology*, New York, Dutton.

Kinder, Marsha (1977) "Reflections on Jeanne Dielman," *Film Quarterly*, Vol. 30, No. 4, pp. 2–8.

King, Noel (1981) "Recent 'political' documentary – notes on *Union Maids* and *Harlan County, U.S.A.*," *Screen*, Vol. 22, No. 2, pp. 7–18.

Klinger, Barbara (1981) "Conference Report" (of the Lolita Rodgers Memorial Conference on Feminist Film Criticism, Northwestern University, Nov. 1980), *Camera Obscura*, No. 7, pp. 137–43.

Kopjec, Joan (1981) "*Thriller*: an intrigue of identification," *Ciné-Tracts*, No. 11, pp. 33–8.

Kovel, Joel (1981) *The Age of Desire: Reflections of a Radical Psychoanalyst*, New York, Pantheon.

Kristeva, Julia (1975) "The subject in signifying practice," *Semiotext(e)*, Vol. 1, No. 3, pp. 19–34.

—— (1976) "Signifying practice and mode of production," *Edinburgh Magazine*, No. 1, pp. 64–76.

—— (1980) "Chinese women against the tide," trans. Elaine Marks of "Les Chinoises à 'contre-courant,'" in Isabelle de Courtivron and Elaine Marks (eds) *New French Feminisms*, Amherst, Mass., University of Massachusetts Press, p. 240.

—— (1980) "Oscillation between 'power' and 'denial'," trans. Marilyn A. August of "Oscillation du 'pouvoir' au 'refus'," in Isabelle de Courtivron and Elaine Marks (eds) *New French Feminisms*, Amherst, Mass., University of Massachusetts Press, p. 165.

—— (1980) "Woman can never be defined," trans. Marilyn A. August of "La Femme, ce n'est jamais ça," in Isabelle de Courtivron and Elaine Marks (eds) *New French Feminisms*, Amherst, Mass., University of Massachusetts Press, pp. 137–41.

—— (1980) "Motherhood according to Bellini," trans. Thomas Gora, Alice Jardine, and Leon S. Roudiez, in Leon S. Roudiez (ed.) *Desire in Language: A Semiotic Approach to Literature and Art*, New York, Columbia University Press, pp. 237–70.

Kuhn, Annette (1975) "Women's cinema and feminist film criticism," *Screen*, Vol. 16, No. 3, pp. 107–12.

—— (1978) "The camera I: observations on documentary," *Screen*, Vol. 19, No. 2, pp. 71–84.

—— (1982) *Women's Pictures: Feminism and Cinema*, London: Routledge & Kegan Paul. (Includes a bibliography.)

—— and Wolpe, Annmarie (eds) (1978) *Feminism and Materialism*, London, Routledge & Kegan Paul.

Lacan, Jacques (1968) *The Language of the Self*, trans. Anthony Wilden, Baltimore, The Johns Hopkins University Press.

—— (1968) "The mirror phase as formative of the function of the 'I.'," *New Left Review*, No. 51, pp. 71–7.

—— (1970) "The insistence of the letter in the unconscious," in J. Erhmann (ed.) *Structuralism*, New York, Anchor Books.

—— (1970) "Of structure as an inmixing of Otherness prerequisite to any subject whatever" (followed by discussion), in Richard Macksey and Eugenio Donato (eds) *The Structuralist Controversy*, Baltimore and London, The Johns Hopkins Press, pp. 186–200.

Lauretis, Teresa de (1978) "Semiotics, theory and social practice: a critical history of Italian semiotics," *Ciné-Tracts*, Vol. 2, No. 1.

Lentricchia, Frank (1980) *After the New Criticism*, Chicago, The University of Chicago Press, and London, The Athlone Press (hardback) and Methuen (paperback).

LeSage, Julia (1974) "Feminist film criticism: theory and practice," *Women and Film*, Vol. 1, Nos 5–6, pp. 12–19.

—— (1978) "The political aesthetics of the feminist documentary film," *Quarterly Review of Film Studies*, Vol. 3, No. 4, pp. 507–23.

—— (1979) "*One Way or Another*: dialectical, revolutionary, feminist," *Jump Cut*, No. 20, pp. 20–3.

—— Unpublished transcript of discussion on pornography at the Conference on Feminist Film Criticism, Northwestern University, Chicago, Nov. 1980.

Lévi-Strauss, Claude (1969) *The Elementary Structures of Kinship*, London, Eyre & Spottiswoode.

Lippard, Lucy (1976) "Yvonne Rainer on feminism and her films," in Lucy Lippard (1976) *From the Center: Feminist Essays on Women's Art*, New York, Dutton.

Lovell, Terry (1980) *Pictures of Reality: Aesthetics, Politics and Pleasure*, London, British Film Institute.

Lyon, Elisabeth (1980) "Marguerite Duras: Bibliography/Filmography," *Camera Obscura*, No. 6, pp. 50–4.

MacCabe, Colin with Eaton, Mike and Mulvey, Laura (1980) *Godard: Images, Sounds, Politics*, Bloomington, Ind., University of Indiana Press.

McCall, Anthony and Tyndall, Andrew (1978) "Sixteen working statements," *Millenium Film Journal*, Vol. 1, No. 2, pp. 29–37.

Maccoby, Eleanor and Martin, John (forthcoming 1983) "Parent-child interaction," in E. M. Hetherington (ed.) *Handbook of Child Psychology*, New York, John Wiley.

McGarry, Eileen (1975) "Documentary realism and women's cinema," *Women and Film*, Vol. 2, No. 7, pp. 50–9.

MacPherson, Don (1980) Introductions to all papers, in Don MacPherson (ed.) *Traditions of Independence: British Cinema in the Thirties* (with Paul Willemen), London, British Film Institute.

Martin, Angela (1976) "Notes on feminism and film," unpublished paper, London, British Film Institute.

Mayne, Judith (1981) "The woman at the keyhole: women's cinema and feminist criticism," *New German Critique*, No. 23, pp. 27–43.

—— (1981–2) "Female narration, women's cinema: Helke Sander's *The All-Round Reduced Personality/Redupers*," *New German Critique*, Nos 24–5, pp. 155–71.

Metz, Christian (1974) *Film Language: A Semiotics of the Cinema*, trans. Michael Taylor, New York, Oxford University Press.

—— (1975) "The imaginary signifier," *Screen*, Vol. 16, No. 2, pp. 14–76.

—— (1976) "History/discourse: Notes on two voyeurisms," *Edinburgh Magazine*, No. 1, pp. 21–5.

—— (1979) "The cinematic apparatus as social institution: an Interview with Christian Metz," *Discourse*, No. 1, pp. 7–38.

Michaelson, Annette (1974) "Yvonne Rainer, Part one: The Dancer and the Dance," *Artforum*, Jan.; "Yvonne Rainer, Part two: Lives of Performers," *Artforum*, Feb.

Millett, Kate (1970) *Sexual Politics*, New York, Doubleday.

Mitchell, Juliet (1974) *Psychoanalysis and Feminism*, New York, Random House.

Modleski, Tania (forthcoming 1983) "The rhythms of day-time soap operas," in E. Ann Kaplan (ed.) *Re-Garding Television: A Critical Anthology*, Los Angeles, American Film Institute.

Mulvey, Laura (1975) "Visual pleasure and narrative cinema," *Screen*, Vol. 16, No. 3, pp. 6–18.

—— (1976–7) "Notes on Sirk and melodrama," *Movie*, Nos 25–6, pp. 53–6.

—— (1979) "Feminism, film and the avant-garde," *Framework*, No. 10, pp. 3–10.

—— (1979) "Women and representation: a discussion with Laura Mulvey," *Wedge* (London), No. 2, pp. 46–53.

—— (1981) "On *Duel in the Sun*: afterthoughts on 'Visual pleasure and narrative cinema,'" *Framework*, Nos 15–17, pp. 12–15.

—— and Wollen, Peter (1974) "*Penthesilea; Queen of the Amazons* – Interview," *Screen*, Vol. 15, No. 3, pp. 120–34.

—— and Wollen, Peter (1977) "*Riddles of the Sphinx*, script," *Screen*, Vol. 18, No. 2, pp. 61–78.

—— and Wollen, Peter (1981) Script of *Amy!*, *Framework*, No. 14, pp. 38–41.

—— See also Flitterman, Sandy and Suter, Jacqueline.

Neale, Steve (1980) "Oppositional exhibition: notes and problems," *Screen*, Vol. 21, No. 3, pp. 45–56.

Nelson, Joyce (1977) "*Mildred Pierce* reconsidered," *Film Reader*, No. 2, pp. 65–70.

Nemser, Cindy (1975) Editorial, *Feminist Art Journal*, Vol. 4, No. 2, p. 4.

New German Critique, special double issue on new German cinema, Nos 24–5 (Fall–Winter 1981–2), eds David Bathrick and Miriam Hansen.

Nichols, Bill (1981) *Ideology and the Image*, Bloomington, Ind., Indiana University Press.

Nizhny, Vladimir (1969) *Lessons with Eisenstein*, New York, Hill & Wang.

Pajaczkowska, Claire (1978) "The thrust of the argument: phallocentric discourse?" in the booklet *Argument*, published by Anthony McCall and Andrew Tyndall along with the film of that name.

—— (1981) "Introduction to script for *Sigmund Freud's Dora* (written by McCall, Pajaczkowska, Tyndall, and Weinstock)," *Framework*, Nos 15–17.

Peary, Gerald and Kay, Karyn (1977) "Interview with Dorothy Arzner," reprinted in Karyn Kay and Gerald Peary (eds) *Women and the Cinema: A Critical Anthology*, New York, Dutton.

Perlmutter, Ruth (1979) "Feminine absence: a political aesthetic in Chantal Akerman's *Jeanne Dielman* . . .," *Quarterly Review of Film Studies*, Vol. 4, No. 2, pp. 125–33.

Place, Janey and Burton, Julianne (1976) "Feminist film criticism," *Movie*, No. 22, pp. 53–62.

Polan, Dana (1982) "Discourses of rationality and the rationality of discourse in avant-garde political film culture," paper presented at the Ohio University Film Conference, April 1982.

Pollock, Griselda (1977) "What's wrong with images of women?" *Screen Education*, No. 24, pp. 25–34.

—— (ed.) (1977) "Dossier on melodrama," with an essay by Geoffrey Nowell-Smith, *Screen*, Vol. 18, No. 2, pp. 105–19.

Rainer, Yvonne (1974) Script of *Lives of Performers*, in Yvonne Rainer (1974) *Work 1961–73*, New York, New York University Press.

—— (1976) Script for *Film About a Woman Who . . .*, *October*, No. 2, pp. 39–67.

—— See also *Camera Obscura* and Carroll, Noel.

Rich, Adrienne (1976) *Of Woman Born*, New York, Norton.

Rich, Ruby (1978) "The crisis of naming in feminist film criticism," *Jump Cut*, No. 19, pp. 9–12.

—— (1980) Review of *Thriller*, *The Chicago Reader*, Vol. 10, pp. 14, 16.

—— (1981) *Yvonne Rainer*, Minneapolis, The Walker Art Center.

Rivette, Jacques and Narboni, Jean (1969) "La destruction la parole," interview with Marguerite Duras, *Cahiers du Cinéma*, No. 217 (November), pp. 45–57.

Rose, Jacqueline (1978) "'Dora' – fragment of an analysis," *m/f*, No. 2, pp. 5–21.

Rossner, Judith (1975) *Looking for Mr Goodbar*, New York, Simon & Schuster.

Rubin, Gayle (1975) "The traffic in women: notes on the 'political economy of sex,'" in Rayna Reiter (ed.) *Toward an Anthropology of Women*, New York, Monthly Review Press.

Ryan, Michael (1981) "Militant documentary: Mai '68 par lui," *Ciné-Tracts*, Nos 7–8.

Saussure, Ferdinand de (1959) *A Course in General Linguistics*, trans. Wade Baskin, New York, The Philosophical Library.

Scrivener, Michael (1979) "Artistic freedom, political tasks," a discussion with Chuck Kleinhans, John Hess, and Julia LeSage, *Jump Cut*, No. 21, pp. 28–9.

Sheridan, Alan (1980) *Michel Foucault: The Will to Truth*, London, Tavistock.

Silver, Charles (1974) *Marlene Dietrich*, New York, Pyramid.

Silverman, Kaja (1981) "Masochism and subjectivity," *Framework*, No. 12, pp. 2–9.

Skorecki, Louis (1977) Review of Jackie Raynal's *Deux Fois*, *Cahiers du Cinéma*, No. 276 (May), pp. 51–2.

Solas, Humberto (1978) Interview with Julianne Burton, *Jump Cut*, No. 19, pp. 27–33.

Stanton, Stephen S. (1957) "Introduction" to *Camille and Other Plays*, New York, Hill & Wang.

Stern, Lesley (1979–80) "Feminism and cinema: exchanges," *Screen*, Vol. 20, Nos 3–4, pp. 89–105.

Stoller, Robert (1975) *Perversions: The Erotic Form of Hatred*, New York, Pantheon.

Strouse, Jean (ed.) (1974) *Women and Analysis: Dialogues on Psychoanalytic Views of Femininity*, New York, Grossman.

Suter, Jacqueline (1979) "Feminine discourse in *Christopher Strong*," *Camera Obscura*, Nos 3–4, pp. 135–50.

"Talking *Reds*: a discussion of Beatty's film" (1982) (between Bell Chevigny, Kate Ellis, Ann Kaplan, and Leonard Quart), *Socialist Review*, No. 61, pp. 109–24.

Todorov, Tzvetan (1977) "Categories of the literary narrative," *Film Reader*, No. 2, pp. 19–37.

Turim, Maureen (1979) "Gentlemen consume blondes," *Wide Angle*, Vol. 1, No. 1, pp. 52–9.

Von Sternberg, Joseph (1965) *Fun in a Chinese Laundry*, New York, Macmillan; London, Secker & Warburg.

Von Trotta, Margarethe, Script of *Die bleierne Zeit*. See Weber, Hans Jürgen.

Weber, Hans Jürgen with Weber, Ingeborg (eds) (1981) *Die bleierne Zeit: Ein Film von Margarethe Von Trotta*, Frankfurt Am Main: Fischer Taschenbuch. (Contains the full script, plus interviews with Von Trotta and others on the production team.)

Weinstock, Jane (1978) "The subject of argument," in the booklet *Argument* published by Anthony McCall and Andrew Tyndall, along with their film of that name.

—— (1981) "She who laughs first, laughs last," *Camera Obscura*, No. 11, pp. 33–8.

Wilden, Anthony (1972) *System and Structure: Essays in Communication and Exchange*, London, Tavistock.

Willemen, Paul (1978) "Notes on subjectivity: on reading Edward Branigan's 'Subjectivity under siege'," *Screen*, Vol. 19, No. 1, pp. 41–69.

—— (1980) "Letter to John," *Screen*, Vol. 21, No. 2, pp. 54–65.

Williams, Linda and Rich, Ruby (1981) "The right of re-vision: Michelle Citron's *Daughter-Rite*," *Film Quarterly*, Vol. 35, No. 1, pp. 17–21.

Wollen, Peter (1976) "The two avant-gardes," *Edinburgh Magazine*, Summer, pp. 77–86.

—— (1981) "The avant-gardes: Europe and America," *Framework*, Spring, pp. 10–11.

—— (1981) "The field of language in film," *October*, No. 17, pp. 53–60.

—— See also Mulvey, Laura.

"Women and film: a discussion of feminist aesthetics," (1978) *New German Critique*, No. 13, pp. 83–107.

Wood, Robin (1980–1) "The incoherent text: narrative in the 70s," *Movie* (UK), Nos 27–8, pp. 33–6.

Zita, Jacqueline (1981) "Films of Barbara Hammer: counter-currencies of a lesbian iconography," *Jump Cut*, Nos 24–5, p. 27.

Name index

Subject index

avant-gardes, the, 86–7, 95, 113, 115;
　see also cinema

Bohemianism, 38, 154

castration, 31, 70, 81, 172, 200, 202,
　203; castrating female, 40, 65
cinema: avant-garde, 9, 10, 85–7, 88,
　114, 138–9, 153–4, 161–2, 171, 180,
　198; avant-garde theory film, 142–70;
　classical Hollywood, 8, definition of,
　11–12, *see also* melodrama and
　narrative; counter-cinema, 10, 33,
　161, 181; documentary, 125–41,
　164–5, 191–3, 194, 195; independent,
　8, 125–41, 195–9; self-reflexive, 86,
　114
cinematic apparatus, 9, 20, 118, 121,
　127, 130, 131, 134, 138, 143, 148,
　166, 174, 194, 197; definition of, 12
classical cinema, *see* cinema
code, 7, 40, 57, 136, 144, 158, 169;
　definition of, 19
counter-cinema, *see* cinema
Cubism, 86

denotation/connotation: definition of,
　18
desire, 7, 8, 27, 29, 38, 39, 40, 41, 44,
　48, 65, 68, 75, 78, 81, 118, 122, 144,
　150, 155, 157, 202, 205
diegesis, 6, 7, 50, 51, 52, 59, 161;
　definition of, 18–19

discourse, 144; definition of, 18–19;
　female, 8, 18, 62, 66, 67; feminist, 82,
　152, 164, *see also* feminism; filmic
　50, 81, 181; male, 96, 98, 100, 105,
　169, 175; phallocentric, 144, 145,
　146, *see also* patriarchy;
　poetic/aesthetic, 132, 134;
　psychoanalytic, 10, 79, 80, 85, 147,
　155, 171, 184
documentary, *see* cinema
dominance-submission, 26, 27, 29, 30,
　74, 202, 205, 206

essentialism, 3, 96, 102, 128, 202, 203,
　204; definition of, 207 (footnote 2)
exhibitionism: definition of, 14
extra-cinematic, 50, 51, 52, 53, 59, 75;
　definition of, 20

family: patriarchal, 34, 42, 44, 55–6,
　57, 59, 60, 79, 88, 164, 167, 182–3,
　188
family romance (Freud), 5, 135, 138,
　148, 149
Father/father, 9, 41, 54, 61, 68, 70, 72,
　80, 82, 93, 109, 144, 151, 155, 175,
　178, 184, 187, 204, 205
female body: as spectacle, 39, 51, 52,
　58, 74, 119, 166, 190; *see also* gaze
female bonding, 5, 8, 55, 57, 58, 59, 78,
　89, 90, 100, 107, 110, 180
female spectator, 2, 8, 31, 33, 49, 50,
　51, 58, 62, 68, 73, 74, 104, 124, 184;